The Basics of Cyber Safety

Computer and Mobile Device Safety Made Easy

The Basics
of Cyber Safety

Computer and Mobile Device
Safety Made Easy

John Sammons

Michael Cross

AMSTERDAM • BOSTON • HEIDELBERG • LONDON
NEW YORK • OXFORD • PARIS • SAN DIEGO
SAN FRANCISCO • SINGAPORE • SYDNEY • TOKYO

Syngress is an imprint of Elsevier

SYNGRESS.

British Library Cataloguing-in-Publication Data
A catalogue record for this book is available from the British Library.

Library of Congress Cataloging-in-Publication Data
A catalog record for this book is available from the Library of Congress.

ISBN: 978-0-12-416650-9

For Information on all Syngress publications
visit our website at https://www.elsevier.com

Working together
to grow libraries in
developing countries

www.elsevier.com • www.bookaid.org

Publisher: Joe Hayton
Acquisition Editor: Chris Katsaropoulos
Editorial Project Manager: Anna Valutkevich
Production Project Manager: Mohana Natarajan
Designer: Matthew Limbert

Typeset by MPS Limited, Chennai, India

Dedication

This book is dedicated gratefully to my wife and children, who were unbelievably supportive and helpful in making this possible. At the time this book comes out, my wife Jennifer and I will have been married 15 years. I love her as much today as when we first got together, and anyone who knows her can understand why.

We have three children who are full of ideas and dreams, and have no reservations in sharing them. Throughout this book, Sara, Jason, and Emily each provided a unique insight about their concerns of cyber safety, showed their interests and individuality, and contributed their own suggestions. Rather than being upset about how little they saw me as I worked on the book, they found their own ways to become a part of it.

Michael Cross

For Lora, Abby, and Rae for making me a truly blessed and lucky man. To my aunt Ruth whose love, support, and encouragement means so much. To my mother Juanita, and my grandmother Grace. For the many sacrifices you made and the example you set … I miss you.

John Sammons

Contents

About the Authors

Michael Cross is a SharePoint Administrator and Developer, and has worked in the areas of software development, Web design, hardware installation/repairs, database administration, graphic design, and network administration. Working for law enforcement, he is part of an Information Technology team that provides support to over 1000 civilian and uniformed users. His theory is that when the users carry guns, you tend to be more motivated in solving their problems.

Michael has a diverse background in technology. He was the first computer forensic analyst for a local police service, and performed digital forensic examinations on computers involved in criminal investigations. Over 5 years, he recovered and examined evidence involved in a wide range of crimes, inclusive to homicides, fraud, and possession of child pornography. In addition, he successfully tracked numerous individuals electronically, as in cases involving threatening email. He has consulted and assisted in numerous cases dealing with computer-related/Internet crimes and served as an expert witness on computers for criminal trials. In 2007, he was awarded a Police Commendation for work he did in developing a system to track local high-risk offenders and sexual offenders.

With extensive experience in Web design and Internet-related technologies, Michael has created and maintained numerous websites and implementations of Microsoft SharePoint. This has included public websites, private ones on corporate intranets, and solutions that integrate them. In doing so, he has incorporated and promoted social networking features, created software to publish press releases online, and developed a wide variety of solutions that make it easier to get work done.

Michael has been a freelance writer and technical editor on over four dozen IT-related books, as well as writing material for other genres. He previously taught as an instructor and has written courseware for IT training courses. He has also made presentations on Internet safety, SharePoint, and other topics related to computers and the Internet. Despite his experience as a speaker, he still finds his wife won't listen to him.

Over the years, Michael has acquired a number of certifications from Microsoft, Novell, and Comptia, including MCSE, MCP+I, CNA, and Network+. When he isn't writing or otherwise attached to a computer, he spends as much time as possible with the joys of his life: his lovely wife Jennifer; darling daughter Sara; adorable daughter Emily; and charming son Jason.

For the latest information on him, his projects, and a variety of other topics, you can follow him on Twitter @mybinarydreams, visit his Facebook page at www.facebook.com/mybinarydreams, follow him on LinkedIn at www.linkedin.com/in/mcross1, or read his blog at http://mybinarydreams.wordpress.com.

John Sammons is an Associate Professor and Director of the undergraduate program in Digital Forensics and Information Assurance at Marshall University in Huntington, West Virginia. He teaches digital forensics, electronic discovery, information security, and technology in the School of Forensic and Criminal Justices

Sciences. He's also adjunct faculty with the Marshall University graduate forensic science program where he teaches the advanced digital forensics course. John, a former police officer, is also an Investigator with the Cabell County Prosecuting Attorney's Office and a member of the West Virginia Internet Crimes Against Children Task Force. He is a Member of the American Academy of Forensic Sciences, the High Technology Crime Investigation Association, and Infragard.

John is the founder and President of the Appalachian Institute of Digital Evidence. AIDE is a nonprofit organization that provides research and training for digital evidence professionals including attorneys, judges, law enforcement and information security practitioners in the private sector. He is the author of best-selling book *The Basics of Digital Forensics* published by Syngress.

Acknowledgments

There are several folks who are well-deserving of my gratitude for this project. This book wouldn't have been possible without them. First and foremost, I'd like to thank my coauthor Michael Cross for lending his time and expertise to this project.

Second, I want to thank the good folks at Syngress particularly Chris Katsaropolis and Anna Valutkevich. Thank you both for your patience and guidance during the creation of this book.

Lastly, (but certainly not least) my wife Lora. I could not do what I do without her.

What is cyber safety?

1

INFORMATION IN THIS CHAPTER

- What Is Cyber Safety?
- Paying Attention to What's Out There
- Privacy
- Encryption
- Monitoring Online Activity
- Identifying the Devices You Use, and Where You Use Them
- Using Different Windows Accounts
- Physical Security

No matter where you go or what you do, safety should always be the primary concern. Any experience becomes a bad one when you or your property is harmed, lost, or in danger. Just as this is true in the real world, it's also true when dealing with cyberspace. Regardless of whether you're new to the Internet or a virtual expert, we'll guide you on how to protect yourself online and off.

WHAT IS CYBER SAFETY?

Cyber safety is the process of using the services and resources of the Internet in a safe and secure manner. It not only involves protecting your data, but also your personal safety. The goal of cyber safety is to safeguard your computer, personal information, and loved ones from attacks and other potential threats. By using the technology in a safe and responsible manner, you'll minimize the risks by managing them.

WHY IS IT IMPORTANT?

The world is a dangerous place, both on and offline. In the physical world, we put locks on doors, use alarm systems, buy insurance, and take other steps to prevent ourselves from becoming victims. It doesn't mean we're paranoid in protecting our assets and families, just that an ounce of prevention is worth a pound of cure. It's better to stop a problem before it starts than deal with the ramifications afterwards.

The Basics of Cyber Safety. DOI: http://dx.doi.org/10.1016/B978-0-12-416650-9.00001-2
© 2017 Elsevier Inc. All rights reserved.

1

The combination of the safety concerns of the physical world and the new risks presented in the virtual world complicate the safety concerns you face when dealing with the Internet. Just like any property, your computer or mobile device might be stolen, lost, or damaged in some way, but connecting it to the Web also means you can be exposed to malware, viruses, hackers, and other threats. While there are thieves, vandals, pedophiles, bullies, and other unwelcome criminal elements in your city or town, the number of people who can be a threat to you exponentially increases with the population of Internet users. Because you're interacting with more people, using new tools, and visiting sites throughout the world, the number of threats you'll encounter also increases.

This information isn't meant to scare you from going online, but is intended to introduce you to potential threats and ways to protect yourself from those threats. There are many ways to mitigate problems, defend yourself, and decrease the likelihood of online risks. Remember, you don't buy a smoke detector because there will be a fire; you get it because one could happen and you want to prevent serious damage. In the same way, we'll show you how to install software, configure settings, and make changes to how you conduct yourself online to help prevent potential damage.

WHAT IS THE INTERNET?

When people talk about the Internet, they often refer to it as a single entity. This is reinforced when they hear other terms like The Web or "The Cloud." *The Cloud* reference comes from the way that the Internet is depicted on network diagrams and flowcharts, which uses an image of a cloud to represent the Internet without showing its actual complexity. In reality the Internet is a complex network of devices that communicate with one another to send your requests or data from point A to point B. When you search Google for cute kittens, this complex system is able to scour its voluminous index of the Internet in fractions of a second and return to you all the cute kitten pictures you could ever want.

From this, you can see how your data may come into contact with numerous devices and programs in this complex Web of computers, cables, and other equipment.

In most cases the system described above consists of actual machines in a physical location but cloud computing has changed that. With cloud computing your information may be hosted at sites all over the world instead of in a group of physical servers. Unfortunately, this means you never know where your email, attached files, or other data is being stored. While this might not seem an issue at face value, it is problematic when you realize that some countries have less stringent data protection and privacy laws than others.

When you visit a site, data is transmitted between the client and server, allowing you to interact with others and/or access content like Web pages, code in pages that perform some function, online apps, file sharing, online games, and so on. Some of the common online threats you might face in doing this include:

- Personal safety issues, such as cyberstalking, cyberbullying, online predators.
- Information security issues, such as phishing, identity theft, and scams.

- Computer threats, such as hackers, viruses, and other malicious software.
- Content issues, such as obscene or offensive content.

KEEP THE FAITH

You might be feeling a little overwhelmed at all the potential threats that are out there, or thinking that you're ill-equipped to deal with them. Don't worry. While many of the articles and news reports sound like someone carrying a sign that says "Repent ... the end of the world is nigh," the reality of cyberspace isn't that grim.

You also might feel unqualified to deal with cybersecurity issues, but don't feel alone. A 2012 survey found that 90% of consumers have had no training or classes on protecting their computer or information (WeLiveSecurity, 2012).

You don't need to be a computer expert to protect yourself. What you do need to do is use the tools and resources that experts have provided. There are a vast number of features, settings, hardware, and software available to prevent an attack, protect your privacy, enhance your security, and/or detect and remove anything affecting or infecting your system. You don't need know everything about computers, but you should know what others have developed to protect you. Everyone feels like an expert on things they know and use regularly but it's important to focus on learning what's needed to keep you safe on the Internet.

PAYING ATTENTION TO WHAT'S OUT THERE

Just as you might read a newspaper to see what crimes are being committed in your city and neighborhood, you should also stay aware of online threats. By paying attention to what the current threats are, you can identify if there are issues that should concern you. Maybe there's a new setting on Facebook that should be changed, or a particular vulnerability that needs you to update a system. You should regularly review your settings to see if anything is amiss, and keep up-to-date about changes to sites and systems you commonly use.

NOT ALL INFORMATION IS VALID

While the Internet is a resource of incredible information, there's also a lot of garbage online. People are often deceived by urban legends, which are stories that are circulated as if they were true. There are rumors and hoaxes that have been passed around for generations, and those that are new to the Web, specifically dealing with certain popular sites, programs, or software vendors.

If you see a story that's particularly humorous, horrifying, or unbelievable, try not to share it with others before doing a little investigation yourself. Copy a line or two and paste it into Google. By surrounding this line in quotes, Google will look for that exact phrase. If the story is a hoax, you'll see a number of results leading to articles that warn it's false. If you see articles verifying its authenticity, then it's probably something you'll want to share with others.

As we'll see in Chapter 5, Cybercrime, there are also misleading, fraudulent Web pages and email, which are designed to fool you into providing details about yourself, give up your username and password, or convince you to give them money. These are often modern versions of old con games, distributed through the Internet in the hopes of fooling more people. In the same way you can investigate an urban legend, you'll often find that organizations and individuals have posted warnings about these swindles.

Whether it's a scam or an entertaining story, don't fall for them easily. There are a number of sites that focus on urban legends and Internet hoaxes, allowing you to verify the information. These include:

- Snopes (www.snopes.com)
- Hoax busters (www.hoaxbusters.org)

Anyone can put up a Web page, create a legitimate sounding social media account, and post and share information that's bogus. By checking first, you can avoid falling for these false stories.

THINK BEFORE YOU CLICK

A major risk when using the Internet can be the links that you click. A *hyperlink* or *link* is a section of text, image, or area of the page that's activated when you click or hover your mouse over it. Clicking the link may take you to another section of the Web page or document, open a new page or document, download a program or file, run code, or send email. Hyperlinks have been the primary method of navigating the Internet, and have expanded to being used in other programs (such as Microsoft Word, PDFs, etc.).

To make a link more user friendly, it may appear as something that says "Contact Us," "Download," or another easy-to-understand word or phrase. HTML or other code in the document informs the program you're using (i.e., a browser, email client) to perform a specific action. Generally, this code will do what you expect, such as taking you to the page you want. However, on clicking it, it could just as easily take you to an untrustworthy site, download malware or a virus, or perform some other action you didn't expect.

You should avoid clicking on pop-up ads or links that seem suspicious. If an email seems to come from a phony source or has elements that seem dubious, don't click any links. If you believe the link came from a known source, such as your bank or a store you shop at, go to the site directly with your browser rather than using the link. You can also inspect most links by hovering your mouse over it. This displays what's referenced in the link (i.e., a website's address or code) in the status bar of your browser or email client. Doing so gives you a better understanding of what that link does and where it will take you.

READING URLs

A *Uniform Resource Locator*, or *URL* for short, is another name for a website's address. URLs are used to instruct Internet clients what resource you want to use on a particular server. It's important to understand how to read a website address so that you understand where you are, where you're going, and how the connection is being made.

A URL is constructed of several different parts. Any URL begins with the *protocol*, which is a set of rules used to determine the communication method that's used between a client and server. Some of the common protocols you'll see in a URL include:

- http://, which is the *Hypertext Transfer Protocol* (HTTP). This is commonly used to download web pages and associated content from a web server, so it can then be displayed in a browser.
- ftp://, which is the *File Transfer Protocol* (FTP), and used to download files from Internet servers.
- news://, which is used to access usenet newsgroups from a news server.
- telnet://, which is used to establish a Telnet session.
- mailto://, which is used to initiate outgoing email.

The next part of a URL is the server you're trying to access. A *domain name* is a friendly name that corresponds to the IP address owned by that particular site. An *IP address* is a unique string of numbers that's separated by dots, and used to identify computers on a TCP\IP network like the Internet. You can think of an IP address like you would your home address. In all the world, there are no two places with your address, city, state, country, and zip code, which is why the mail (usually) is sent to the correct address. Because an IP address like 192.168.0.1 would be difficult to remember and type in a browser, we use domain names that correspond to the IP address. When you type in a URL like http://www.microsoft.com, it goes to a DNS (Domain Name Server) that translates this to the correct IP address, so you can then go to the correct site.

You'll notice that each domain name consists of a hostname (i.e., the name of the server) followed by a dot, and the domain that it's a part of. Originally, there were only a few domain suffixes (.com, .org, .net, .mil, etc.), but this expanded to use country codes (.ca, .ru, .tv, etc.), and then expanded further to use market-related or custom domains (.coffee, .dentist, etc.). In looking at this, you'd think that the country codes would indicate the location of a server, but this isn't the case. It only identifies under what country the site's owner registered the name.

After the domain name, you may also see a slash followed by another word. This may indicate a particular resource you're accessing, such as a default web page with the file extension of .asp, .htm, or .html. If you went to www.fda.gov/default.htm, you're telling the browser to load the web page default.htm on that site. Alternatively, the resource you're accessing may be in a folder, so the URL may show the path. If you went to www.fda.gov/Food/default.htm, you're telling the browser to open the file default.htm that's located in the Food folder on that site. Fig. 1.1 depicts the parts of a typical URL.

Faking sites with URLs

Now that you have a good understanding of how URLs work, we'll show you how they can be manipulated. Legitimate sites will often use subdomains to split apart a

FIGURE 1.1

Parts of a URL.

site into logical parts called subdomains. If you started a site called www.myfakesite.com, you might want to split it apart. While your main site is on myfakesite.com, you might have a store on a subdomain called shop.myfakesite.com, or support for using your products on support.myfakesite.com. Each of these are different sites on one or more servers.

Cybercriminals may try and misdirect you by naming a subdomain after a different site you're expecting to visit. You may get an email about your Amazon account, with a link that goes to amazon.myfakesite.com. When you glance at the URL, you might think you're on Amazon's site, but you're really on a bogus site designed to look like the real thing. As we'll see in Chapter 5, Cybercrime, this is a common trick to fool you into logging on and "verifying" information.

When reading a URL, read the domain name from right to left. In doing so, you may see a country code indicating its possible location (remember, this isn't always the case), its name, and any possible subdomains.

Another possible problem you may encounter is when you see URLs that have been shortened. Using a service like TinyURL (www.tinyurl.com) or Google URL shortening service (https://goo.gl/), you can enter a long website address, click a button, and have it shortened to a shorter URL. This is useful when sharing URLs on sites that have character limits, or you're suggesting people visit a site with an incredibly complex address. When the person clicks on the link, it contacts the service, which then refers your browser to the address you want them to go to. It's so useful that Twitter and Facebook have their own URL shorteners, so that any tweets containing long URLs are automatically shortened.

The problem with shortened URLs is that you don't know where it's taking you. Maybe it's taking you to a legitimate site, or maybe it's leading you to a site where malware will be downloaded. To make sure you're going where you expect, use a site like LongURL (www.longurl.org/) to expand shortened URLs. After entering a shortened URL in the box, click the **Expand** button to see the full URL. At this point, you can decide to visit the site, or ignore it for safety's sake.

NOTE

A Fun Way to Shorten URLs

There are some fun URL shortening services on the Web. ShadyURL (www.shadyurl.com) allows you to enter a website address, and have it converted to something that may be longer and looks like it should be avoided. Essentially, this is the opposite of what you'd want, but it can be funny seeing a URL like www.google.com "shortened" to something like www.5z8.info/michaelangelo-virus_u9f8wg_mercenary.

PRIVACY

Internet privacy is a growing concern. When you visit a site, save a file, or provide information online, you should be secure in the knowledge that only you and authorized users have access to it. Unfortunately, that's not always the case.

EXPECTATIONS AND REALITY

When you use the Internet, you should take some time thinking about the level of privacy you expect from different sites, how the information you post online is used, and who can see where you go and what's stored. This will determine the settings you select, the sites you visit, and the browser, apps, and search engines you use.

Many times, your expectations of privacy are clearly outlined on a site, although few people actually read it. Often when you visit a site, there's a link to a Terms of Use or Privacy Policy page that outlines whether data is shared with third parties and how it may be used. Similarly, when you install an app on your phone or tablet, it will say what personal information and data is being accessed by the app. The problem is that many of us either don't understand or ignore this information. We want to use the app or site, so we click on an Accept button. Taking the time to read this information will however help you understand your rights, and help set your expectations.

Because of how much they have to gain, advertising firms have considerable interest in Internet privacy issues. Once advertisers understand what you're looking for, they can focus the site's ads to sell items and services you're interested in. This is done in a number of ways, including:

- As we'll see in Chapter 2, Before connecting to the Internet, small files called *tracking cookies* may be stored on your computer as a means of monitoring the sites you visit.
- Search engines may store information on your searches.
- Online surveys may be used to get you to provide details about shopping habits, etc.

Questionnaires and online surveys are useful tools for gathering information, but you should be careful of how much you reveal. You may sign-up with a site to fill out a survey in exchange for rewards, or take it out of interest or concern. In such situations, you might create a profile or sign-in with your real name and email address, which lets the site know who you are and associate you with what's entered on the survey. If you've ever used an online questionnaire to help diagnose a potential medical or psychological issue, it can be even worse since you've provided personal, private, and medical information to a group of strangers. If you post comments and questions in a support site afterwards, then knowledge of the medical issue is even more public; it's visible to anyone who uses the site and possibly accessed in search engines results.

Often, some of the most personal bits of information are facts that we've posted about ourselves. Posting your date of birth, address, phone number, where you work or go to school, and other personal details online can expose your private life to strangers. The same applies to information in profiles, online resumes, and albums, which should be set so that only those you trust can see it. When using the Internet, the goal is to keep private information private.

The other issue with privacy comes in the form of governments. While conspiracy theorists said for years that the US government was monitoring telephone and Internet communications, it came to most people's surprise that there was some truth to it. In 2013, Edward Snowden (a former government subcontractor) leaked top secret documents that showed numerous surveillance programs were being conducted by the National Security Agency (NSA) and other intelligence agencies. Snowden began stealing documents about how the NSA was conducting domestic surveillance on millions of citizens, monitoring their calls, and Internet use. The validity of the information was essentially verified when the US government charged Snowden under the Espionage Act (The Washington Post, 2013).

According to information provided by Snowden, the NSA used a program called PRISM to collect real-time information. While it supposedly only gathers information on American citizens, it apparently wasn't the only one in use. When you consider that much of the world's communications goes through the United States, it's logical to assume that the network traffic being monitored isn't just the data being generated by its citizens.

While a number of countries have laws and regulations dealing with Internet privacy, most do not. Even when such laws exist, there can be difficulty enforcing them when a citizen is in one country and the server is in another. While international privacy enforcement authorities have cooperated with one another, and even taken initiatives to examine websites, there are so many sites around the world that it's difficult (if not impossible) to ensure online privacy is being adequately protected.

You are the greatest defender of your privacy. Throughout this book we'll show you various privacy settings you can configure to prevent others from seeing your data. When using a site, determine if it has a privacy policy, and if there's contact information for addressing privacy questions or concerns. Similarly, if you're using an app, read the warnings that inform you of what information will be sent and what will be shared with third parties. If you're not comfortable with those policies, then don't bother using the app.

WHO HAS OWNERSHIP?

Just because you posted something, it doesn't mean it's necessarily yours. You may have read an article, made a poignant comment, and in posting your thoughts, transferred your rights to them. If an online newspaper, media outlet, or other site has set conditions on being able to review or respond to the article, they may have included a clause of who owns those comments once they're submitted. The reviews and feedback you give may become the property of the site or blog that you responded to.

When you sign-up for a new account or use a site, you agree to the Terms of Service. The site may say in using the site, you've agreed to the conditions, or they may have you click a button to explicitly agree to them. The Terms of Service will explain your rights, and let you know whether you retain ownership of your intellectual property, transfer it to them, or allow them to use it. These conditions should be reviewed periodically just so you're aware of any changes. Some of the terms you might see on commonly used websites include:

- On Facebook (https://www.facebook.com/terms.php), you own all of the content that you post.
- Although other sites may pull reviews from Amazon (www.amazon.com), you own the reviews you've posted.
- *The New York Times* has a different view on user-generated content. They state in their Terms of Service (www.nytimes.com/content/help/rights/terms/terms-of-service.html#discussions) that "you waive any rights you may have in having the material altered or changed in a manner not agreeable to you" and you grant *The New York Times* or any third-party designates "a perpetual, nonexclusive, world-wide, royalty free, sub-licensable license."

You may have seen people posting disclaimers on Facebook and Twitter that state any material they've created is protected by copyright, is their intellectual property, and belongs to them. However, posting a disclaimer doesn't override the Terms of Service you've agreed to when setting up an account. That being said, it may be advisable to post a disclaimer if you have anything of value posted online, but not because you think the site's policies may change. If you're a photographer or an artist, the sale of pictures is your livelihood, and posting copies online may be your way of advertising. Posting a disclaimer may dissuade others from using your content on their own blogs, intranet sites, or other venues.

If you're using a site where your comments do become the property of someone else, this doesn't mean you aren't liable for any derogatory or inflammatory comments made. Posting something that goes against their community standards or user agreement may result in deletion of your account. If you threaten or post statements in relation to some other crime, the site may release it to police so you can be prosecuted.

Another situation where ownership becomes an issue is in the workplace. Many organizations have policies that state anything created with company-owned equipment, during work hours, and/or using their resources becomes their property. Perhaps they don't want you creating a work-related product and later claim it's your intellectual property, or they want to prevent you from running your own business from work.

Businesses also commonly have policies that state, because anything with company-owned devices or services is theirs, they have the right to check your work email and the contents of any computer, tablet, or device you use. This means that any emails you send, files you save, or sites you visit are not private. A company may remotely check your laptop or mobile device, log activity, or read through any emails sent or received using your work account.

WHERE ARE YOUR FILES STORED?

You've probably realized by now that the location of your data plays a big part in your expectations of privacy. While there are risks saving files to your local hard disk there are serious considerations when they're stored online, a corporate network, or devices owned by the people you've texted, emailed, or sent files to.

If you've used any computer or mobile device for a time, you've probably sent someone a photo. You might not consider that the photo is now on your device and the other person's. The other person could now share it with his or her friends, post it online, or do something else that's out of your control. If either device was lost, stolen, or hacked, the photo is now in the hands of someone else. If the photo was saved to the Cloud, then it's also on an Internet server. You're trusting that the storage is secure, anyone who works there won't access it, and that your account won't be hacked, meaning another complete stranger might publish it on different sites. As we'll see in Chapter 8, Protecting yourself on social media, the type of storage you choose will depend on your needs, and how secure it is will often rely on you.

You should be aware of where your data will reside, so you can understand what may happen to it. If you're a decent, law abiding person, then it's pretty remote that law enforcement will serve a warrant to search your computer. If files are stored on the Cloud, or data has been entered into a site's database, it resides on a server. If a government entity decided to seize the servers as part of an investigation, your files and data may not be immune to being searched.

Organizations may shy away from the Cloud for corporate needs is because it isn't clear where the servers reside, or if they reside in a foreign country. Imagine what would happen if a police department kept criminal records on the Internet, and the server was in another country. Antiterrorism laws in that country might allow their government to have access to the data, or data protection laws there may be lax or nonexistent. Just as a company protects the privacy of customer and client data, you should be concerned about yours.

HOW IMPORTANT IS YOUR DATA?

While we've talked a lot about protecting sensitive information, you should also consider what the data is and its importance. When looking at what's being posted or saved online, consider the relevance of the information. Would you really be embarrassed or care if it got out? While your medical and financial information require the highest levels of protection, does it matter if a hacker or the government gets ahold of your Aunt Martha's peach cobbler recipe?

When saving to the Cloud, sending as an attachment, or posting on social media, look objectively at the information. Try to determine its importance, and how it may affect you if it went public now or in a few years. This not only tells you if it's suitable to share, but also whether it requires higher levels of protection.

ONCE IT'S OUT THERE, IT'S OUT THERE

It's important to realize that information you post online may be there permanently, or at least what seems like forever. Many sites will keep articles, posts, and other data online indefinitely, allowing others to view what you said or did years later. While this can be useful if you want to look at old pictures or events on your Facebook page, it can be problematic when there's information you'd rather others not see.

Just because there are laws to protect your privacy, they may be somewhat fuzzy where the Internet's concerned. For example, credit bureaus and financial institutions can't reveal details like bankruptcies after a certain number of years, but an article or post that mentions it may be online indefinitely. Newspapers and media outlets regularly report people who are arrested, but rarely tell you the outcome if the case is thrown out of court. You might be charged, but there might never be a follow-up article saying it was all a big mistake. The long-term effects of this can be catastrophic, because there isn't an expiration date for content on the Internet.

If you're concerned about your reputation, then you should be careful about what you put on the Web. This not only includes what you've explicitly shared with others, but also what's been stored on the Cloud. While efforts are made to make online storage as secure as possible, it doesn't mean a server on the Net is impenetrable. In 2014, hackers used phishing and brute force password attacks to acquire the usernames and passwords of people using iCloud (Ars Technica, 2014). The Apple Cloud services breach lead to hundreds of private photos belonging to celebrities being accessed, which were then shared on other sites. When using the Cloud, you're trusting that the best possible security measures are in place, but that means you're trusting someone who works for that service to have your best interest in mind, to have made no mistakes, and to have left no security holes in the system.

The same applies to the data you enter into websites. This became painfully obvious to users of Ashley Madison (www.ashleymadison.com), an online dating service for people who are married or in "committed" relationships. In July 2015, hacker(s) calling themselves *The Impact Team* stole the website's customer's data, including personally identifying information (names, addresses), financial information (credit card numbers), and details of their sexual fantasies and interests. The hackers posted this information on Pastebin (www.pastebin.com) when Ashley Madison didn't meet their demand to shut down the company's websites. Some of what was posted showed that even though people requested (and even paid) to have their data deleted, it still existed in the hacked servers (The Register, 2015).

As we'll see in Chapter 11, there are some methods and tools to remove your content from the Internet. You can request it be removed from websites, search engines, and in a number of cases remove them yourself. However, this doesn't mean that it's completely gone. Sites may have a backup of files, someone out there has a copy of it, or the sites made your data so it isn't visible but haven't actually removed it.

What's the best way to prevent others from seeing something you don't want them to see? Never post it at all.

ENCRYPTION

Encryption is a process of encoding messages so that only those who are authorized to view the data can read it. Without encryption, the message is referred to as *plaintext*, but when an algorithm is applied the message becomes scrambled and is called *ciphertext*. There are different kinds of encryption that may be used to protect the data stored on a computer or sent over a network, including:

- **Symmetric Cryptography**, which is also called *private-key cryptography*, uses a key (which may be a password or digital certificate) to encode the message into ciphertext, and the recipient uses the same key to decrypt it. To use this type of encryption, the same key must be shared among anyone accessing the data. If you and I don't use the same key, you'll be unable to decrypt what I've sent to you. Common symmetric encryption methods include Advanced Encryption Standard, International Data Encryption Algorithm, and Data Encryption Standard.
- **Asymmetric Cryptography**, which is also called *public key cryptography*, uses a private key and a public key to encrypt and decrypt messages and data. While the public key is available to anyone to encrypt messages, the private key is used by the recipient to decrypt the message. Common asymmetric encryption methods include Diffie-Hellman and RSA.
- **Hashing**, in which a unique fixed-length signature is created for a message or data set with an algorithm. Because the signature is unique to the message, even a slight change to its content can create a drastically different hash. It's different from the previous methods, because once hashed, it isn't decrypted to its original form. Instead, it's compared to other data, so you can determine if both hold an identical message. This makes it useful for password verification, digital signatures, and other situations where one message or data set is compared to another, because you can determine if both sets hold the same data. Common hashing algorithms include Message Digest 5 and Secure Hashing Algorithm.

As we'll see throughout this book, there are many different ways in which encryption is used. In Chapter 2, Before connecting to the Internet, we'll discuss how encryption is used on networks, like the Wi-Fi network in your home, work, or school. This prevents others from seeing passwords, usernames, and other packets of data being sent to-and-from your computer. As we'll see in the sections that follow, encryption can be used on your computer to prevent others from viewing your files, and also used on the Internet to prevent others from viewing transactions and other activities between your computer and a secure server.

ENCRYPTING STORAGE

A simple way to access someone's data is to plug their storage device into another computer. While removing an internal hard drive from a computer is slightly more difficult and considerably more noticeable than walking off with an external hard drive or USB flash drive, once attached to a different computer, a thief is able to access your files without ever entering an account name or password. This is why file encryption is so important.

Encryption makes any data on a storage device useless to a thief. If one were to steal an encrypted drive, they would only be able to access the data using a key (such as a password), or by using the original computer that encrypted it. There are a number of free and commercial products that can be used to encrypt individual files, folders, or entire hard disks, including VeraCrypt (https://veracrypt.codeplex.com) and CipherShed (https://ciphershed.org/). In addition, some operating systems include features to encrypt local and removable drives.

BitLocker is an encryption tool that's included with Windows Vista and higher versions. It will not encrypt individual files and folders, but it will encrypt entire drives. This not only includes drives on your computer, but also any external hard drives or USB flash drives you might have. In the following example, we'll show you how to encrypt an USB stick:

1. Open File Explorer, and in the left-pane right-click on the drive letter for your USB stick.
2. Click **Turn on BitLocker**.
3. When the wizard appears, click on the checkbox to **Use a password to unlock this drive**. If you use a smart card, you could also use that feature to unlock the drive, which would require you to insert your smart card and enter your PIN to unlock the drive. If you were encrypting a fixed drive, you would select the option to automatically unlock when you log into Windows. After selecting to use a password, enter a password into the **Type your password** box, and then type it in again in the **Retype your password** box to confirm. Click **Next**.
4. On the *How Do You Want To Store Your Recovery Key* page, click **Save the recovery key to a file**. When the *Save BitLocker Recovery Key* dialog box appears, choose a location to save the file and then click **Save**. You have the option of using this to print the recovery key (password) when needed.
5. Click **Next**, and on the *Are You Ready To Encrypt This Drive* page, click **Start Encrypting**.

When Bitlocker encrypts the USB flash drive, it will add a program to it called bitlockertogo.exe, which is the BitLocker To Go Reader. This program is used to unlock the drive so you can read the data. If the drive is encrypted with a password, it will prompt you for it, and upon clicking the **Unlock** button, you're then able to access the files.

The BitLocker To Go Reader is not required for reading an encrypted local drive, as the BitLocker feature on the operating system will handle this for you. If you've encrypted a local drive, and want to move it to another computer, you would need to decrypt the drive before installing it on another machine. To do this, you would right-click on the drive letter, click **Turn Off Bitlocker**, and follow the prompts.

To see which drives are encrypted on your machine, you can use the BitLocker Drive Encryption program in Windows. In Windows 8*x* and 10, you would search for "bitlocker" and then click BitLocker Drive Encryption. In Windows 7, click **Start**, click **Control Panel**, click **System and Security**, and then click **Manage Bitlocker**. Once it appears, you will see a list of your drives, and have the options to turn bit-locker off on encrypted drives, or turn it on when you want to encrypt a nonencrypted drive.

Encrypting mobile devices

In addition to encrypting computers, you can also encrypt mobile devices and the SD cards you've inserted for extra storage. It's common for devices to require you to set a PIN, passphrase, or swipe pattern to unlock your phone prior to setting encryption. If this isn't set, the options for encrypting SD cards may not be available in your settings. Once you've set a PIN, password, or swipe pattern to unlock the screen, you would then go into your **Settings** menu to encrypt the card.

- On an Android phone, you tap **Settings**, tap **Security**, and then decide on the option to encrypt an external SD card or **Encrypt Device**. If you encrypt the device, you'll need to enter your password each time you turn your phone on, so it can be decrypted. If you have an SD card that you want encrypted, you would select **Encrypt external SD card** on the *Security* screen and follow the prompts to either encrypt the entire card, or new files that are added.
- On an iPhone, iPad, or iPod Touch, you would set a passcode to access your phone, which will instruct you that *Data protection is enabled*.
- On a Blackberry, you would tap **Settings**, tap **Security and Privacy**, tap **Encryption** and then move the slider to the **On** position for what you want to encrypt. You can select to turn **Device Encryption** and/or **Media Card Encryption** to either encrypt the device and/or an SD card.

SECURE COMMUNICATION ON THE INTERNET

Secure Sockets Layer (SSL) is a protocol used to transmit communications over networks like the Internet, so that any data is encrypted. Sites use SSL to ensure confidential communication, especially in situations when account information, passwords, credit card numbers, financial transactions, or other sensitive information is being sent between you and the server. Email programs and mail servers may also use SSL to ensure that data can't be captured and viewed during transmission. Some sites also use *Transport Layer Security*, which is an updated version of the previous standard, and provide the following security measures:

- **Client authentication**, which means that the client can identify the server, and verify that any data being transferred will be secure.

FIGURE 1.2

Site using HTTPS.

- **Data encryption**, so that any data being transferred will be indecipherable if it's captured en route. In doing so, the server can decrypt any messages the client has sent, and vice versa, but anyone else would only see it as a scrambled message.
- **Integrity checks**, which verifies that the data hasn't been altered in any way while in transit.

As seen in Fig. 1.2, it's easy to identify if your browser has a secure connection by looking at the address bar of your browser. If the site begins with *https://* then you can see that SSL is being used. Also, to the left of this in Chrome and to the right in Internet Explorer, you'll see information about the site's certificate. By clicking on it, additional details are displayed, allowing you to see who verified the certificate, and the type of encryption being used.

It's important to look at the address bar and see when SSL is being used. Even if you're using HTTPS to do business on a site, the initial logon to the site may be using HTTP, meaning your username and password will be sent unencrypted. Just imagine the implications of signing onto a banking site, where everything after the initial logon is encrypted, but the username and password may have been captured by an unknown party.

You can force a browser to use HTTPS by typing *https://* in front of every URL you enter into the browser's address bar. You can also install *HTTPS Everywhere* (www.eff.org/https-everywhere) on your Chrome, Firefox, or Opera browser. Once installed, the browser will try to use HTTPS to connect to any website you visit. If HTTPS isn't supported, then the browser will try using HTTP.

MONITORING ONLINE ACTIVITY

A good way to recognize if you have a security breach is to monitor your online activity. As we'll see in Chapter 6, Protecting yourself on social media, there are a number of ways to keep track of when someone last logged onto your social media accounts. Some provide automatic email notifications when someone logs in from an unfamiliar machine or unsuccessfully tried to logon. Sites often provide a date and time of your last logon attempt.

If some of the sites you use don't provide these abilities, then review previous posts you've made, and periodically check your account. If you see any changes or unfamiliar activity, change your password immediately.

If there are sites you don't use anymore, delete the accounts. Even though you don't use it, walking away from an account without deleting it means the profile information is still there, and so is any content you posted. This means it's a potential target for hackers and a possible source of intrusion for you.

MONITORING YOUR BANK ACCOUNT

It's common for people to use game systems, apps, and websites to make online purchases. What should be equally common is checking your financial account in the days following a purchase. By routinely logging onto your bank and credit card accounts, you can review past purchases and see if you've been overcharged, or charged for items and services you never agreed to buy. It only takes a few minutes to sign-in and look at recent activity, so it shouldn't be a burden. If you see a purchase you don't agree with, dispute it and contact the bank or credit card company to report a possible problem.

IDENTIFYING THE DEVICES YOU USE, AND WHERE YOU USE THEM

It's wise to take an inventory of the devices you have, so you understand what connects to the Internet and what devices you need to manage. By having a list of devices, you won't inadvertently miss one when you change a Wi-Fi password for your home network, update settings, or when troubleshooting which device may be causing a network problem or security risk. Making a list isn't that difficult, but it should include any PCs, mobile devices, game systems, smart TVs, or other devices using your home network or the Internet.

When making the list, you should include any important identifying information, such as its make, model, serial number, and so on. This will be helpful if you ever need to report it stolen, and can help police in returning it.

SEPARATING HOME AND BUSINESS COMPUTERS

When you inventory which devices connect to the Internet, try and make a distinction between those used for personal use, and those used for work. As we saw earlier in this chapter, businesses often have policies stating that anything on a company-owned machine belongs to the organization. This includes email, files, and any other work you've created. Your employer can search any device they've issued you, at any point, and without your permission.

Another reason to separate home and business is support. Because your phone, tablet, laptop, or other device is owned by the business, it's up to them to maintain it. If something breaks, you won't pay to fix it yourself, but would bring it to your IT department. In doing so, you should be aware that they may inspect the machine, and see any files you've saved, email that's been sent, or browser activity. Depending on what's on your machine this could be embarrassing or cause problems in your job.

When you use a business device for personal use, the question arises of who's responsible for any damage. You might find that because you've installed personal apps, let your child use it, or done something else related to the problem, you may be responsible for paying for any repairs. Companies often have policies on proper computer use, and violating them may result in you being responsible for any repairs or replacement.

Bring your own device

To lower the cost of paying for new equipment and decrease training, many companies allow you to *Bring Your Own Device* (BYOD) to the workplace. This can include tablets, laptops, smartphones, and other devices that you pay for, but can use for work-related purposes. When they allow this, the organization will often draft a policy that outlines who's responsible for repairs, support, and so on. Often, only the business-related elements (i.e., network connectivity, corporate email) are supported. In other words, don't expect help from the IT department because Angry Birds isn't working.

Because the device needs to be setup to function with the business' systems, you'll need to bring your personal device to the IT department, so they can configure it to work with their email system, access the corporate network, and install any software needed to adhere to keeping their network secure. This may involve configuring the device with passwords, prohibiting certain types of applications from being installed, ensuring that encryption is used, and so on. To ensure this hasn't changed, they may ask you to bring in the device, so they can audit it.

Although it's convenient to use your own devices at work, you should really consider what's happening here: someone is accessing your device, installing software, changing settings, and possibly limiting your ability to manage it. Depending on the security policies, you might be blocked from visiting certain sites, or unable to install certain apps. The company may also give themselves the ability to remotely wipe your device, which may be required if you quit or get fired. If that happens, not only will you lose work-related information and files, but your personal ones as well. Even if you're not fired, accidents happen, so make sure you regularly back up the device to minimize the loss.

BYOD may also draw you into some strange situations. Many companies have an acceptable use policy, and this may extend to your own device. While it may seem strange having an employer tell you what you can and can't do with your own device those rules exist to protect both you and the employer from inappropriate or potentially dangerous Internet activities. It may get trickier when you also have your own business and save that work on the device used in the BYOD program at your other job. The employer may challenge you on what data on the device belongs to them, what belongs to other clients you have, and what material is your intellectual property.

If you're going to bring your own device to work, consider using one that's only for business use. While it would still give you the benefits of having your own device, it would avoid many of the problems you'll encounter in a BYOD program, and keep your personal files and activities separate.

COMPUTER USE IN PUBLIC PLACES

Not every computer you'll ever use is yours. You may be using a computer in a school laboratory or one at work, one in a library, or borrow someone else's phone or tablet. When using any system that's not yours, you should take steps to prevent your data from being left behind:

- Delete any phone number from the recent calls list on a phone you've borrowed.
- Don't save any logon information. If prompted to save a password on the browser, always click no, as this can be used by someone else to later log in automatically. When logging into a website, ensure that there are no checkboxes checked stating you want the site to remember you. Always log out of any websites you visit.
- Don't save files locally, as these will remain on the computer.
- Don't leave the computer unattended. Walking away from a machine while its logged in may leave sensitive information displayed on the screen.
- You should use InPrivate or Incognito browsing so that details of your browsing activity isn't saved on the machine.
- As we'll see in Chapter 2, Before connecting to the Internet, disable any features that stores passwords.
- Don't use the computer for anything that may reveal financial or sensitive information. You don't know if someone installed a keylogger or other monitoring software, which we will discuss in Chapter 5, Cybercrime.

If you have your own mobile device, you're probably thinking this isn't a problem. After all, you're the only one using your phone or tablet, and you've taken all the necessary precautions to secure it. However, even though the device is yours, any public Wi-Fi (such as hotspots in coffee shops, restaurants, and other public places) won't be under your control. As we'll see in Chapter 2, before connecting to the Internet, there are risks to using someone else's Wi-Fi, and steps you can take to protect yourself.

MOBILE DEVICES

A *mobile device* is any small, portable computing device, such as tablets, smartphones, and other handheld computers. Even though they're small, they have processing power and storage that is greater than many of the computers you might have used years ago. For many people, they've also replaced the desktop computer and other devices they may have had in the past.

Because mobile devices have an operating system, applications, and Internet connectivity, they also have vulnerabilities to threats previously associated with a home PC. This includes virus and malware infections, hacking, privacy issues, and other potential threats discussed throughout this book. If you haven't already configured your mobile device to be more secure, you should do so as we go from chapter-to-chapter.

Mobile apps

Mobile apps are applications that are developed to run on a mobile device. They are often lightweight versions of software created for your home PC, and may be created to perform a single function or a group of related functions. Others are designed with mobility in mind, or exclusively for certain devices.

When you first install an app, you're provided with a screen that tells you what permissions the app is requesting. This may include access to shared files, being able to view your location, being able to read your phone state, and so on. For the application to work, it may need some very deep permission, but you should always review and question what it wants.

First, look at what the app is for, and what you expect it to do. If you downloaded a weather app, it might have a need to access your current, network-based location. After all, it would need to know your current location to tell you what the weather in my area will be like. However, if it's asking for access to shared files, you'd rightly wonder why it would ever need that.

You should also be concerned when an app combines permissions. For example, if you had a free app, it might ask for permission to the Internet so it could display the advertising that funds its development. If the app also asked permission to access the contents of your SD card, you should be concerned. The app would be able to post data from your device (including any photos you have on a phone or tablet) to the Internet.

Certain apps may also want to access your online accounts. For apps provided by Facebook, Twitter, or other social media sites, this is required for basic functionality, so you can post or tweet. As we'll see in Chapter 6, Protecting yourself on social media, there are settings related to your security and privacy that you can configure while using such apps. However, if an app hasn't been developed by the site you're using, you should question whether to install it. Just like anything, you can always read online reviews about the app, and decide if it's okay to use.

In many cases, you can adjust permissions prior to installing, but for some it's a take-it-or-leave-it situation, and you're left with the choice of not installing it or trusting that it's okay. Once an app is installed, you can view it's permissions through the App Manager on your phone or tablet, and adjust the permissions from there. If you do deny an app the permissions it requests or needs, it may not function as expected.

Information shared and collected by apps

One way to view the permissions and privacy of apps installed on your phone is by installing Malwarebytes Anti-Malware Mobile. While we'll discuss the primary purpose of this app (scanning for malware) in Chapter 3, Software problems and solutions, as seen in Fig. 1.3, it also provides an App Manager to view the apps that are running and installed. By clicking in an app on the list, you can close it, view details about it, clear its cache, and view its permissions. If the app is locked up, you can force it to stop, and if it's problematic or no longer needed you can uninstall it.

FIGURE 1.3

Malwarebytes app manager.

The mobile version of Malwarebytes Anti-Malware also includes a Privacy Manager. As seen in Fig. 1.4, you can scan the device to see a list of apps that can cost you money, track your location, has network access (i.e., can connect to the Internet), reads personal information, accesses settings, monitors calls, and other areas of concern. You can also click on the **Security Audit** button to see a list of recommended actions to make your device more secure.

Location feature

Many apps use a location feature that can track where your phone or tablet (and presumably you) are. The feature is useful if you're using GPS software on the device, or other apps that use location-specific information. For example, perhaps you have an app that provides coupons, alerts you on sales, or some other function that needs to know what stores are nearby. If you use such apps, you should leave the location feature on your device turned on, and then review what other apps have permission to see your location. If you don't use any apps that require permission to see your location, then turn it off. To turn off locations services:

- On an Android, tap **Settings**, tap **More**, and then slide the **Location** slider to **Off**.

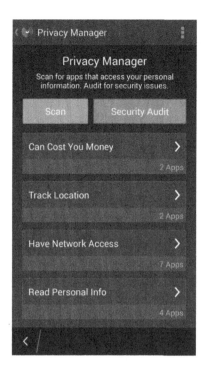

FIGURE 1.4

Malwarebytes privacy manager.

- On an iPhone, tap **Settings**, tap **Privacy**, tap **Location Services**, and then slide the **Location Services** slider to **Off**.
- On a Blackberry, tap Settings, tap Location Services, and then slide the **Location Services** slider to **Off**.

SMART TVs AND GAME SYSTEMS

Internet access has extended from computers and mobile devices to other types of systems. *Smart TVs* are televisions that have integrated features to connect to the Internet, allowing you to surf the Web, stream video, and install various apps. Even if your TV doesn't have these features natively, you may have similar functionality through game systems like Sony PlayStation, Microsoft Xbox, and Nintendo Wii. Because the devices are exposed to the Internet, and have the functionality to browse sites, install software, and perform different functions through various apps, you should be concerned about how vulnerable these devices are, how they're used, and the privacy of information exposed through them.

You should regularly check your system settings, and use any update features to ensure the firmware is up to date. Firmware is a program or set of instructions that's been programmed on to a piece of hardware. The system may also provide notifications instructing you to update it. Any apps and games that you've installed may also check to see if new versions are available. For example, if Netflix is installed, you'll be notified when you open it that you need to upgrade to a new version, and be forced to install it. This fixes any security problems, and may provide new features that weren't previously available.

INTERNET OF THINGS

The *Internet of Things* refers to devices that have the ability to connect to the Internet or local Wi-Fi networks. To do this, the device is assigned an IP address, uniquely identifying it on a network. A washer and dryer might have features that allow it to connect to Wi-Fi to send a message to smartphone apps, allowing you to monitor wash cycles and status. Similarly, a refrigerator might have a panel similar to a tablet on the door, which can be used to keep an inventory of food, and how long it's been there. In addition, there are heart monitors that can connect to a medical specialist's computer, transponders to keep track of livestock, and other devices that use the Internet to communicate and acquire updates.

It's important that you're aware of the devices you own, who supports them, and whether you're responsible for any updates. In the case of a heart monitor, you would obviously leave any maintenance to a specialist, but there may be some you're responsible for. If we were to look at the washer/dryer that connects to the Web to tell an app on your phone about its status or if there's a problem, you would need to update the app when new versions are out. Because there probably isn't antivirus software or other programs available to protect your device, you'll want to ensure your home network itself is secure (as we discuss in Chapter 2, Before connecting to the Internet).

USING DIFFERENT WINDOWS ACCOUNTS

Have you ever considered setting up a single Facebook account for your entire family and allow guests to use it when they visit your house? Of course not, and most people would (rightly so) be shocked at the suggestion. Guests and family members could change settings, compromise your security and privacy, and cause all sorts of problems. As absurd as a shared account sounds, many fail to apply the same logic to accounts on a home computer.

It's common to see home PCs setup so that everyone logs in using the same account, allowing everyone access to files and settings on the computer. It's even worse when it's an administrator account and has full control over the machine. User accounts separate people using the computer into different profiles, allowing them to choose different backgrounds, screensavers, locations to store photos and other files, and have different settings applied to each person. They may also be necessary if you'll be using some of the tools we'll discuss in this book, such as when you want to monitor or apply parental controls to a kid's account.

While you can create multiple user accounts in Windows, the account has to be set as a certain type, which determines the level of control they have over a PC. These are:

- **Standard account**, which provides access but doesn't allow the person to make changes that will affect other users. Almost all of your accounts should be a standard account.
- **Administrator**, which has full control and can install software, create and delete accounts, and make changes to settings that affect everyone. You should only have one administrator account on a machine, and this should only be logged onto when you need to make changes. You shouldn't name any account of this type "Administrator" or "admin" as hackers know these are commonly used. Instead, give the account a different name that doesn't indicate its purpose.
- **Guest**, which should only be used when people need temporary access. It's advisable that you disable any accounts on the machine named "Guest," as it's a common account name. Instead, if you want to provide guest access, create a new account with a different name.

As we'll see in Chapter 10, Protecting your kids, there are also child accounts that you can setup in Windows, which work with parental control features. When a child account is setup on machines using Microsoft Family Safety, you can set time limits that control when and how long a person can use the computer, what kinds of games they can play, allow or block specific programs on the computer, and other settings to protect a child.

The steps involved in creating and managing a user account vary between versions of Windows. If you're using Windows 7, you would do the following:

1. Click on the **Start** button and click **Control Panel** in Windows 7.
2. Under *User Accounts and Family Safety*, click **User Accounts**, and then click **Manage another account**.
3. Click **Create a new account**.
4. Enter the name you want to give the account, which could be the name of the person using it, and select the type of account. In most cases, you'll want to create the account as a **Standard user**.
5. Click **Create Account**.
6. When you've returned to the *Manage Accounts* screen, the new account will appear in the list of existing accounts. By clicking on the account, you can then manage the account, and create a password, change the account type or delete the account.

Setting up a user account in Windows 8x and 10 is a little different, and you'll notice that they try to steer you into creating an online account. It will try to set you up with a Microsoft account, which you would use to logon and use Microsoft services. It also allows you to sync your settings, so that any computer you use will have your profile picture, apps, and other settings when you logon. Despite this, you can still setup a local user account on your PC. To setup a local user account, you would do the following:

1. In Windows 10, click on the **Start** menu, click **Settings**, and then click **Accounts**. In Windows 8*x*, click **Settings**, and then click **Change PC Settings**.
2. Click **Accounts**.
3. In Windows 8*x*, click **Other accounts**. In Windows 10, click **Other user accounts**.
4. Click **Add an account**, and then click **Sign in without a Microsoft account**.
5. Click **Local account**.
6. Enter the username for the account. For simplicity, this can be the name of the person who will use the account.
7. Enter a password, and then reenter it to confirm it. In the **Password** hint box, you can optionally give a hint that will help the person remember their password. When entering a hint, don't reenter the password, or give such an easy hint that anyone reading it will be able to guess the password. Click **Next**, and then click **Finish**.
8. Once finished, you'll see the new account in the listing. By clicking on it, you can then manage the account, and change the password, account type, and modify other aspects of the account.

BIOMETRICS

As we discuss in Chapter 2, Before connecting to the Internet, any password you create should be a strong one that's difficult to guess, and will be harder for password cracking software to break. However, passwords aren't the only way to login to a system. You can also use biometrics.

Biometrics is the process of identifying who you are based on certain characteristics. By looking at unique features like fingerprints, facial features, and so on, a system is able to identify who you are and provide access. If you have a child who may find it difficult remembering a password, or want to save time typing out lengthy passwords, biometrics provides a good solution to securing a system.

A number of operating systems support biometrics. Apple uses fingerprint scanning in iOS devices, while Android supports facial recognition and finger drawn patterns. Windows also supports the ability to logon to the operating system using fingerprint, iris, and facial recognition.

Fingerprint readers prove your identity by scanning an image of your fingerprint, and saving a copy of it to the system. When logging into Windows or a website, you would press your finger on the reader, and it would compare it to the fingerprint on file. There are a number of laptops that come with a built-in fingerprint reader, but you can purchase them separately and install them on your computer.

Windows 10 also provides built-in biometric login features, called *Windows Hello*. With this feature, you can use face, fingerprint, or iris recognition to logon. *Facial recognition* involves the system recognizing your face by reading characteristics, such as the distance between your eyes, ears, and so on. *Iris recognition* involves the system looking at the pattern in one or both of the irises in your eye. When you sit in front of the camera on your computer, the characteristics of your face or eye are compared to what's on file. If it's a match, you're logged in.

To use these features in Windows 10, you would click **Start**, click **Accounts**, and then click **Sign-in** options. Once on this screen, you'll see several options for setting up face, fingerprint, or iris. However, you'll only be able to use these if your computer has a fingerprint reader or camera that supports it.

PHYSICAL SECURITY

When people think of protecting computers, so much is said about software and settings that it's easy to forget someone might easily walk off with a device. Laptop computers, tablets, smartphones, monitors, printers, and even desktop computers are smaller and lighter than ever before, making them easy to steal. This is especially true in public or semipublic areas that can't be or haven't been secured, and situations where your device is unattended.

Thefts are often crimes of opportunity. Generally, a burglar or thief won't target a person. They don't care about you, only that you've made it easier to get what they want. For example, every year police will get calls from people who were outside, left their door unlocked, and later found they were burgled. The thief simply went door-to-door, checking until they found an unlocked house. While you're gardening at the side of the house or mowing the backyard, someone walked out the front door with your laptop, phone, wallet, and other possessions. The lesson here is to make your belongings secure, so it isn't worth the thief's trouble and he or she will move on to another potential target.

While a lock may not seem like much of a deterrent, it's often enough. Laptops and other small devices are often stolen from offices while their owners have taken a quick break or gone to a meeting. Students in dorms may also find things stolen by someone who simply walked in and took it. Keep any USB sticks, music players, or small devices in locked desks, and keep the room, apartment, and house locked so that no one can enter while you're not there.

The usefulness of many modern devices is that they're portable, allowing you to take them with you to class, work, shopping, or any other place you're heading. It also expands the area where they can be stolen. You should never leave devices unattended. Leaving your wallet and tablet in an open purse, setting your phone on a store counter, or walking away from a laptop in a lecture hall presents a tempting target to thieves.

Another place where these devices are often left unattended is in cars. You might think you're your laptop bag or phone is safe on the backseat, but it's visible to anyone walking by. Someone with a slim jim or coat hanger could unlock the car, one of several doors may be unlocked, or smashing the window would allow them to get it. You might think leaving your belongings in the trunk is an option, but this causes another problem: temperature. Laptops, phones, and other devices are susceptible to heat and cold. Leaving your device inside an idle car or trunk means that it can get extremely hot or cold, damaging the device to the point it's irreparable. The same applies to any source of heat or cold that has direct or close proximity to the device.

Impact damage is another common cause of devices being broken. When traveling, keep them on your person or as carry-on luggage. You also should avoid setting them down on the floor, such as when you're waiting in a walkway or lecture hall and decide to set a laptop bag on the floor. Not only can someone easily pick it up and walk away, someone may accidentally kick or step on it. Similarly, avoid setting your devices on any vibrating surfaces, such as machines in a factory setting, as the shaking can jostle connections loose or cause other damage. To avoid damage from impacts and vibration while traveling from place-to-place, use a bag or case that's padded and designed to protect laptops, tablets, or other devices.

LOCKING DOWN HARDWARE

There are a number of ways to prevent hardware from being lost or stolen. Starting at the smallest device, USB sticks or thumb drives are able to store an incredible amount of data, but are small enough to misplace or be taken without noticing right away. If you can't keep them in a locked drawer while not being used, you should have them on your person. Attaching them to your keychain on a lanyard makes them portable and hard to lose. It will be easier to notice it's missing if you leave the USB stick in a computer once you're done.

Many laptops, desktop computers, and larger external storage devices like removable hard drives and CD\DVD drives have built-in slots that are designed to connect with a cable lock. The cable connects to the devices, locks in place, and the other end can be attached to something stable and difficult to move. If the steel cable is attached to a desk leg or an anchor that's affixed to a wall, it makes it almost impossible to steal the device without doing damage or being noticed. The way you release your device is with a key or combination. If you're thinking this might be an expensive way of securing a device, think again. Cable locks are available online and at computer stores for around $30.

SUMMARY

In this chapter we introduced you to some basic elements of cyber safety, and also showed you some of the potential threats you might face in protecting yourself and your devices. We saw how important it is to keep private information private, and showed you some ways to review settings and secure your computer and mobile devices. Now that we've touched on some basics, let's move on to Chapter 2, Before connecting to the Internet, and discuss some of the steps to take before connecting to the Internet.

FURTHER READING

<www.welivesecurity.com/2012/10/10/study-finds-90-percent-have-no-recent-cybersecurity-training/>.

<http://www.theregister.co.uk/2015/08/25/us_class_action_ashley_madison/>.

<http://arstechnica.com/tech-policy/2014/09/fbi-apple-investigating-celebrity-photo-hacks/>.

<https://www.washingtonpost.com/world/national-security/us-charges-snowden-with-espionage/2013/06/21/507497d8-dab1-11e2-a016-92547bf094cc_story.html>.

Before connecting to the Internet

2

INFORMATION IN THIS CHAPTER

- Securing Your Web Browser
- Wi-Fi Security and Safety
- Passwords
- Firewalls
- Physical Security
- Identifying the Devices You Use, and Where You Use Them

When people get a new computer, they often set up an Internet connection and begin having fun. This is a mistake, because the tools you're using to visit sites may not be as secure as you hoped. If you're already using the Internet, then you should review your settings, and ensure that your home network is as secure as you hoped.

SECURING YOUR WEB BROWSER

A browser is your window to the Web, and likely the most used program you'll use on the Internet. Internet or Web *browsers* are programs with a graphical user interface (GUI) that display HTML files (web pages), images, and other content found on the Internet. Using this tool, you're able to navigate the Internet, and view different websites, as well as the various resources and services available through them.

The most popular Web browser used today is Google Chrome (www.google.com/chrome). According to sites like StatsCounter (http://gs.statcounter.com), statistics on the browsers being used by people show that Chrome is used by dramatically more people than any other browser, followed by

- Internet Explorer (IE) (http://windows.microsoft.com/internet-explorer)
- Firefox (https://www.mozilla.org/firefox)
- Safari (www.apple.com/safari)
- Opera (www.opera.com)

Of the various browsers available, Safari is for Apple computers, and comes preinstalled on your Mac. Similarly, IE comes preinstalled with Windows. Although IE was once the major browser on the Web, its popularity has been in steady decline for

The Basics of Cyber Safety. DOI: http://dx.doi.org/10.1016/B978-0-12-416650-9.00002-4

years, as more and more people switching to other browsers like Chrome. Microsoft's new Edge browser (https://www.microsoft.com/en-us/windows/microsoft-edge) is also included with Windows 10, but appears to be catching on slowly with users (0–4% usage, depending on the country) according to StatsCounter. However, as with Safari, IE is installed on your computer when you first buy your computer or install the operating system. As such, many people will simply use what's already installed, enjoy using the preinstalled browser, or use it at least once to download a different browser like Chrome.

NOTE

Being Married to a Specific Browser

Despite your browser preferences, there may be specific reasons as to why you'll want to use IE. Many organizations are "Microsoft shops" and only use their products, and it can be easier for the company's IT department to support one browser. Also, if a business uses Microsoft SharePoint for their Intranet, browser support is limited and users have the best experience using IE. While support for other browsers in Sharepoint 2013 was improved, there are still some features that will only work with IE. That being said, you generally won't need to worry about configuring your browser at work, as these will be set through policies and other methods by the IT department.

Regardless of the browser being used, you should always review its privacy and security settings to make sure you're comfortable with the default settings. Even though the default settings may be what's recommended, you should know what it is or isn't protecting you from, and whether or not those settings are right for you. While we'll be discussing settings throughout this book, in the sections that follow we'll show you a number of settings that should be configured as soon as you start using a browser.

COOKIES

One of the settings you'll want to review and possibly disable involve cookies. *Cookies* are text files sent to the browser by a Web server, and used to store information about your visit to a site. For example, the first time you visit a site, you may be asked to fill out a form and provide information about yourself, or your preferences in using the site. In doing so, when you revisit the site, or move from page-to-page on a site, you won't need to provide this information again, because the browser can provide saved information through the cookie. There are *session cookies*, which are stored temporarily, and deleted once you close the browser, and *persistent cookies* (also called *permanent* or *stored cookies*) that remain on your computer indefinitely or until a specific date is reached when the cookie expires.

Often, cookies don't present a problem, and are beneficial to your experience on the Web. It would after all be annoying to set your preferences (such as safe search options being set to high or off) each and every time you visited a search engine like Bing or Google. While these types of cookies are innocuous, there are certain kinds of cookies that present a risk to your privacy.

Tracking cookies are used to record information and report it back to where the cookie's designer wants the information to go. They record your online activities (i.e., the sites you visit), and send this information to a third party where it's stored with data collected from millions of other people. The data can then be analyzed for marketing and statistical analysis, and may be used to target advertising that appears on different websites you visit. Ever wonder how a particular website seems to have ads that are relevant to you? Now you know. If the tracking cookie is designed to gather names, addresses, and other personal information, you may see ads mentioning your name, or showing businesses close to your location (Fig. 2.1).

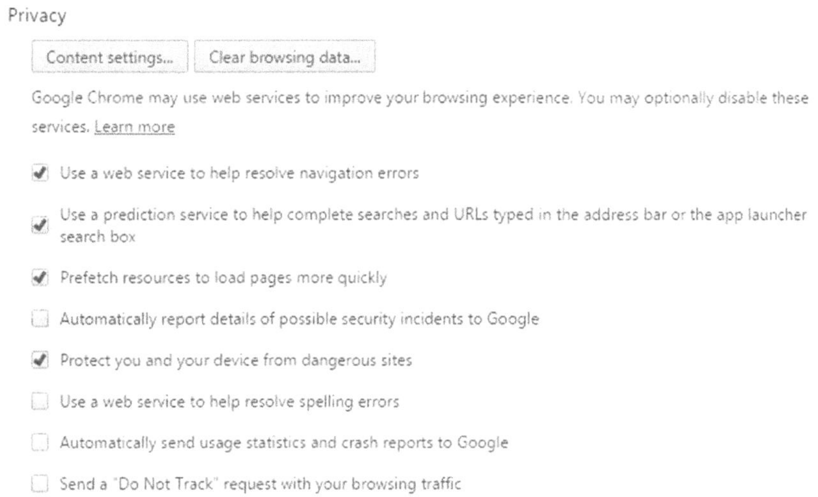

Privacy

| Content settings... | Clear browsing data... |

Google Chrome may use web services to improve your browsing experience. You may optionally disable these services. Learn more

☑ Use a web service to help resolve navigation errors

☑ Use a prediction service to help complete searches and URLs typed in the address bar or the app launcher search box

☑ Prefetch resources to load pages more quickly

☐ Automatically report details of possible security incidents to Google

☑ Protect you and your device from dangerous sites

☐ Use a web service to help resolve spelling errors

☐ Automatically send usage statistics and crash reports to Google

☐ Send a "Do Not Track" request with your browsing traffic

FIGURE 2.1

Chrome privacy settings.

To manage and delete cookies in Chrome, you would perform the following steps:

1. Click on the Chrome menu ☰ , which is located in the upper right-hand corner of the browser.
2. Click **Settings**.
3. Scroll to the bottom of the page and click **Show Advanced Settings**.
4. Scroll to the *Privacy* section of the page (shown in the following figure), and click the **Content Settings** button.
5. To disable cookies, click **Block sites from setting any data**. If you only want to block third-party cookies, then leave the recommended setting to **Allow local data to be set**, but click **Block third-party cookies and site data** so the checkbox appears checked.
6. To view and\or delete any existing cookies, click on the **All cookies and site data...** button.
7. Review the cookies that appear in the dialog box, click on a cookie that you want to remove, and then click the **X** that appears to the right of that entry. To remove all of them, click the **Remove All** button at the top right of the dialog box.

8. Click **Finished**.
9. To request that sites don't track you, click on the **Send a "Do Not Track" request with your browsing traffic** so the checkbox appears checked.

In IE, you can also manage and delete your cookies. In IE 11 for Windows 7 and 8*x*, you would delete cookies by doing the following:

1. After opening IE, click on the gear-shaped Tools icon ⚙ in the upper right-hand corner, select **Safety**, and then click **Delete browsing history**.
2. Click on the **Cookies and website data** checkbox so it appears checked.
3. Click **Delete**.

To adjust your settings for cookies, you would do the following:

1. After opening IE, click on the gear-shaped Tools icon ⚙ in the upper right-hand corner, and click **Internet Options**.
2. On the *Privacy* tab, adjust the slider in the *Settings* section to a level that you feel comfortable with. Information on what occurs with each setting appears to the right of the slider. Moving the slider to the top will block all cookies.
3. To override the settings and block third-party cookies completely, click on the **Advanced** button. When the *Advanced* dialog box appears, click **Override automatic cookie handling** so the checkbox appears checked. Under *Third-party cookies*, click on the **Block** option. Click **OK**.
4. Click **OK**.

TRACKING PROTECTION

Earlier in the chapter you learned how to set one option in Chrome that has the browser send a request to sites to not track you. In doing so, your browsing activities are kept more private. You can (and should) also set Tracking Protection on IE to help prevent browsing information from being sent to third-party sites, which are sites that are external from the one you're actually visiting. To start, you need to add a tracking list, which is essentially a blacklist of sites that provide third-party content, and collect information about your browsing activity.

Using IE 11, you would add a tracking list by doing the following:

1. After opening IE, visit the *Internet Explorer Gallery* (www.iegallery.com/en-us/trackingprotectionlists), and click **Add**.
2. Click **Add List** when prompted.
3. Repeat this for any additional tracking lists you want to add.

Now that you have one or more tracking lists installed, you need to turn on Tracking Protection. If you're using IE 11 on Windows 7 or 8*x*, you would follow these steps:

1. After opening IE, click on the Tools icon, select **Safety**, and then click **Turn on Do Not Track request**.
2. When prompted, click **Turn On**.

If you're using IE 11 on Windows 10, you would follow these instructions:

1. After opening IE, point your mouse at the lower right-hand corner of the screen, and then move the mouse pointer up. Click **Settings**.
2. Click **Privacy**.
3. Turn *Block content on sites from services that could track my browsing* to **On**.
4. After setting Tracking Protection on IE, you'll need to restart your browser.

DISABLING AND MANAGING POP-UPS

A *pop-up* is a small window or other display area that opens when you click or move your mouse over a link or a particular area of a web page, or when you first open the page itself. The pop-up is generally smaller than the initial window you were in, and may be used to display a small web page, text, an image, or a GUI interface that allows you to provide input. It may appear in a different window, or overlaid on the page you're currently viewing. Pop-ups can be aggravating when surfing the Web when you have multiple pages displaying advertisements, and taking you to sites that you had no intention of going to. At worst, the pop-up may be used to automatically run malicious code, download viruses or malware, or gather information about you.

Despite the inherent dangers and annoyances of pop-ups, they aren't all bad. There may be some sites where pop-ups are used for basic functionality. For example, if you were to visit a chat site, you might click on a link to enter a particular forum, or open a pop-up that allows you to chat with one or more people. In doing so, the pop-up might be running a Java applet or some other kind of program that allows you to chat with others in the new window. Because you went there to chat, and the design of the site requires pop-ups to be used, you expect this behavior to use the basic functionality of the site.

Now that you're aware of the potential problems and benefits of pop-ups, you should configure your browser to block most pop-ups, except the ones on sites that you explicitly allow. To disable and/or manage pop-ups in Chrome, you would follow these steps:

1. In Chrome, click on the Chrome menu in the upper-right hand side of the browser.
2. Click **Settings**, scroll down to the bottom of the page, and click **Show advanced settings**.
3. In the *Privacy section*, click the **Content settings** button.
4. When the dialog appears, scroll down to the *Pop-ups* section, and click **Do not allow any site to show pop-ups (recommended)**. By default, this will be selected.
5. To specify which sites are allowed to use pop-ups, click on the **Manage exceptions** button
6. When the dialog appears, enter the web address (URL) of the site that's allowed to use pop-ups in the box. To allow any page or subsite under a particular website to show pop-ups, add [*] at the beginning of the Web address. For

example, if you wanted anything under delphiforums.com to use pop-ups, you would enter "[*].delphiforums.com." To the right of the box, click on the dropdown box and select **Allow**.

7. To remove a previously added site from using pop-ups, click the **X** to right of the entry.
8. Click **Finished**.

IE also has settings that allow you to disable and/or manage pop-ups. To configure IE, do the following:

1. In IE, click on the **Tools** button, and then click **Internet Options**.
2. Click on the **Privacy** tab, and under the *Pop-up Blocker* section, click on the **Turn on Pop-up Blocker** so that the checkbox appears checked.
3. If there are some sites you want to allow pop-ups, click on the **Settings** button. The *Pop-up Blocker Settings* dialog box will appear.
4. To ensure you're notified of when a pop-up is blocked, look at the settings in the *Notifications and blocking level section*. If the **Show Notification bar when a pop-up is blocked** checkbox is unchecked, click on it so it appears checked.
5. Review the settings in the *Blocking level* section. By default it is set to **Medium**, which blocks most automatic pop-ups. This is sufficient for most people, but if you want to block all pop-ups, click on the dropdown list and select **High**. If you want to allow all pop-ups for secure sites, set it to **Low**, but be aware that this is the least secure setting.
6. To enable pop-ups on certain sites, enter the website you want to allow pop-ups to work in the **Address of website to allow** box, and then click **Add**. The site will now appear in the listing of *Allowed sites* below this box.
7. To remove a site you previously allowed, click on the site in the *Allowed sites* listing, and then click the **Remove** button at the right of this list.
8. Click **Close**.
9. Click **OK**.

WI-FI SECURITY AND SAFETY

When you sign-up for Internet access with an Internet Service Provider (ISP), you may have had a technician come to your home and setup devices, or you may have set them up yourself. In many cases, it probably allowed you to connect your computer, phone, or other devices wirelessly, giving you a home network. Before you purchased Internet service, you may have even had a home network already installed. This question is whether this network is secure, and keeps others out.

If you have a smartphone or other mobile devices, you've probably searched for open networks, which will allow you to use another person's Internet connectivity. In using it, you become a part of that person's network, acquire an IP address, and can surf the Web on their dime. The problem is that you would have to pay additional fees if others caused you to exceed a monthly data transfer limit (i.e., the maximum amount you can download and upload), and experience performance problems as bandwidth limits were reached. If a hacker gained access, they might gain access to your computer or monitor the traffic going across your network to view unencrypted passwords and other data. If someone downloaded movies, music, or other pirated material from a site, or visited sites with illegal content (such as child pornography), it would appear to the ISP that you were the one downloading or accessing those sites. As you can see, it's important that your wireless network is secure, and allows access to only the computers and devices that you control. Before we go into the steps involved, let's first look at what makes up your network.

A BASIC UNDERSTANDING OF COMPONENTS USED TO CONNECT TO THE INTERNET

When you connect to the Internet, there are a number of components involved. Moving forward from you, there is the device you're using. Whether it's a computer, smartphone, tablet, or another device, it connects to the Internet using a combination of hardware (physical components) and software (programs). Generally, it will use a network card that allows it to communicate over a *network*, which is a series of interconnected computers and devices. A network cable may be plugged into an *Ethernet* port with the other end plugged into a router (which we'll discuss next), or the device may have a chip or card that allows it to connect wirelessly. This wireless connection is called *wifi* or *Wi-Fi*.

A *router* is used to connect several computers or devices together. This allows you to have a home network, and enables multiple devices to use a single Internet connection. You may plug the network cable directly into the router, but if you have a wireless router, you'll generally connect without using cables.

The router may connect into another device called a *modem*. The modem is used to connect to the Internet, and communicate across a particular medium. For example, if you have dial-up access, a telephone modem is used. Similarly, if you subscribed to a DSL service, it will connect over the phone line using a DSL modem. Other mediums will use different kinds of modems. If you have cable access to the Internet, a cable modem is used, while satellite service will use a satellite adapter. The kind of modem you use depends on the type of service you purchased, which the modem will connect to, allowing you to access content and services on the Internet.

Because technology has the tendency to converge, you may be thinking that you're missing something in how you connect to the Internet. There may be only one device that you connect computers and other devices to, which then allows you to connect to the Internet. This is because the router may be built into the modem. Instead of separate modems and routers, a multipurpose device may be used, which consists of a router and modem in one.

CONFIGURING YOUR ROUTER

At the most basic level, you or a technician will use a browser to logon to the router, and set the required information that allows devices on your home network to connect to the Internet. Aside from that, once you're on the Internet, everything just seems to work. You may think you're done, but all you may have is an insecure network that provides you, your neighbors, and anyone close enough to connect with free access to the Web. What you need to do now is make your Wi-Fi secure by configuring the wireless router properly.

Changing the administrator username/password

One of the first things you should change on a wireless network is the password and (if possible) the username of the administrator account. A *password* is a string of characters that is used to verify access, while a *username* is the name of an account that determines what access you have to a system. In this case, the administrator account is used to logon to the router and change its settings.

Routers come with a default username and password that allows you to logon after you first install it, and it isn't difficult to hack into a router that hasn't had this changed. If you know the manufacturer and model of the router, you can look up the specific default account name and password online at sites like www.routerpasswords.com, and if you don't have this information, it's still easy to guess. For example, if it's a Linksys router, you can logon as the administrator on most models using the username *Admin*, and a blank password.

If you check your installation instructions, or look up your router's make and model on the Internet, you should find that there's an IP address that you can enter into your browser to access the router's settings. For example, for a Linksys router, you would enter http://192.168.1.1 into the address bar of your browser, and then enter a default username and password. In the case of our examples and figures, we'll use a Linksys router, which is commonly used on home networks. If you're using a different router, similar options should be available.

After logging in, you'll see a screen as shown in Fig. 2.2. By clicking on the **Administration** tab, and then clicking **Management**, you'll see two boxes where

FIGURE 2.2

Changing default password on Linksys router.

you can enter a new password and then reenter it to confirm that its typed correct. After entering the new password, click the **Save Password** button at the bottom of the screen.

Service set identifier

The next step is to change the name of your wireless network, which is also called an SSID (Service Set Identifier). This is a unique identifier that's 32 characters, and will be broadcast to people looking to connect to a network. Generally, when you first install the router, it's set to the name of the manufacturer or ISP that you purchased or rented it from. For example, it may be *Linksys*, *ComCast*, or *Dlink*. This is a problem, because it shows the type of modem you're using or the name of your ISP, which provides a starting point for hackers. If I have this, and you haven't made other configuration changes, I can look up on the Internet and see what the default username / password combination is, as well as other useful information about your router.

To change the name, you need to navigate through the router's interface to find the area where the name is set. For example, on the Linksys router, you'll generally find this by clicking on the **Setup** tab, and then clicking **Basic Setup**. On this page, you'll see a section that specifies the router's name. Change this to a unique name, which is what will appear when looking for a Wi-Fi network to connect with.

Security mode

The next area to configure is the security mode and passphrase that will be used to connect to the network. A *passphrase* is similar to a password in that it's used to verify authorized access, but is longer and can contain multiple words. The security mode determines whether encryption is used to protect any data that's transmitted between your computer or mobile device and the router, and requires that someone connects using a Wi-Fi password (discussed in Section SSID Passphrase). If no encryption is used, then someone could use a tool to capture network traffic (as we'll see in chapter: Cybercrime), and see usernames, passwords, and other data being passed over the network.

On a Linksys router, you set the security mode by clicking on **Wireless** and then clicking **Wireless Security**. You'll generally see a dropdown box of various security modes that can be set for connecting to the router. You will want to set it to the most secure method that will support the devices connecting to your network. Some of your options will include:

- None or Disabled, which provides no encryption whatsoever.
- WEP, which stands for *Wired Encryption Protocol*, was the first encryption available for wireless networks. As its name states, it was designed to provide the same security as wired networks, but it has a number of security flaws and isn't difficult to break.

- WPA, which stands for *Wi-Fi Protected Access*, was created as an interim measure to deal with the vulnerabilities of WEP. It is more secure than WEP, but less secure than its successor.
- WPA2, which is the second version of WPA, uses the Advanced Encryption Standard (AES) for encryption. As we discussed in the previous security mode, you may see WPA2-Personal and WPA2-Enterprise, which are designed for home and enterprise networks, respectively.
- Because some of these modes require additional servers and configuration, you'll want to use the most secure method of connecting (WPA2). If you have older wireless clients, you'll probably want to set your router to use WPA2/WPA Mixed Mode. With this setting, the router will use AES if possible, but also allow older wireless clients to connect with WPA. Using this mode, you can have clients using WPA or WPA2 to coexist on the same SSID, so you won't need multiple routers with different security modes on your network.

To enable clients to use encryption, you'll need to set an associated passphrase, which we'll discuss further in the next section. The passphrase not only grants access to the wireless network, but is also the encryption password. It is a preshared key that is used in the process of encrypting and decrypting packets of data sent between a computer or other device and the router.

SSID passphrase

As mentioned, routers generally work right out of the box, so there won't be a passphrase to connect to the network when it's initially setup. To force a person to provide a password, you need to set one. On different routers, this is called a SSID password, Security Key, WPA Key, Pre-Shared Key, or Passphrase. This is different from the administrator password we discussed earlier. When a person attempts to connect to your Wi-Fi, they'll be asked for this password, and will join your network as if they were wired directly to the router. Because it can be saved on the person's computer or device, they don't need to reenter it each time, so you should feel free to make it as long and difficult to guess as possible.

On a Linksys router, you set the passphrase on the same page where you set the Security Mode (clicking on **Wireless** and then clicking **Wireless Security**). Below the Security Mode you selected, you'll see a box to enter a passphrase. Upon entering this passphrase, click the **Save Settings** button at the bottom of the screen.

USING OTHER PEOPLE'S WI-FI

There are always risks in connecting to a wireless network that isn't your own. Even if you've gone to exceptional effort to secure your own Wi-Fi, when you use someone else's, you trust that a complete stranger has done the same. There is no guarantee that they or others using the Wi-Fi aren't running software to capture network traffic going over that connection.

If you're using open Wi-Fi networks like the ones you'll find at coffee shops, restaurants, airports, and libraries, the connection generally isn't encrypted. You'll be able to tell because the icon for that Wi-Fi connection doesn't have a lock symbol on it, and you didn't have to enter a passphrase. Any unencrypted web pages, forms, or logons you connect to over the Wi-Fi will be visible to anyone using the right tools (which we discuss in chapter: Cybercrime) without you ever knowing.

As we discussed in Chapter 1, What is cyber safety?, you should always pay attention to the URL of the site you're connecting with, and see whether it's using HTTPS. If you're doing something sensitive, you'll want to ensure that the browser is going to encrypted pages whenever possible. You should also avoid using the insecure Wi-Fi for any business that could be used by others for financial gain, or cause significant problems for you. This would mean avoiding any online banking, checking credit card balances, and so on.

If you're connecting using a laptop running Windows, you'll be prompted the first time connecting to a network to choose the network location. You should always select **Public network** for any insecure networks in public places. This prevents others from seeing your computer on the wireless network, and will also configure the connection so that you're better protected from any malicious software while surfing. This setting automatically locks down many of the settings on your computer, providing you with the best level of security. In using it, Windows automatically turns off file sharing, network discovery, and public folder sharing. The only other time you'll want to specify a connection as Public is if you're using a mobile broadband connection, or you don't use a router and connect directly to the Internet.

You should also be aware that just because a public wireless hotspot appears to be free Wi-Fi provided by a business or some other legitimate source, this may not be the case. A hacker can easily setup a honeypot network. When searching for Wi-Fi networks, you may see something that says "Public Wi-Fi" or another name related to a business that offers free Internet, but it's actually a hotspot created to entice people into connecting. Once connected, your security is compromised because you're part of a network that's sole purpose is to monitor traffic, capture data, and possibly infect or hack into computers that have joined it. When possible, ask the business for the name of their free Wi-Fi, so you know you're connecting to the right network.

SHARING YOUR WI-FI WITH OTHERS

It's not uncommon for people to share their Wi-Fi with others, but doing so carries its share of risks and concerns. While we discussed some issues with insecure networks, there are potential problems when sharing your Wi-Fi with anyone. If you've used encryption on your Wi-Fi, then it's important to be careful about handing out the SSID passphrase. Think of the passphrase like a key to your house, and only give it to those you trust.

Once someone has the passphrase, it can be saved to the device and used anytime they're in range of your Wi-Fi. If that person lost their phone, tablet, etc., anyone who found it could then get into your network. This might seem not worth worrying about until you consider that when someone connects to your Wi-Fi, their device could see other computers, as well as printers, shared files, and other resources on your network. Unless you're careful about what's shared on a computer, and the locked down systems they shouldn't have access to, you may be making more than just your Internet connectivity available to them.

Another problem is if the person's computer or mobile device is compromised. Just because you're running antivirus and antimalware scans doesn't mean everyone does. Allowing infected systems onto your network could leave you open to malicious software, worms, viruses, and other threats.

While most people give access thinking it will be temporarily, this isn't always the case. If you're living in an apartment, perhaps you and your neighbor decided to split the cost of Internet connectivity. Maybe your neighbor is out-of-work, and you decided to be the Good Samaritan and given them your SSID passphrase until they're back on their feet. In both these cases, the ISP would probably view the extra household as stealing Internet. If the neighbor was visiting, got the password to check email on a phone, and then went home and setup everything to use your Wi-Fi, you'd probably feel the same. If the terms of service with your ISP prohibit this, you could be penalized or have your service dropped.

If you're concerned about someone piggybacking on your Internet, or the possibility of an unknown person gaining access through a stolen device or learning the password, there is an easy solution. Simply change the password. You can go into the router and change passphrase for your Wi-Fi at any time, which forces anyone attempting to connect to provide the new passphrase.

Setting up a guest network

A way to avoid many of the problems caused by people accessing your Wi-Fi is to setup guest access. In doing so, they are using a separate wireless network, and visitors won't have access to your main network.

When a computer or device connects to a guest network, the person always needs to enter the guest password before they can access the Internet. The password can and should be different from the SSID passphrase you set for your main network, and you'll often find that people use a shorter, more user friendly password than the complex passphrase used for setting up devices on the main network.

On a Linksys router, you can setup guest access by logging into the router, as we saw earlier, and then clicking on the **Wireless** tab and then clicking **Guest Access**. On this page, look for the option to *Allow Guest Access* and click on the **Yes** option. Click the **Change** button to set the *Guest Password*, and then enter a new password. In the *Total Guests Allowed* dropdown, set the total number of devices that can be connected at any given time. You should keep this number low. Finally, to prevent everyone from seeing the name of your guest Wi-Fi, click **Disabled** in the *SSID Broadcast* section. This final step doesn't provide much security, but it will prevent people from easily seeing that the guest network exists. Anyone attempting to connect to your guest network will know it exists, and need to manually add it as a wireless hotspot.

Some routers also provide the ability to set a separate security mode for guest access. If a Security Mode option exists on your router for guest access, you can select what type of encryption to use for the separate network, and even use a different security mode from what's used on your regular network.

NOTE

Supporting Older Devices

Guest Wi-Fi is also useful if you have older devices (e.g., a Nintendo DSi game system) that can't connect using stronger encryption like WPA2 or WPA, and can only connect with WEP. In such situations, you can have your main network using stronger security, while the guest Wi-Fi is less secure. If your router doesn't support using a different security mode for a guest network, then you may want to consider purchasing a separate router to support the older devices rather than compromising your main network with lessor encryption. It is strongly advisable to use the strongest encryption possible.

PASSWORDS

As we discussed earlier, *passwords* are strings of letters, numbers, and/or special characters that are used to verify your identity, while *passphrases* are longer and can consist of multiple words. Whether you're logging onto your computer, a social media site, an application, or other systems and applications that require you to prove that you're authorized to have access, passwords and passphrases serve as a basic line of security.

STRONG PASSWORDS

There are a number of factors that can make a good or bad password. Strong passwords are more complex, more difficult to guess, and will take longer to crack using software. To create a strong password, you should include the following characteristics:

- The length should be at least 8 characters, with 12–14 characters being a better target to shoot for. The rule here is that longer is better.
- A mix of uppercase letters (A, B, C,...), lowercase (a, b, c,...)letters, numbers (0, 1, 2 ,...), and special characters (` ~ ! @ # $ % ^ & * ( )_ - + = { } [ ] \ | : ; " ' < >, . ? /)
- It should not contain any dictionary words (e.g., password, monkey,...). This includes complete words merged together like *LetMeIn!*

Even when following this criterion, you can still create a weak or mediocre password. For example, *P@$$w0rd* would follow all these rules, but a tool to crack passwords would recognize that you're using symbols to replace letters and crack it easily. Avoid using characters that look like letters as a replacement for letters.

The best way to determine if you have a strong password is to test it, such as by using the password checker tool at Online Domain Tools (http://password-checker. online-domain-tools.com/). If you enter a password on this page and click the **Check!** button, it will analyze its strength, provide information about the properties of the password (such as length, number of upper and lower case letters), and whether it is a frequently used password used by others. It will also provide estimates as to how long it would take to crack it using brute-force password cracking tools, which we discuss in Chapter 5, Cybercrime.

CHANGING PASSWORDS

Nothing good lasts forever, including good passwords. Just because you've created a strong password you can remember, you shouldn't keep it indefinitely. Even a strong password can be compromised, and if someone else has it, they can use it to access your account. If you change your password every 30–180 days, it will limit how long the password is useful to anyone who has it.

NOTE

Cracking Passwords

If you think it's difficult to crack a password, think again. The most basic way of getting someone's password is *shoulder surfing*, where you simply watch what they're typing: noticing each of the keys they strike. Even if it's a complex password, you can often figure out the password if you watch someone enter it a few times.

Any passwords you create should be different from previous passwords. Some people rotate through several passwords, so if a hacker knew a previous password, he would only need to wait until you reused it. This is why systems will often keep a history of previously used passwords to prevent you from reusing the same passwords.

Making the password significantly different is also important. If someone guessed your last password, making a minor change would mean the guesser had most of your password. Increasing a number in your password (such as changing *YbSane1?* to *YbSane2?*) or making other logical increments (like changing *January1!* to *February1!*) might fool a system into seeing the password as different from previous ones, but lots of people change passwords in this way. It wouldn't fool a hacker, especially if he knew you had a habit of doing this.

PASSWORD POLICIES

Companies enforce how their employees create and change passwords through policies on the network. In doing so, they can set how frequently you must change the password, how long it must be, how often it can be reused, and how complex it must be. Depending on the operating system you're using, you can also use policies to

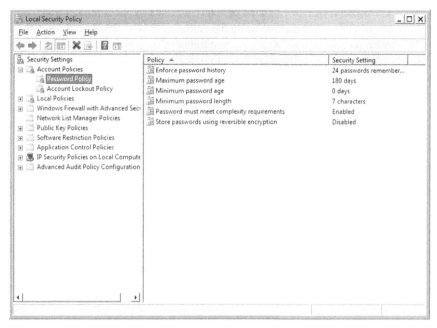

FIGURE 2.3

Local security policy.

control passwords used on your personal computer. In doing so, you can ensure that any of the accounts logging onto an account on that machine uses strong passwords.

If you're using the nonhome versions of Windows 7, 8x, and 10, and logged on with an Administrator account, you can also enforce passwords using the Local Security Policy. In Windows 7, you can start this tool by clicking **Start**, typing *secpol.msc* in the **Run** dialog, and then clicking **OK**. In Windows 8x and 10, you can type *Local Security Policy* in the start menu search, and then press the **Enter** key on your keyboard. As shown in Fig. 2.3, once the tool appears, you can then click in the left pane to expand **Account Policies**, and then click **Password Policy**.

To change any of the policies regarding passwords, double-click on the policy in the right pane, and then modify the setting. The available options are as follows:

- **Enforce password history**, which enforces the number of unique passwords that must be used before an old one can be reused. You can set this to a value between 0 and 24. At the very least, change it to 1 so the user can't "change" their password to an existing one.
- **Maximum password age**, which is the number of days before users must change their passwords. You can set a password to expire after 1–999 days. If set to 0, passwords never expire. Microsoft recommends that you set this to 70 days, but the important thing to remember is not to set it so high that it

provides hackers with an extended period of access to your computer and network, or so low that anyone using the computer has to change it frequently.

- **Minimum password age**, which is the number of days that the password is used before a user can change it. If set to 0, a user can change it immediately. Otherwise, you can set it to a value less than the maximum password age (unless that value has been set to 0). You should set this to a value of at least 1 day, so that users can only change the password once a day.
- **Minimum password length**, which sets how short a password can be. It can be set to 1–14 characters, or set to 0 if no password is required. You should set this to a value of 8 or higher.
- **Password must meet complexity requirements**, which can be enabled or disabled to enforce that passwords must not contain the username, any part longer than two characters of the user's full name, be six or more characters in length, and contain at least three of the following: uppercase letters, lowercase letters, numbers, and special characters that we described earlier. This should be enabled.
- **Store passwords using reversible encryption**, which saves a user's password without encryption (i.e., as plaintext). You should leave this disabled unless otherwise required.

As you should expect, these settings only affect the passwords used by user accounts on the computer, and have no effect on passwords on websites or applications.

SETTING UP SECURITY QUESTIONS

When you setup your account, you're often required to provide answers to security questions, which are later used if you forget your password. These questions are often the same, regardless of whether it's a social media site, online retailer, or your bank. You might be asked for your mother's maiden name, the town you were born in, or some other seemingly innocuous question. The problem is when others know these answers. If a hacker can see a maternal uncle's name on a list of Facebook friends, he's got your mother's maiden name. If you've mentioned where you were born, he's got that answer too. The hacker can now click on the "Forgot Your Password" option, reset your password, and take over your account. Even if they access one account, the problems and embarrassment they can cause can be significant.

If this seems unlikely, consider what happened during the 2008 US presidential election, when Sarah Palin's online email account was hacked. The hacker looked up details about the vice presidential candidate on Wikipedia, and then used information about the high school she attended and her birthdate in Yahoo!'s account recovery. Clicking a link to indicate a forgotten password, he answered the questions, accessed her account, and then posted her emails on another site (Zetter, 2008).

Obviously, it's best to restrict who has access to your information, but that's easier said than done. To get someone's birthdate, simply look at their Facebook wall and see how many people wish the person a happy birthday, and mention which birthday it is. Some simple math will reveal their birthdate.

Some sites have recognized the problem, and allow users to create their own custom security questions. When presented with this option on a site, don't simply recreate one of the standard security questions we've been discussing. Instead, try and come up with a question and answer that is unique to you, and isn't something people would normally know. The food your mom made for Sunday dinners as a kid, or the person you hated most in grade 3, might be something no one else knows. Using difficult to answer questions, relating to things you'd never admit to or mention online, are the kind of security questions that will really make your account secure.

Another way to deal with the security questions is to make up false answers. There is no reason that you have to give your actual personal information to answer these questions. When asked about the name of your first pet, or the make and model of your first car, give the name of your favorite pet or favorite car instead. Using an easy-to-remember lie can sometimes be better than the truth. If however you're worried you'll forget, you could include the answers in a password list, which we'll discuss next.

REMEMBERING PASSWORDS

Passwords can be difficult to remember, which is a reason why so many people develop bad habits when creating passwords, or reusing the same passwords on multiple sites. There are however a number of tricks and tools that can be used to manage your accounts and passwords.

The best kind of password is one that is long and random, or at least appears to be random. A trick to creating a strong password is to think of a phrase that's meaningful, and will be one you can remember. For example, if you took the phrase "My daughter's birthday is on Oct 18, 2015!", you could change it to *Mdb-dayionOct18!*. Although it's a strong password, it would be easy for you to remember, so long as you remember the phrase.

Another way to remember passwords is to take the strong password, and try and read it phonically. For example, if your password was *dRzorm!In9egs*, you might recite it in your mind as "Dr. zorm! I need 9 eggs" each time you typed it. The more you typed it this way, the easier it will be to remember.

Because you should use a different password for each site and application you use, you should consider creating a password list. This doesn't mean a set of sticky notes on your monitor, or a piece of paper tucked in the top drawer of your desk. In companies, it's common for IT departments to keep a list of all administrative usernames and passwords stored in a safe, which can be retrieved in the event of a disaster. The list may be printed, or stored on a USB stick. Even if you don't have a safe, you probably have a secure location in your house where you keep a copy of your mortgage, insurance policy, and other important documents that the list can be kept with.

As we'll see in the sections that follow, there are apps available for mobile devices and computers, which allow you to keep track of the various usernames and passwords you use. The password management software allows you to store this information into a central location, referring to it as needed and/or using features to automatically log onto a site. When using these tools, your credentials may be saved on the computer or mobile device, meaning that if it's lost or stolen, your passwords are gone as well. This is a reason why you'd want to keep that password list in a secure location, so you'll still be able to get into your online accounts and change the passwords when needed.

You should also remember to keep it up-to-date. A common problem with changing passwords is that many people forget their passwords a short time after changing them. Give yourself time to get used to the new password, and remember to update any entries you make in a password list or any password management software you use. You'd be surprised how many calls a company's Help Desk will get from people who changed their password and forgot it by the time they got back from lunch.

TOOLS

There are a number of tools for creating, storing, and generating new passwords. They take a lot of the guesswork out of keeping an account secure and keeping track of your credentials. However, as we'll see, not all of the features and tools that are available for password management should be used, or used in all circumstances.

Password generators

A password generator is a tool that automatically creates a random password. Some products will include such a tool with its other products, but if you don't have one, there are free ones you can download and online generators you can use. When choosing a password generator, make sure you're using a trustworthy site, and not the one that's going to gather information about the sites you're using, your interests, and so on.

A good password generator is available on the Norton website (https://identity-safe.norton.com/password-generator/), which can be used online or downloaded and run from your computer. When visiting this tool, you'll see that you can specify the criteria for your password (i.e., length, whether to include letters, numbers), and the number of passwords to create. After clicking the **Generate Password(s)** button, your new password(s) will be presented to you.

Password vaults

Password vaults or *password managers* are programs that keep your passwords in a secure location. When you use this software, the passwords are encrypted, and you use a single master password to access them. Depending on the tool being used, these passwords may be stored on a secure website, or on your local computer. In using it, you only need to remember one password to view the database of other passwords for various sites and apps. Some of the password managers available include

- LastPass (https://lastpass.com)
- RoboForm (www.roboform.com)

FIGURE 2.4

RoboForm.

Each of the above-mentioned tools are free, although premium versions can be purchased. Both have versions available that work with mobile devices and Windows computers, while RoboForm also has a version that works with Macs. By installing an extension to your browser, you navigate to a site, enter your username and password, and have the option to save it to the password manager. After this, you can navigate to the bookmarked sites and automatically login.

At any time, you can view and edit the logon information you've saved. As shown in Fig. 2.4, tools like RoboForm also provide additional fields, where you can add additional notes about the account.

Password management tools also provide a number of other common features. It's common for them to have password generators that can be used to create strong passwords. Many also have the ability to automatically fill out Web forms, such as online job applications, order forms on retail sites, and contest forms. By entering your contact information into the tool, it can then pass your name, address, and other contact information into fields on whatever Web form is loaded in your browser. With a click of a button, you can fill out most or all of a form.

When using password management software, there are serious considerations you need to make. If the tool saves passwords on the local computer, then all of these may be lost to you if the computer itself is stolen. As such, many provide the ability to print a list of your passwords, which you can then keep in a safe place. If it's stored on the cloud, then this isn't a concern, unless you've used a weak password to access your other passwords. If you have, someone could enter the easy-to-guess password or easily crack the password to gain access to all of your account credentials.

Passwords stored in IE

Even without a password manager installed, browsers commonly provide the ability to save passwords. When you logon to a site for the first time, you're prompted whether you'd like to save the password. If you choose yes, the next time you visit the site and enter your username, the browser will automatically fill in the password field. This can be dangerous if you're using a public computer, or someone else is browsing under your Window's or Google account. If you're using someone else's computer, never agree to save the password.

Saving passwords is not without its vulnerabilities. For example, when you save a password in IE, it's encrypted and stored in the Windows Registry. While this might seem secure, as we'll see in Chapter 5, Cybercrime, there are tools that can easily view the username and password being used to logon to a site. These potential threats should always be considered when you're deciding whether to use a third-party password management system or the native features of a browser. If you are going to use third-party software, you should disable the browser's ability to save passwords.

IE has AutoComplete features to save passwords, and fill in information on forms automatically. When you visit a site and begin entering your username, it will provide a dropdown list of possible data to fill into that field, and after selecting an account from the list, it will fill in the password. To enable or disable IE's ability to save passwords on Windows 7 and 8x, you would do the following:

1. In IE, click on the gear-shaped **Tools** button, and then click **Internet Options**.
2. Click on the **Content** tab, and in the *AutoComplete* section, click the **Settings** button.
3. To delete all your previously saved passwords, click the **Delete AutoComplete History** button.
4. To prevent IE from saving passwords, click on the **Usernames and passwords on Forms** checkbox so it appears unchecked. To allow IE to save passwords, click this checkbox so it appears checked, and then ensure the **Ask me before saving passwords** checkbox is also checked.
5. Click **OK**.

On Windows 10, you would disable the ability to save passwords by doing the following:

1. After opening IE, point your mouse at the lower right-hand corner of the screen, and then move the mouse pointer up. Click **Settings**.
2. Click **Options**, and in the *Passwords* section, turn **Offer to save passwords when I log into sites** to **Off**.

In Windows 8x and 10, you can also view and remove stored passwords for sites by going to **Control Panel**, and then clicking on **Credential Manager**. Once open, click on **Web Credentials** and a list of passwords for sites will appear on the screen below. By clicking on the down arrow beside an entry, you can view information on the account and password used for that site. To view the password, click the **Show** link beside the password field, and then enter your Window's password. To remove the stored password, click on the **Remove** link below it, and then click **Yes** on the dialog box that appears.

Passwords stored in Chrome

When you visit a site in Chrome on your computer, you're also presented with a dialog that asks if you want to save the password. You can click **Save Password** to save the password, **Nope** to not save it, or **Never for this site** to never be asked again when visiting that site. Mobile devices are presented with simple **Yes** or **Never** options. To manage passwords in Chrome, or disable Chrome's ability to store passwords, you would do the following:

1. Click on the Chrome menu that appears as three horizontal bars in the upper right hand side of the browser.
2. Click **Settings**.
3. Scroll to the bottom of the page and click **Show advanced settings**.
4. Scroll to the *Passwords and Forms* section. If you want to turn off the ability to save passwords, click on the **Offer to save your web passwords** checkbox so it appears unchecked. Otherwise, to leave it enabled, leave the box checked.
5. Click **Manage passwords**.
6. When the *Passwords* dialog box appears, you will see a listing showing the site, username, and a series of dots indicating the password. To view the password, click on the password field, and then click the **Show** button that appears.
7. Enter your Windows password. The password will now appear.
8. To remove a password, click the X at the right of the site that you want removed.

If you remove a password, the browser will not be able to log onto the site using a stored password. You would again need to reenter the password, and then save it.

Google smart lock

Google Chrome and Android devices that use Google Smart Lock for Passwords provide the ability to save passwords, and have them associated with your Google account. When you save a password with Google Smart lock, it's associated with your Google account, so you can then sign onto your Google account on any machine, and then sign into any site or app you've previously saved. To manage passwords saved with Smart Lock, do the following:

1. After logging into Google, go to https://passwords.google.com.
2. If you don't want passwords for Android apps to be saved, click on the toggle beside **Smart Lock for Passwords** so it is set to the left and appears white. If you want passwords for these apps to be saved, click on the toggle so that it is set to the right and appears blue. By default, this is turned on.

3. In the Auto Sign-In section, review the listing of saved passwords. To remove a password, click on the X to the right of a site or app. To view the existing password, click on the eye icon to the right of the Passwords field.
4. If you don't want to be able to automatically sign in to apps and sites, click on the toggle so it is set to the right and appears white. Otherwise, click on the toggle so that it is set to the right and appears blue.

FIREWALLS

A *firewall* is a software or hardware that works as a barrier between your computer and the outside network. It allows your computer to communicate on a network, while blocking unauthorized access to your computer. On larger networks, such as those used by a company, the settings for firewall software on your computer may be set using policies. On your home computer, you may use a firewall like the one that comes with Windows, or install software like ZoneAlarm (www.zonealarm.com) or other firewalls included with security suites that we'll discuss in Chapter 3, Software problems and solutions.

1. To ensure Windows Firewall is running, click on the **Start** button and click **Control Panel** in Windows 7. Right-click on the **Start** button in Windows 8.1, or right-click on the taskbar in Windows 10, and then click **Control Panel**.
2. On Windows 7 and 8x, click on **System and Security**, and then click **Windows Firewall**. On Windows 10, click **Windows Firewall**.
3. In the left pane, click on **Turn Windows Firewall on or off**. On the screen that appears, shown in Fig. 2.5, ensure that the **Turn on Windows Firewall** option is selected under *Private network settings* and *Public network settings* sections. Click on the **Notify me when Windows Firewall blocks a new app** under both sections, beneath the option to turn on Windows Firewall.
4. Click **OK**.

You should not turn off Windows Firewall unless you've installed another product that provides this security. Once you've installed another firewall product, you would control the settings through it, and not the Windows Firewall settings in Control Panel.

FIREWALL ON A ROUTER

You should also have a firewall on your router that protects the entire network from outside networks like the Internet. For example, if you own a Linksys router, you would log onto it as we discussed earlier in this chapter, and then click to the **Security** tab to be presented with the screen similar to that shown in Fig. 2.6.

In looking at this screen, you'll see that there are a number of options. The ones that you should always have enabled are **IPv6 SPI Firewall Protection** and **IPv6**

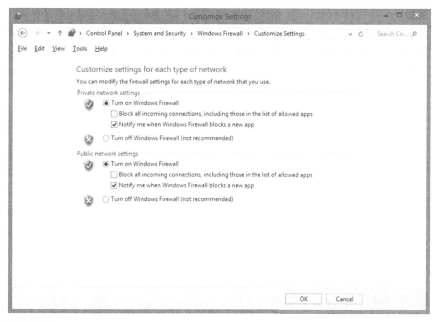

FIGURE 2.5

Windows firewall.

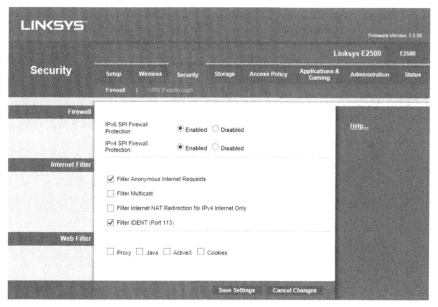

FIGURE 2.6

Linksys firewall.

SPI Firewall Protection. These will protect you from incoming Internet traffic. The other options include

- Filter Anonymous Internet Requests, which should be enabled to hide your network ports, prevent your network from being detected from Internet users, and basically make it more difficult from Internet users from getting into your network.
- Filter Multicast, which prevents others on the network from multicasting, in which multiple transmissions can be sent to specific computers.
- Filter Internet NAT Redirection for IPv4 Internet Only, which will use port forwarding to block access to local servers from local computers.
- Filter IDENT (Port 113), which prevents scanning of port 113.
- Web Filter, which provides checkboxes that allow you to disable Internet Proxy Web servers, Java, ActiveX, and Cookies. Depending on the checkboxes that are checked, sites that use Java or ActiveX content on pages won't work, and the use of cookies will be disabled.

SUMMARY

In this chapter we saw that you have a lot of control over your privacy and the security of your network, computer, and other devices. These settings are available to protect systems from unwanted attacks, ways to keep others from gaining access to your accounts, and tools that will help you in generating and managing passwords. Now that you've looked at the various security and privacy settings available on browsers, routers, and operating systems. We'll move on to show you how to protect yourself from some of the most ruthless threats on the Internet: viruses and malware.

REFERENCE

Zetter, K. (2008, September 18). *Palin E-Mail Hacker Says It Was Easy*. From Wired. <https://www.wired.com/2008/09/palin-e-mail-ha/> Accessed 16.05.16.

Software problems and solutions

3

INFORMATION IN THIS CHAPTER

- Malware and Viruses
- Antivirus
- Antimalware
- Staying Up-To-Date
- Disaster Recovery

There are threats that are directed against your personal safety, and those against your computer. When your system becomes infected with software designed to damage data, alter security settings, or take over your system, it can compromise your digital assets, privacy, and ability to use your computer. If the software is designed to capture financial or personal data, or coerce, extort, or blackmail you into sending money to someone, it can devastate you.

While having an attacker inflict this kind of damage is increasingly common, it isn't the only risk to your property. A natural disaster or human mistake can destroy your computer and devices with equal or greater efficiency. In this chapter, we'll discuss these dangers, how to protect yourself, and what to do after damage has been done.

MALWARE AND VIRUSES

Malware is a term that's short *for malicious software* and describes any type of code that's designed to compromise the functions of a computer by bypassing access controls, stealing, and\or damaging data, or otherwise disrupting its normal operations. Note that we said that it's designed for this purpose. If you install a bad piece of software (such as a buggy update) that causes problems on your computer, this doesn't necessarily make it malware. After all, software developers are humans, and humans make mistakes. What makes it malware is that the software was designed with a malicious intent and/or with the purpose of causing that problem.

The other thing to understand about malware is that it's an umbrella term, used to describe a number of different software threats. One type of malware you've probably heard of is a virus. A *virus* is a type of program or code that spreads from

The Basics of Cyber Safety. DOI: http://dx.doi.org/10.1016/B978-0-12-416650-9.00003-6

one system to another by attaching itself to other files. When you open a document, execute a program, or run a script file that's been infected with a virus, it often makes a copy of itself and can attach itself to other files on your system. When you share one of those files with other people, such as by sending an infected document as an attachment via email or saving it to a network where someone else can open it, other computers then become infected. Code in the virus determines what the virus will do to a system, inclusive to damaging data or stealing information.

When you hear people talk about viruses and malware, they often use the words interchangeably, but that's not the case. Viruses have been around for decades, gaining significant media attention in the 1990s when the Internet became commercial and people first began using it on home PCs. The term was seared in the public mindset and people began to refer to any kind of malicious software threat as a virus. While they're still a real danger to your computer, there are many kinds of malware that are not viruses. Now that you have a good understanding that all viruses are malware, but not all malware are viruses, let's look at some other types of malicious software.

TYPES OF MALWARE

There is no way to know how much malware is on the Internet, because new ones are always being developed and undiscovered. In the Q2 report for April–June 2015 by PandaLabs (www.pandasecurity.com/mediacenter/reports/), it was stated that during this period they saw "an average of 230,000 new types each day and a total of 21 million new threats during those three months." A majority of these were variants of existing malware, which are changed to avoid detection.

In addition to new forms of malware being developed, there is *polymorphism*, in which a virus or other unwanted program is designed to replicate itself with modifications, which makes it harder to detect. Sometimes these variants are identified as new malware, and later recognized as being part of the same family.

Because of the sheer volume of unwanted programs that exist, they're grouped into different categories so it's easier to understand their function and characteristics. Some of these categories include:

- **Adware** is short for *advertising-supported software*, and is designed to deliver advertisements. You've probably experienced pop-up ads on websites or advertisements in free programs (*freeware*) or those offered on a trial basis (*shareware*). In these cases, the site or software's creator gets money through the ads displayed or clicked on, which helps fund his or her endeavors. While this is a legitimate use of adware, it becomes malicious when its bundled with spyware (which we will discuss later) that gathers information about you, and sends it to a third party.
- **Backdoors** are methods to gain unauthorized access to a system. A software developer may write a backdoor into a program so that he or she can troubleshoot problems, which may also be used by hackers to gain access.

Malware may also be used to install a backdoor to a system by taking advantage of some vulnerability in the software. For example, *Remote Access Trojans* are used to create such backdoors, allowing the attacker access to your system from a remote location. Once in, the attacker has access to your system, and can operate the computer as if he or she was sitting at your keyboard.

- **Bots**, which are short for *robots*, are programs that perform a specific task or operate in a way that simulates human activity. They can be used to gather information, deploy additional malware, or used in collections called *botnets* as part of a larger attack. We will discuss these more thoroughly in Chapter 5, Cybercrime.
- **Browser hijackers**, which attack Internet browsers, prevent you from navigating to an intended site. This may prevent you from using search engines properly, visiting antivirus sites to get additional help or download removal tools, and may direct you to sites to steal information or download additional malware.
- **Exploits** are designed to take advantage of system vulnerabilities, such as a security hole in an operating system. It may use a known vulnerability that the vendor has decided to fix later, exists because a patch hasn't been released yet, or is still a problem on your computer because you haven't kept your system updated. There are also *zero day exploits*, which take advantage of vulnerabilities that are unknown to a vendor.
- **Password Stealers and Monitoring Tools** are used to monitor your system and record information on your activities. They can record passwords as they're entered, access ones stored in a browser, and (in the case of *keyboard loggers*) capture anything else you type on a keyboard. We'll discuss these in greater detail in Chapter 5, Cybercrime.
- **Ransomware** is a kind of malicious software that prevents access or performs some other action that either locks your computer or devices or encrypts your data, essentially holding your computer/data hostage until you pay the malware's creator to release it. We'll discuss this in greater detail in Chapter 4, Email safety and security.
- **Rootkits** are programs designed to hide on your system and perform specific actions programmed or configured by the attacker. After the rootkit installs, it will reside there until the attacker uses it to gain remote access to your system, install additional malware, or control the computer as part of a botnet. They are difficult to detect, and may need to be removed manually or with special tools available on antivirus and antimalware sites. We will discuss these in detail in Chapter 5, Cybercrime.
- **Scareware** is a malware that's designed to scare you into visiting websites that will install other malicious software, or tries to get you to purchase software to remove viruses or other threats that don't actually exist on your system. We'll discuss this in greater detail in Chapter 4, Email safety and security.
- **Spyware** is a software that's designed to monitor your activities and report them in some way. Spyware may be used to track your browsing activities, log

what's entered on a keyboard, and send this data to a particular email address or server. *Tracking cookies* may be used to store information about the user on the person's own computer, and send this information to advertisers or other third parties. In addition to being a threat to your privacy, it may also modify security settings, interfere with network connections, or cause other problems that you may attribute to your operating system or software you're running. It may be hidden in legitimate software you install, or Trojan Horses that have infected your computer.

- A **Trojan Horse** (or *Trojan*) is a malicious software that's hidden inside or disguises itself as a seemingly harmless program, document, or other file. For example, you might download a flashlight app for your mobile phone. Once installed or executed, it then runs malicious code that harms your system, downloads other malware, or performs some other harmful function. Trojans are the most common form of malware.

- **Worms** are another common type of malware, and can cause serious problems for computers and networks. They are selfreplicating, and can fill up computer memory and/or consume bandwidth across a network, causing performance issues and errors. They may also include a *payload*, which is a program that's released to perform some other action, such as stealing or damaging data, create botnets, and so on.

ANTIVIRUS

A primary defense against malware is using a good software to protect your system. While there are a number of antivirus programs on the market, the one you choose should be established with a good reputation. The software should focus on this type of protection, and not a program that includes antivirus features as an afterthought. Whichever one you choose, the antivirus should constantly run in the background, so it can check for viruses, Trojans, and other threats while you're using the computer, and can be scheduled to run regular scans of your file system.

In choosing antivirus protection, cost doesn't necessarily have to be a concern. There are a number of reliable programs available that are free. The companies that provide free versions make their money by selling premium versions that include additional features and enhanced protection against threats. When deciding on what software to use, you should review what each version offers so you're getting the protection you expect and not paying for features you won't use. Some of the free antivirus programs available include:

- **AVG** (http://free.avg.com/) is a free antivirus software that runs on Windows, Macs, and mobile devices running Android. While the free version also protects against spyware and malware, a premium version is available that includes a firewall, antispam protection, and other features.

- **Avast** (www.avast.com) is a free antivirus and antispyware software that runs on Windows, Macs, and mobile devices running Android. Premium versions are also available that includes a firewall, antispam protection, and other features.
- **Windows Defender** is an antivirus and antispyware tool that's included with Windows 8*x* and 10. It replaces **Microsoft Security Essentials** (http://windows.microsoft.com/en-us/windows/security-essentials-download), which can be used on Windows 7 machines.

In addition to these free tools, there are also products that only come at a price, but provide a wide range of features. These include:

- **McAffee** (www.mcafee.com), which provides protection for devices running Windows, Mac and iOS, and Android.
- **Panda** (www.pandasecurity.com), which has a number of products for securing Windows, Mac and iOS, and Android devices.
- **Symantec** (www.symantec.com), which provides protection for computers, servers, and devices running Windows, Linux, Mac, and Android. They provide security suites and tools inclusive to **Norton Anti-Virus** (www.norton.com) and Symantec Endpoint Protection.

If price is an issue, you should check with your Internet Service Provider (ISP), school, and employer to see what they offer. Some ISPs provide free antivirus products when signing up for Internet service. Universities, colleges, and companies may also provide free or discounted versions of the commercial product they use for home use. The logic is that by installing protection on your home computer, there is less chance that you'll bring virus-infected documents or other files to work or school and infect their systems.

WINDOWS DEFENDER

Windows Defender is probably the first tool you'll use to protect yourself from malware, because it comes installed with Windows 8*x* and 10. When it was first released, it was antispyware software, but evolved into protecting against a wider range of threats. The current version of the product was upgraded to protect your computer against viruses, providing real-time protection, and protects your system from files downloaded with Internet Explorer or Edge. When a file is downloaded with one of these browsers, Windows Defender will scan it to block any malicious software or virus-infected files from being installed on your system.

In looking at its interface, you'll see that there are a number of settings and features that are common to any program that protects against malware. To open Windows Defender in Windows 8*x*, you would type "Windows Defender" on the start screen, and then click **Windows Defender**. In Windows 10, you would click **Start**, select **Settings**, click **Update & Security**, and then click **Windows Defender**.

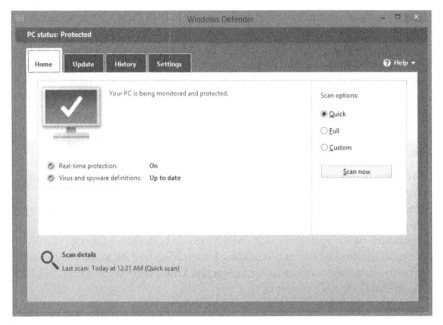

FIGURE 3.1

Windows defender.

As seen in Fig. 3.1, the *Home* tab provides information about whether the virus and spyware definitions (used to detect and remove threats) are up-to-date, and if real-time protection is turn on. It also provides three options for scanning your system:

- **Quick**, which scans areas of your computer that are most likely to be infected.
- **Full**, which scans files on your hard disk(s) and programs that are running.
- **Custom**, which allows you to select what drives and folders will be scanned.

After selecting the type of scan to perform, you would click the **Scan now** button to start the scan. If you selected a Custom scan, you'll be prompted to select the drives and folders to be scanned first. Once started, a quick scan will only take a few minutes, but a full scan may take hours to complete.

The *History* tab is used to view a list of items you've allowed to run on your computer, quarantined items, and all items that were detected on the machine. Quarantined items are infected files, malware, and potentially dangerous items found on your machine, which have been removed so they can't cause additional damage. Once quarantined, the files can't run on your computer, but they haven't been removed. You're given the options on this tab of deleting them, or restoring the ones you feel were quarantined by mistake to their original locations.

As seen in Fig. 3.2, the **Settings** tab is where you can configure Windows Defender to perform the way you want. By clicking on categories in the left pane,

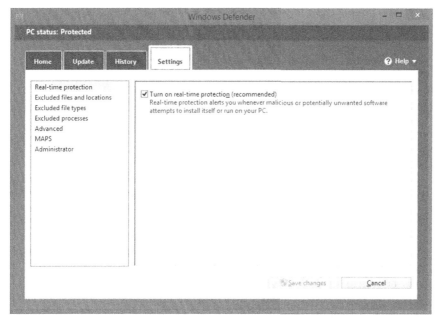

FIGURE 3.2

Windows defender settings.

you can view and set options in the right pane. The various categories of options you can configure include:

- **Real-time protection**, which allows Windows Defender to warn you when malware or potentially unwanted programs (PUPs) attempt to install themselves on your computer. The checkbox for this option should be checked.
- **Excluded files and locations**, which allows you to set what files and folders should be ignored during scans. You might need to set particular locations so that Windows Defender doesn't quarantine any programs or files that may be seen as a threat, but you want to keep. For example, you may have downloaded or installed monitoring tools, password recovery utilities, and so forth that could be a potential threat if the wrong person installed and used them.
- **Excluded file types**, which allows you to set which file extensions should be ignored during a scan. This should not be used unless you have a specific reason for excluding a file type.
- **Excluded processes**, which allows you to specify processes (programs running in memory) that should be ignored in the scan.
- **Advanced**, which provides a number of settings that we'll discuss shortly.
- **MAPS**, which allows you to provide Microsoft with information on malware and other PUPs that were found on your computer. If privacy is a concern, then

click the **I don't want to join MAPS** option. Otherwise leave the option set to the default membership, so that the latest virus or spyware definition can be automatically downloaded when a problem is detected.

- **Administrator**, which has an option to turn Windows Defender on or off. Unless you have another antivirus program that is actively running, the checkbox for this option should be checked so that Windows Defender is turned on. You may need to turn it off at times temporarily, such as when you're installing certain tools that may be recognized as a threat and need to set files and locations to exclude from a scan. If you do disable it temporarily, remember to turn it back on as soon as possible.

The *Advanced* section of the Settings tab provides a number of options that can be used to improve how Windows Defender scans your system. These include:

- **Scan archive files**, which will have any zip or cab files scanned for viruses and malware. You should have this checkbox checked.
- **Scan removable drives**, which will scan USB flash drives and removable disks that you've attached to your system. Unless you're going to install a tool that may be seen as a potential threat, it's advisable to have this checkbox checked.
- **Create a system restore point**, which (as we'll discuss later in this chapter) will create a point that you can restore your system to prior to removing, running, or quarantining detected items. The benefit of this is that you can restore the computer to the state it was in prior to when any items were removed. However, it also presents an opportunity for you to accidentally restore the system to when it had malware installed. By default, this checkbox is unchecked.
- **Allow all users to view the full History results**, which enables anyone who uses the computer to see items that others have been quarantined. By default, this checkbox is unchecked so that user privacy is respected.
- **Remove quarantined files** after is an option that provides a dropdown box that allows you to set when quarantined files are deleted. By default, it's set to 3 months.
- **Send file samples automatically when further analysis is required** is a setting that gives your permission for the computer to automatically send samples of items that may be malicious. This helps Microsoft to identify threats and is enabled by default. If privacy is a concern, then uncheck this box. Otherwise, you'll be prompted whether a file can be sent if Windows Defender determines it may contain private information.

UPDATING

Signature files or *definitions* are an important part of how antivirus and antimalware software works. These files contain information about different viruses and malware, which is used by the software to detect, clean, and remove detected threats. If you haven't updated these files, then your antivirus software isn't nearly as effective.

In Windows Defender, these files are automatically updated as part of the Windows Update process. By clicking on the **Update** tab, you can see the last time antivirus and antispyware definitions were downloaded by your system. To manually update them, you can click the **Update** button.

SCHEDULING REGULAR SCANS

Many antivirus programs provide an option to schedule when scans are to be performed. This allows you to configure a time when a scan runs, the frequency (daily, weekly, etc.), and what should be scanned. The software may provide real-time protection, and may protect your files when you're not using the computer, but regular full scans of your system are advisable.

Windows Defender does not have the option to schedule scans in the program, but uses a different tool in Windows for this purpose. To schedule when a scan occurs:

1. Search for **Schedule Tasks**, and open the program.
2. In the left pane, click on the arrow beside **Task Schedule Library** to expand it, and then repeat the process to expand the **Microsoft** and **Windows** nodes.
3. Double-click on **Windows Defender**.
4. In the top middle pane, double-click on **Windows Defender Scheduled Scan**.
5. When the dialog box opens, click on the **Triggers** tab, and then select **New**.
6. Set the frequency of the scan and what is to be scanned, and then click **OK**.

ROGUE ANTIVIRUS

As we'll discuss further in Chapter 5, Cybercrime, it's important to be aware of fake security alerts that may appear while surfing the Web, or which appears on your screen from previously downloaded malware. A pop-up may be designed to appear as if it's a genuine warning, telling you that your computer has been infected or that you need to update your antivirus, but it's actually a link to lure you into downloading bogus software or install malware. You may also expose yourself to installing such malware when searching for antivirus software, and clicking on a link to a site that automatically downloads malicious code and/or provides a link to download their product.

You can limit the risk of installing such software by having up-to-date antivirus and antimalware protection on your computer, using firewall protection, and using nonadministrator accounts on your computer to limit its ability to be installed. Another key factor in avoiding these scams is to be wary of clicking on such links, and becoming familiar with how your antivirus and antimalware looks, as well as the messages they present. Most of these pop-ups aren't exact duplicates, so if it doesn't look right, don't click on it.

ANTIMALWARE

If viruses are a type of malware, and antivirus software also protects against other kinds of malware, then you're probably wondering why you need antimalware software. It's true that the antivirus software discussed previously will protect you from most of the threats on the Web. According to the Q2 report by PandaLabs (www.pandasecurity.com/mediacenter/reports/), systems infected between April and June 2015 by different types of malware were as follows:

- Trojans 75.25%
- Viruses 1.53%
- Worms 2.63%
- Adware/Spyware 5.43%
- Other types of malware 14.39%

By looking at this, we can see that Trojans are by far the biggest malware threat facing computer users. Since antivirus software focuses on protecting against Trojans, viruses, and worms, you definitely need one installed. However, while antivirus software prevents, detects, and removes a majority of infections, it will not catch everything. Companies that specialize in antimalware protection often focus on certain types of threats (such as spyware and adware), with some providing superior protection against zero-day or zero-hour malware that was previously unknown. While you need antivirus software running constantly in the background, you should also run antimalware software to catch threats your antivirus hasn't detected. Some of the antimalware available include:

- **Ad-aware** (www.lavasoft.com) is a free antivirus and antispyware tool, which also has premium versions that provide features like parental controls that prevent access to adult websites, email protection, and more.
- **Spybot—Search & Destory** (www.safer-networking.org) is a free antimalware and antispyware tool, which also has premium versions that provide antivirus protection and additional features.
- **Microsoft** (http://www.microsoft.com/security/pc-security/malware-removal.aspx) also provides an antimalware tool that is available on their site and is downloaded automatically as part of Windows Updates.
- **Malwarebytes Anti-Malware** (www.malwarebytes.org) is a free antimalware tool that's designed to remove malware and spyware from your computer. The premium version has additional features that provide additional scanning features and stop malware from activating. They also have additional free and premium tools to protect systems from exploits. Versions are available for Windows, Mac, and mobile devices running Android.

While Microsoft deploys an antimalware tool to detect and remove known threats, you shouldn't rely on this as your only means of defense. While included in your Windows Update once a month, this utility can't compare to tools like Malwarebytes

Anti-Malware, which updates itself on a recurring basis throughout the day to find the latest threats. Therefore, think of Microsoft's utility as one layer of protection, but not the only one. Use other tools that can be scheduled to run daily or weekly or on-demand, in addition to a good antivirus program that runs in the background.

DON'T FORGET YOUR MOBILE

While people may install antivirus and antimalware protection on their computers, it's easy to forget that your mobile devices are vulnerable to the same threats. There are mobile versions of many popular antivirus and antimalware tools, which can be installed to scan your device and provide real-time protection against threats.

When looking at possible antivirus and antimalware apps, you should only install ones that you trust. There are apps that promise protection, but are actually malware. Use apps developed by reliable companies, such as Avast, AVG, and Malwarebytes, and look up the reviews of people who have used any of the apps you're considering installing.

STAYING UP-TO-DATE

When a software company releases their final product, it's not exactly final. Operating systems, games, apps, and other software may be released with known issues or have problems that are discovered after being released. For example, previous versions of Windows have been released with thousands of known bugs, with Microsoft deciding it better to fix the problems later than delay the release and face poor user adoption. In addition, security vulnerabilities, bugs that effect performance or functionality, or other issues are often discovered after it's on the market. To remedy these problems, vendors will release software to install on your system that repairs the problem(s).

There are many different names to describe software that updates the existing software, including *updates*, *fixes*, *bugfixes*, *hotfixes*, *patches*, and *updates*. If several updates are combined into one, you'll hear it referred to as a *cumulative update*, or if it's a major update to the system it may be called a *service pack*. Regardless of the name, they are designed to repair issues that have been identified, and/or provide new features that weren't available previously.

It's important that updates get applied, so that any security holes or other problems with the software are repaired, and the system works as expected. If not, it's a vulnerability that allows a hacker to gain access to your system that's like having the front door to your house open, and refusing to close it.

TYPES OF UPDATES

There are different kinds of updates that may be applied to a system. Mobile apps and other systems may simply provide an update that upgrades the application or OS to a new version, while others will modify parts of the code and replace certain files. Different terminology may also be applied to describe the updates. Microsoft operating systems and products will separate updates into different types, including:

- **Security updates**, which are designed to fix vulnerabilities in the software. These may be further rated based on the severity of the vulnerability as critical, important, moderate, or low. It is important to install any security update rated as critical.
- **Critical updates**, which are nonsecurity updates that address certain bugs found in the software.
- **Service packs**, which are cumulative sets of updates, as well as certain changes or features to the software. Once installed, previous recommended updates may no longer be offered, because they've already been applied through the service pack, and new ones that are designed to fix problems found after the service pack was released may be offered.

You may also see other updates offered, such as ones that will upgrade your browser to a new version, optional updates for drivers, or new software that can be installed on your system. Important updates that you should install relate to fixing privacy or security issues, and you should always consider installing them as soon as possible.

To see if there are updates available for a computer, you can visit their website. If you're running a Mac, you can visit www.apple.com/ca/support/osx/software-updates/ to view recent updates for OS X. In the same way, when visiting a software manufacturer's site, you'll often see a Support or Download section that provides information on downloading and installing any patches that have been released. To check for updates on Windows machines, you would follow these steps:

1. Click on the **Start** button and click **Control Panel** in Windows 7. Right-click on the **Start** button in Windows 8.1, and then click **Control Panel**. In Windows 10, Windows Update is no longer in the Control Panel, so you'll need to click **Start**, select **Settings**, and then click **Update & Security**.
2. Click on **Windows Update**.
3. Click the **Check for Updates** button.
4. After checking, you'll be informed if there are no updates available for your computer, or if you're using Window's 7 or 8x, you'll be provided with a list of available updates specifically for the operating system you're using. You can then select the updates you want to install, and follow any instructions that might be related to the installation on your screen. In Windows 10, you're not given the option to pick individual downloads, and they'll install automatically.

AUTOMATIC UPDATES

Some systems will automatically check for updates, and either notify you or automatically install them for you. The benefit of having the OS automatically install updates is that it takes the bother of checking for updates out of your hands, which can also be a problem. Sometimes, updates can cause new issues, and may have new bugs or introduce new vulnerabilities. This is why many organizations wait before installing them. By not immediately installing a patch or service pack, you can see if others have had problems, and gives the vendor time to retract any buggy updates.

In Windows, you can turn automatic updates on or off by doing the following:

1. Click on the **Start** button and click **Control Panel** in Windows 7. Right-click on the **Start** button in Windows 8.1, and then click **Control Panel**.
2. In the left pane, click **Change Settings**.
3. Under **Important Updates**, click on the dropdown list and select one of the following:
   a. **Never check for updates**, which turns automatic updates off. If you choose this, you'll need to manually check for updates. This is not a recommended setting.
   b. **Install updates automatically**, which sets Windows to check for updates and install them automatically. Depending on the update, you may still be prompted for some input. This is the setting recommended by Microsoft, and works for most users.
   c. **Download updates but let me choose whether to install them**, which gives you the option of which updates to install, so updates aren't installed immediately. The benefit of this is that you're given more control on what's being installed on your computer.
   d. **Check for updates by let me choose whether to download and install them**, which is similar to the last option, but Windows won't automatically download them to your computer.
4. To schedule how often Windows checks for updates, click on the **Install new updates** dropdown lists. You should have Windows check for new updates every day to insure critical or security updates are applied (or, depending on your update settings, that you're aware they exist). You can also select the time that Windows will check. If your computer is in hibernation mode when it's time to check for updates, Windows will check when you start your computer, and prompt you if you want to postpone installation.

Updates in Windows 10

Windows 10 handles updates differently from previous versions. You have less control, and the operating system will update you automatically, with little control over what's being installed. The updates on Windows 10 also modify the usability of the system. Rather than holding back new features until the next version of Windows, updates are automatically installed to deploy new features and remove old ones that Microsoft feels you don't need anymore.

As we saw earlier, the update feature in Windows 10 is no longer in the Control Panel. To manually start an update, you need to click **Start**, select **Settings**, click **Update & Security**, and then click **Windows Update**. If updates are available, this screen will inform you. Clicking the **Download** button will download them immediately.

To control what happens when updates are installed, you would click the **Advanced Options** at the bottom of this screen. You'll immediately notice that your options are significantly limited, and the **Choose how updates are installed** dropdown list only allows you to choose whether your system restarts automatically or will schedule a reboot when you're not using it.

You are however given a checkbox to **Give me updates for other Microsoft products when I update Windows**, which when checked will update Microsoft Office and other programs on your system that are made by Microsoft. Generally, people will leave this checked so that everything is updated at once, but if you want to disable such updates, click on the box to uncheck it.

If you're using the Professional, Enterprise, or Education versions of Windows 10, the *Advanced Options* screen also provides a **Defer upgrades** checkbox. It's used to prevent feature updates from being installed for several months, but will not prevent any security updates from being installed. This ensures that organizations running the Professional, Enterprise, or Education editions will have stable systems that don't have new features suddenly appearing. In doing so, trainers won't be surprised by a new feature they don't know about, and IT support staff won't have to field calls on features that didn't exist the day before. If you're using the standard edition however you won't see this checkbox. To delay upgrades, you would click on the **Defer upgrades** checkbox, so it appears checked.

A benefit of the automatic feature updates is you get new features without having to buy a new version of Windows. However, if you feel like a bit of a guinea pig used for testing, you're not exactly wrong. The Defer upgrades option gives a business time to test features before they're deployed company-wide and any problems with features will be experienced by home users, giving Microsoft time to fix or remove the feature in future updates. Another potential issue is that you may get used to using a feature at home, but not see that feature on your work computer for months.

A problem with Windows 10 forcing updates to be installed is when there's a glitch in the update, or other issues prevent it from being installed properly. Take what happened in August 2015 as an example, when people had the frustrating experience where an update would partially install, reboot the computer, and fail (Gibbs, 2015). Windows 10 would roll back the installation, but the next time you logged onto your computer, it would again try to install the update and the problem would repeat itself. This didn't just happen once, but with three different cumulative updates released that month (KB 3081424 on August 5, KB 3081436 on August 12, and KB 3081438 on August 14). It wasn't until August 19 when people reported the updates weren't installing properly. Added to this was the problem that Microsoft began providing vague descriptions about their updates, merely stating that "This update includes improvements to enhance the functionality of Windows 10." Without knowing what the update fixes or does to a system, you can't decide whether you really need it or not.

While Windows 10 doesn't provide an option to prevent automatic updates, there is a sneaky way of doing it. Later in this chapter, we'll show you how to control updates when using a mobile Internet connection, and show how setting a connection as *metered* will prevent any automatic updates that aren't marked as being a priority. So, to prevent automatic updates, simply mark the connection to your home wireless network as metered. By setting the connection as metered, you'll receive a message stating that Windows will download the updates when you've connected to Wi-Fi. When you're ready to receive updates, you can unmark the Wi-Fi connection so it is no longer metered or manually download the updates as we showed you earlier.

Windows 10 peer-to-peer updates

A new feature in Windows 10 involves how updates are downloaded from the Internet. It uses a peer-to-peer (P2P) method to distribute updates, similar to that used for torrents. Microsoft makes updates and Windows Store apps available by turning the computers that have them into servers, so these files are shared and available to others wanting to download it.

Traditionally, your operating system would connect to Microsoft's servers, or you would visit their site using a browser, and directly download any updates from their servers. This would be done on each computer on your home network. In Windows 10, you can download the update once, and the machine downloading it could then share it with other computers on your local network. This is beneficial because it saves wasted bandwidth as each machine no longer needs to download the same files over the Internet.

NOTE

How P2P Works

As we'll discuss in Chapter 11, P2P file sharing involves downloading a shared file from multiple sources. Each computer (peer) that has the file makes it available to others. If you want to download it, you may be getting the entire file from one computer, but you'll often find that you're downloading small bits of it from hundreds of different computers. After your computer has the entire file, it then makes it available to your peers on the network.

The problem with this delivery method is in the default settings for the P2P updates, as it allows your computer to share any installed updates with users on the Internet. While this arrangement benefits Microsoft, in that fewer customers are chewing up bandwidth and potentially overloading their servers, it does not benefit you. The P2P file sharing will eat up some bandwidth, possibly slowing your Internet connection and drawing you closer to any data transfer limits (i.e., how many GB of data you can upload/download per month) set by your ISP. The issue of how much data is being transferred is particularly important if you're using a mobile hotspot, such as one in your vehicle or created with your phone.

To configure how updates are delivered, and disable updates being sent to the Internet from your computer:

1. Click **Start**, select **Settings**, and then click **Update & Security**.
2. Click **Windows Update**.
3. On the *Advanced Options screen*, click **Advanced Options**.

4. To turn off the P2P updates completely, slide the option that allows your PC to send parts of previously downloaded Windows updates and apps to **Off**. If you want to allow Windows to share these files, slide the option to **On**. If set to *On*, you can then choose one of the following options:

a. If you want to allow your computer to share and get updates from other computers on your local network, click the **PCs on my local network** option. This is beneficial, as any computer on your home network will get an update from the first computer to install it. This saves time and bandwidth, as each computer in your home won't need to connect to the Internet to download the same file from Microsoft.

b. If you want to allow your computer to share and get updates from not only computers on your local network but also computers on the Internet, then click the **PCs on my local network, and PCs on the Internet** option. As we'll discuss later, it is recommended that you don't select this option if there's a concern of how much bandwidth it will use, especially when using a mobile hotspot.

MOBILE DEVICE UPDATES

Mobile devices like smartphones and tablets also need to have updates applied to them. Although they're different devices, the way you check and install updates on them is similar to one another.

- On the Blackberry 10 OS, you would go to **Settings**, tap **Software Updates**, and then tap **Check for Updates**.
- On the iOS for an iPhone, iPad, or iPod touch, you would tap **Settings**, tap **General**, and then tap **Software Update**.
- To update the OS on an Android smartphone or tablet, tap **Settings**, tap **About Phone** or **About Tablet** (if you have a tabbed settings menu, this appears on the General tab), tap **Software Update**, and then tap **Software update check**.

Regardless of the OS you're using, if an update is available, follow the onscreen instructions to download and install. When doing an update, you should always have your mobile device plugged in and charged. If you lost power during an update, it could corrupt the OS or cause other problems because the update failed without completing.

You should also check for any updates that might be available for apps installed on your mobile device. These too could have patches available to fix vulnerabilities or other issues. To update your apps, do the following:

- On the Blackberry, you should receive notifications when a new version of an installed app is available. Opening the notification reveals an option to open, and then update. You can also manually check for updates by tapping **Blackberry World**, swiping right to reveal the navigation menu, tapping **My World**, and then tapping **My Apps & Games**. A list of available updates will be displayed.

Tapping the icon beside an app's name will update that particular app, while tapping the **Update All** option will update all of the listed apps.
- Mobile devices running iOS can check for app updates by tapping **App Store**. Upon opening, it will check for any available updates. You can then click the **Update** button to update each app separately.
- On Android devices, tap **Play Store**, tap the menu icon (which appears as three horizontal bars), and then tap **My Apps**. Select that app that's labeled "Update," and tap **Update**.

OTHER DEVICE UPDATES

As we discussed in Chapter 1, What is cyber safety?, it's important to be aware of all the devices connected to the Internet. You may also have game systems (such as an X-Box, PlayStation 3, or 4), a Smart TV, or apps on those systems (e.g., Netflix and Hulu) that require occasional updates. The systems may require you to update when you first start them, or you may need to check the settings to check for updates manually. By looking in the user guides for those systems and devices, you should find instructions on the steps involved in checking for upgrades and installing them.

> **NOTE**
>
> **Tethering and Disaster Recovery**
> Tethering can be useful in a disaster, when you want to look up information on how to recover. While it should go without saying, you never want to restore your system from an online backup by tethering your computer to a phone, and using your data plan to restore the backup. Backup files and system images are extremely large, and you'll find that you'll go over your monthly data limit very quickly if you try this.

DISASTER RECOVERY

Disaster recovery involves methods that protect your data from natural or human-induced disasters. A disaster may be a fire, earthquake, flood, or some other natural occurrence, or intentional acts or mistakes caused by a person (such as a hacking attack, viruses, malware, dropping a mobile device in water, or accidentally reformatting a hard disk). If you've been adversely affected by such an event, you want to get yourself up and running with as little permanent loss as possible.

Businesses will have sets of policies and procedures to protect data, software, and hardware, so they can recover in the event of a disaster and resume normal functions. However, this doesn't mean that you shouldn't take steps to ensure your personal data, software, and devices aren't protected from the same or similar problems that can cause damage. By taking steps to protect yourself, you'll be able to recover the digital photos, documents, and other assets stored on your computer, laptop, or other mobile devices.

KEEPING A COPY OF PASSWORDS

As we discussed in Chapter 2, Before connecting to the Internet, an important part of disaster recovery is keeping a list of accounts and passwords in a safe place. If anything happens to your computer, you may not be able to logon or access accounts, encrypted folders, and so on without a necessary key or password. You may not even remember all the sites you used.

Any list you have should be stored in a safe, locked firebox, or another secure location. Regardless of whether it's a printed sheet or a document saved on a USB stick, you don't want others having access to it. You also want it protected so that if there's a fire or flood, the list is protected and usable.

BACKING UP FILES

A *backup* is a copy of files on your computer saved to a single file. These can be only certain folders that you select, or everything on a hard disk. When you create a backup of your computer, a system image can also be made, which can be used to restore the computer if it crashes and no longer works properly.

When you backup a drive, its strongly advised not to save the backed up files to the same drive or computer. If you have a home network, you could backup to another computer. However, you should remember that the price of storage is cheap, and buying an external hard disk is relatively inexpensive. An external drive is a hard disk that comes in a case that connects to your computer with a USB cable. This allows you to add and remove a particular disk as needed, or have multiple external drives connected to your system. To backup a Windows 7 machine, you would do the following:

1. Click **Start**, and then click **Control Panel**. Under *System and Security*, click **Back up your computer**.
2. In the *Backup* section, click **Set up backup**.
3. Select a destination where the backup files are to be saved by double clicking on a drive letter.
4. On the next screen, you can select what to backup. Your options are **Let Windows choose**, which will have the system backup files in your libraries, the desktop, and Windows folders for each user account on the computer. It will also create a system image. If you choose **Let me choose**, then only the files you choose are backed up. Generally you'll select the first option that's recommended, but for the purposes of this exercise, we'll have you choose the latter.
5. When the next screen appears, you will see a list of libraries belonging to users on that computer, which are checked by default. This backs up all libraries for each user, but you can click on a library to expand it and then select only certain libraries belonging to a particular user. A list of local and external hard disks also appears in the listing. To backup an entire drive, click the checkbox beside a particular drive letter. If you only want certain files, then navigate to the

folders you want to backup, and click the checkbox beside the folder. To make a system image of the drive where Windows is installed, ensure the **Include a system image of drives** checkbox is checked. Click **Next**.

6. To automate the backup so it runs on a recurring basis, click **Change schedule**.

7. Ensure the **Run backup on a schedule** checkbox is checked. In the **How often** dropdown list, select whether the backup should run Daily, Weekly, or Monthly. In the **What day** dropdown list, select the day it has to run on. If you selected a weekly backup, you would select the day of the week, but if you selected monthly, you'd choose a number corresponding to the day of the month. Finally, in the **What time** dropdown list, select the time the backup should run. Click **OK**.

8. Review the summary of your choices, and then click **Save settings and run backup**.

9. In Windows 8x and 10, backups are done slightly differently. Windows 8x still provides a link to the **Windows 7 File Recovery** tool, which is the backup tool we just discussed. The new backup feature is called Fire Recovery in Windows 8x and 10. Using this, you can have Windows save copies of files so that they can be retrieved if they're deleted or damaged. It also provides the ability to create an image backup, where a copy of the drives containing files that Windows uses are backed up. To use File History, you need to do the following:

   1. Right-click on the **Start** button, click **Control Panel**.
   2. Click **File History**.
   3. Click **Turn On**, and File History will be activated on the computer.
   4. To control how often your files are backed up, click **Advanced Settings**.
   5. Click the **Run** backup on a schedule checkbox so its checked. In the **How often** dropdown list, select the frequency that your files will be backed up (e.g., Daily, Weekly), and in the **What day** dropdown list, select the day of the week these backups are to run. Click **OK**.

To perform an image backup in Windows 8x and 10, you would also use the File History app in Control Panel, but would do the following:

1. Click System Image Backup.
2. When the wizard starts, select where you want to save the backup. While you can backup to blank DVDs or a network share, for these steps, you would choose On a hard disk. As we mentioned, this should not be a local drive, but an external hard disk. Click Next.
3. Confirm your settings, and then click Start backup.

Online backups

While backing up files to an external drive is a commonly used solution, it won't help you if something happens to both your computer and external drive. If a fire, flood, or some other disaster happened in your home, there's a good possibility that you'd lose both your computer and any backups because both are kept in the same place.

Offsite storage involves keeping a copy of your data in another location. Larger companies will have backups copied across a network to a remote server and/or store backup tapes at another building or secure storage facility. Since most of us don't have such options, a simple solution is to use an online backup service.

There are a number of different companies that provide large amounts of storage space on a secure Internet server. The price ranges depending on the company you use, the amount of space you need, and the number of computers you'll be backing up. A number will also provide a trial evaluation period, so you can test the services for a limited time without paying. Some of the online backup service providers you might choose include:

- Carbonite (www.carbonite.com)
- Barracuda Cloud Storage (www.barracuda.com)
- CrashPlan (www.crashplan.com)
- Mozy (www.mozy.com)

When you use one of these services, you backup and restore your computer using the tools they provide, which are designed for various platforms like Windows, Mac, Linux, and mobile devices. You can schedule regular backups, or use continuous backups so that any changed files are automatically copied to one of their servers. If you ever have a problem, you can restore individual files or the entire hard drive on your machine.

If you are going to backup your device to the Cloud, security should be your primary concern. There is a difference between making a backup that copies your files and settings to some free storage space on the Cloud, and using a business that is focused on providing secure online storage solutions. While you should always check what such companies offer, ones like Carbonite encrypt your data as it's transferred between your device and their servers, and encrypt the files so that they're inaccessible without a key (i.e., password).

Backing up phones and tablets

While backing up computers has been stressed as a vital process since long before the Internet, many don't consider the need to backup data on mobile devices. If you think of the number of photos and documents on your phone or tablet, you can see how much you could lose if the phone was lost, stolen, or seriously damaged.

One method of backing up the files on your mobile device involves connecting it to your computer, so it's accessed as a removable drive. After connecting your phone to the computer using a USB cable, you would select the prompt on your phone to allow access to your SD card, or go into the phones settings and allow it to connect as USB Mass Storage. For example, on an Android device, you would swipe down from the top of the screen to view the main menu, tap **USB connection**, tap **USB Mass Storage**, and then tap **OK**. Once your SD card and storage on the phone appear as new drives (removable disks) on your computer, you can then copy the files to a new location on your computer. You could then include the folder containing these files in any backups you do of the computer.

Some devices also include software for your PC, so you can backup and restore your mobile device to a computer. For example, Blackberry devices allow you to install a program called *Blackberry Blend*, which includes a Backup & Restore feature. In using it, you can backup and restore your settings, phone history, saved searches, messages, browser bookmarks, organizer data, fonts, and media files. If your phone doesn't include such an application, there are third-party backup solutions that provide similar functionality.

Other devices like iPhone provide the ability to backup the phone to iCloud. You can also set the phone to make automatic backups while connected to a Wi-Fi network, or do it manually. Once you're connected to a Wi-Fi network, you would tap **Settings**, tap **iCloud**, and then tap **Backup**. You would need to make sure that the **iCloud Backup** slider was turned on, and then tap **Back Up Now**.

Companies that specialize in secure online backups commonly provide backup solutions for popular mobile devices, such as those running iOS and Android, as well as Windows Phone. Using these tools, you can backup and restore your mobile device, and access and restore files from a backup using a mobile app. As we mentioned earlier, with online backups, you should always ensure that encryption is used to transfer and store your data, so that you're the only one who can access it.

SETTING AND RESTORING RESTORE POINTS

A *checkpoint* or *restore point* is essentially a snapshot of your system at a given point in time. When you create a restore point, information about your computer is stored, and can later be used to restore Registry settings, system files, and programs that Windows needs to run properly. If a problem occurs, you can used the restore point to restore your system to its previous state, so it's exactly like it was when the restore point was made.

Restoring a system in this way is useful when a serious problem occurs. If a change was made to Windows, such as a bad update being applied or malware infecting your computer, a system restore can help make it the way it was before the problem occurred. This may sound like a backup, but it's different in that you can't select individual files to restore, and your personal files are never affected. It just restores Windows.

Restore points are automatically created by Windows on a weekly basis, and also when a significant change occurs, such as a program being installed. You can also create restore points manually. To create a restore point:

1. In Windows 7, click the **Start** button, right-click **Computer**, and then click **Properties**.
2. Click on **System Protection** in the left pane.
3. When the *Systems Properties* dialog box appears, ensure the *System Protection* tab is selected. Click the **Create** button.

To restore your system to a specific point in time, you would do the following:

1. In Windows 7, click **Start**, click **All Programs**, click **Accessories**, click **System Tools**, and then click **System Restore**.

2. When *System Restore* opens, click **Next**.
3. Select the most recent restore point from the list. To view additional restore points, you would click on the **Show more restore points** checkbox so it appears checked. Click **Next**.
4. Click **Finish**.

SUMMARY

The best way to deal with a disaster is to avoid it. Following the advice outlined here will go a long way to ensure your data is protected. As we saw in this chapter, while there are a number of threats on the Internet (inclusive to malware, viruses, and vulnerabilities that can be exploited) there are also tools that can be used to protect systems from being infected. That being said, sometimes you can't avoid a serious problem, and it might just take your system down. That's why you need to prepare.

By being ready for the possibility of a problem, you're better able to recover from it. Backups, recover points, keeping copies of passwords, and having the ability to get additional help can help you recover from a disaster. As we saw, by backing up your computer and mobile devices, you can then restore it to a previous state, and minimize your loss.

REFERENCE

Gibbs, S., 2015, August 11. Windows 10: Broken update forces some users into endless reboot loop. From The Guardian. <https://www.theguardian.com/technology/2015/aug/11/windows-10-broken-update-endless-reboot-loop> (accessed 16.05.16.).

Email safety and security

4

INFORMATION IN THIS CHAPTER

- Email Protection
- Limiting What Your Email Reveals
- Choosing an Email Client
- Free Email Sites
- Security Settings on Email Sites

Email is a term that's short for electronic mail, and a common method of exchanging messages over the Internet. You'll use an email client, like Google mail or Outlook, installed on a computer, an app on your mobile phone, or a website to create and read the messages. The email is sent to a *mail server*, which is a computer that's used to store and forward messages.

To demonstrate how this works, let's say that you're going to send me an email. If you have an email client installed on your computer, you'll write a message to me and click the send button. That message is sent to a mail server, which may be one provided by your Internet Service Provider (ISP). If I had an email account with another ISP, or a free email service like Gmail, the mail server would forward that email onto the mail server that I use. It would be stored in a *mailbox*, which would be an area on the mail server that's designated for mail going to my account. When I retrieve the mail online, I would be accessing that *mailbox*, and see your email in an area for mail I've received called an *Inbox*.

As we'll see in the sections that follow, there are a lot of potential problems with using email, but there are settings and decisions you can make to protect yourself. You may have information of some kind included with the email called an *attachment*, which could be virus infected. It could have links in the email that may take you to a site to fool you into providing sensitive information or automatically download and infect your system with malware. By knowing what to look out for, and configuring your email client properly, you can safeguard yourself and minimize these and other threats.

The Basics of Cyber Safety. DOI: http://dx.doi.org/10.1016/B978-0-12-416650-9.00004-8

EMAIL PROTECTION

Depending on what you plan to do on the Internet, it's advisable to setup separate email accounts for different types of online activities. By this, we're not saying that you should have different email addresses for each of the sites you commonly visit. The kind of email accounts you have will be based on what they'll be used for and your need for privacy. Some of the ones you might have include:

- A generic account, which is often the first one you have when you sign-up for Internet Service. This will be the one you commonly give to friends, family, and others you want to stay in contact with.
- Work email, which is used for business purposes. This may be one created for you by your employer, and should only be used for work-related purposes.
- Social media email, used for sites like Facebook, Twitter, and so on.
- Email account(s) for chat, instant messaging, shopping, promotional sites, or other sites where you want additional privacy.

There are many reasons why you'd want separate accounts. One is that you should never use work email for personal reasons. Many companies have policies dealing with proper use of technology, and using corporate email to sign up on sites, chat, or simply sending personal messages could result in disciplinary actions or even termination of employment. As we saw in Chapter 1, What is cyber safety?, companies own any email account issued to you, meaning that they can access your mail, and you should have zero expectations of privacy.

Another reason to have multiple accounts is that it compartmentalizes what you send and receive, and can limit the amount of SPAM and notifications going to your primary account. Personal messages go to a generic account, work email to a corporate account, and notifications and messages from social media sites, chat sites, and so on would go to their own account.

LIMITING WHAT YOUR EMAIL REVEALS

Generally, when you sign up with an ISP, you're issued an email address that includes your name in it or your first initial and last name. For example, my email address might be michaelcross@domainname.com or mcross@domainname.com. In looking at it, you can see that all or part of my name is included in the address. As we'll see throughout this book, these little tidbits of information can be used with other information gathered about you, and reveal more than you want to know.

Before setting up any accounts on social media sites, chat rooms, and so on, you should seriously consider setting up one or more email accounts with less revealing information. In doing so, the name used for the email account should include nonidentifying information. For example, using an email address like snickers@domainname. com may indicate you're a happy person, but it doesn't reveal who you actually are.

> **NOTE**
>
> **Understanding the Importance of Nonidentifying Email**
> Keep in mind that your family and friends already know your full name, but many of the online "friends" or connections you make are actually strangers. You never want to reveal more to a complete stranger than necessary, and one of the biggest identifiers of a person is their name. To illustrate a problem with revealing email addresses, let's say you used a chat site, discussion board, or instant messaging (which we discuss in chapter: Beyond technology—dealing with people) to meet new people and have online discussions. When you set up an account to use any of these, you're probably given the option of creating a username or alias, so that when you're chatting other people would see you as "Big Bob" or some other name you came up with. Now, consider that one of these people decided to check your account profile, and saw your email address. If it included your real name, the stranger now knows who you are, and the anonymity and protection provided by an alias or username is lost.

Depending on your needs for the account, you should also limit any information included in a signature in messages. For work email, you might include your work number, extension, company website, business address, and so on. However, you do not want to include this in other emails being sent, unless there is a specific and exceptional reason to do so. Even if you send personal information in an email to someone you trust, there is no guarantee that they won't forward it, or include others in the reply that would show the original information you sent.

CHOOSING AN EMAIL CLIENT

There are a number of good email clients available, but the one you choose will often depend on the operating system you're using, and the amount of money you're willing to pay. The email client you use may be one that's installed on your computer, or an online version that you access through a browser. Some of the email clients that can be installed on a computer include:

- **Microsoft Outlook**, which runs on Windows and Apple and is commonly used by businesses. It's included with Microsoft Office or Microsoft Office 365.
- **Apple Mail**, which is Apple's email client.
- **Thunderbird**, which is available for Apple, Linux, and Windows machines.

Securing Thunderbird

In this section we'll go through a number of common settings found in email clients that are installed on your computer, using Thunderbird as an example. *Thunderbird* is a popular, free email client from Mozilla that can be installed on Windows, Apple, and Linux machines, and has a number of features that can be configured to improve your

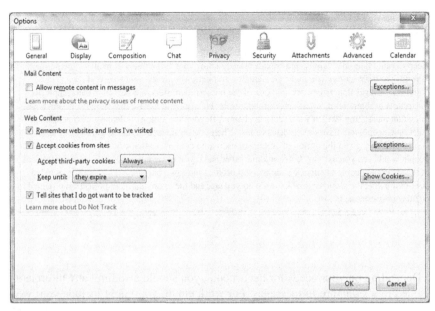

FIGURE 4.1

Thunderbird privacy settings.

security and privacy. If you're using another email client on your computer, similar features should be available under the client's settings. To configure Thunderbirds Privacy and Security settings:

1. After opening Thunderbird, click on the **Tools** menu, and then click **Options**.
2. When the *Options* dialog appears, click on the **Privacy** icon at the top to display a screen similar to that shown in Fig. 4.1.
3. Click on the **Allow remote content in messages** so it appears unchecked. This will prevent any images or other content from being automatically viewed in the email. We'll explain more about why it's important not to allow this in a section that follows.
4. In the section dealing *Web Content*, if you don't want cookies (which we discussed in chapter: Before connecting to the Internet) to be used, you can click on the **Accept cookies from sites** checkbox so it appears unchecked. You can then click on the **Exceptions** button to specify which sites are always or never allowed to use cookies. To view the cookies on your machine, click the **Show Cookies** button, where you can then remove them as desired.
5. Click on the **Tell sites that I do not want to be tracked** checkbox so that it's checked. This will send a request not to track your activities, opting you out of any tracking systems on a site you're accessing, so that tracking cookies aren't sent to your computer.

To modify the security settings in Thunderbird, you would click on the **Security** icon at the top of the Options dialog. Upon doing so, you'll be presented with several tabs of options, where you can make the following modifications:

1. On the **Junk** tab, you can configure settings to train Thunderbird to detect junk mail or SPAM, and specify what happens to email. You can flag an email as junk mail in Thunderbird by right-clicking on a message, selecting **Mark**, and then clicking **As Junk**. On this tab, you should do the following:
   a. Click on **When I mark a message as junk** so the checkbox appears checked, and then either select the option to move it to a junk folder. This will automatically move any junk messages to the account's "Junk" folder. Alternatively, you can click on the **Delete them** option, so that your junk mail is automatically deleted.
   b. Click on the **Mark messages determined to be junk** as read checkbox so it appears checked. In doing so, the message won't appear as unread, meaning there's less chance of you accidentally opening it.
   c. Click on the **Enable adaptive junk filter logging** so the checkbox appears checked.
2. On the **Email Scams** tab, click on the **Tell me if the message I'm reading is a suspected email** scam so the checkbox appears checked. If the email has known elements of being a scam, you'll be presented with a warning.
3. On the **Anti-Virus** tab, click on the **Allow antivirus clients to quarantine individual incoming messages** so it appears checked. This will allow your antivirus software to remove any infected messages before you read them.
4. On the **Passwords** tab, click the **Use a master password** checkbox so it appears checked. After checking this, you'll be prompted to provide and confirm a password. The next time you open Thunderbird, you'll need to enter the password, preventing anyone else from opening Thunderbird and reading your email. To change the password afterwards, click on the **Change Master Password** button on this tab.
5. Click **OK**.

WHY IS IT IMPORTANT TO BLOCK REMOTE CONTENT?

When an email is opened, or viewed in the message pane of an email client, it's possible for content from a server to appear in the message. If the email is in an HTML format, then you're viewing a message that's written in the same language as a web page. Any external content can be displayed in the message as if you've visited the sender's website. Your email client will load any images, including ones that have an executable (Malware) embedded in it, and other content from an external server. While allowing remote content allows you to view any graphic content automatically, it isn't a secure option.

Another problem with allowing remote content is that it can be used to verify your email address. If I send you a SPAM message, when you load the remote content, your client is contacting my server and requesting that the content be sent. I can now see that you made that request, and can see that it's a legitimate email account that's still in use. In verifying that email, I know to contact you further with either additional email, or (as we'll see in chapter: Cybercrime) attempts to phish additional information out of you.

Also, additional information about you is sent with the request to a Web server for images and other content. The browser or email client will identify the application being used and the operating system its running on, which could be used by a hacker to identify possible vulnerabilities or target distribution of malware. The request will also include your IP address, which can be used to get a rough idea of your location.

When you block remote content and open the email, images and other external content don't appear in the message. If I want to view the blocked content, I can click on a link at the top of the message to display images and other content, or if I trust the sender to always allow remote content from that sender.

HIDING THE MESSAGE PANE

A common feature in email clients is the Message Pane, which allows you to view the contents of any emails that you select in your inbox. It is a little deceptive in making you think that you haven't opened the email, as you haven't double-clicked on it so it opens in a new window. However, the Message Pane does open and display the contents of your email, and (depending on your settings) will display any of the images or external content used. As we mentioned, because emails can be written in HTML, the email client is acting like a browser, and you're loading the equivalent of a web page with all the potential threats one can provide.

Hiding the message pane allows you to review the subject, sender, and other information listed in your inbox, but won't show its contents when you click on it. This allows you to select different emails that seem suspicious or appear to be SPAM, and delete them as needed without opening them. To remove the message pane from Thunderbird, click on the **View** menu, select **Layout**, and then click **Message Pane**.

THE DANGERS OF AN ATTACHMENT

The message in an email is only one of the potential threats to your system. Files can also be attached to a message, and these have the same potential risks of files that you download from sites. Documents may be virus infected, and executable files (such as those with an .exe extension) may be attached to install malicious software on your computer. Even though the attachment is with the file, they only pose a threat if they're activated.

Never open any attachment if you don't know the sender, or the email seems suspicious. Even if you know the sender, it's possible that the message and attachment was sent automatically by malware, and the actual person the email says it's from doesn't know that the email was sent. To avoid many of the known problems with attachments, ensure that the settings to allow your antivirus program to scan and quarantine email is enabled. If your antivirus can catch and remove infected messages, there's less chance you'll open a file that will infect your system.

FREE EMAIL SITES

You could contact your ISP to have additional email accounts setup for various purposes, or you could set them up yourself through an online service. There are a number of sites available for setting up additional email accounts that are free, including:

- Gmail (www.gmail.com), which is a free email service from Google.
- Outlook (www.outlook.com), which was is Microsoft's email service formerly called Hotmail.
- mail.com (www.mail.com), which provides the ability to choose different domain names in the email address.

These free email services allow you to store and access your email online, using a web-based interface to read and compose messages. Some of these have almost unlimited storage, while others require you to pay for premium accounts that allow you to store mail and attachments over a certain limit. These sites may provide additional features and services that may be useful, such as online calendars and file storage.

When looking at the features of free online email, you want to ensure that the service provides virus checks and good SPAM filtering. As we have seen in Chapter 10, Protecting your kids, antivirus protection will prevent unwanted code from corrupting your data or system, while SPAM filtering will keep unwanted advertisements, scams, and other inappropriate, dangerous, and/or unwanted email from getting into your inbox. Even if you have antivirus software installed on your computer, it's important to realize that it will not scan and protect email and attachments stored on one of these sites. The email is stored on the email service's server, so you need to ensure that they provide adequate protection before you download or open anything that's been sent to you.

SECURITY SETTINGS ON EMAIL SITES

The security settings on free email sites vary. All of them will allow you to change your password, which as we saw in Chapter 2, Before connecting to the Internet, should be done on a recurring basis and use strong passwords. Beyond this, the features you encounter will vary.

While it would be impossible to cover the settings in every online email service, looking at a couple of popular sites will give you a good idea of what's offered, and how to configure it properly. In the following sections, we'll look at Mail.com and Gmail. For any email service, you'll generally find the security and privacy settings for your email under your account settings.

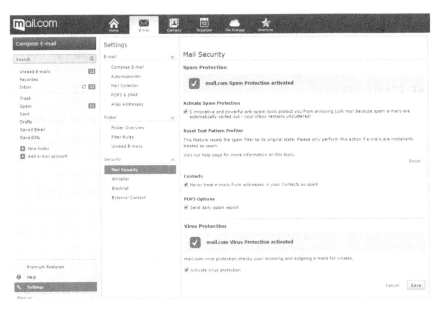

FIGURE 4.2

Mail.com security settings.

Mail.com security

If you're using mail.com as a free email service, you would login and see a link in the left pane of the screen called **Settings** (as shown in Fig. 4.2). Clicking this, you would then click on the **Mail Security** link under *Security*. Doing so provides you with a number of options, which when checked will activate the related feature:

- **Spam protection activated**, which will prevent SPAM emails from being added to your inbox.
- **Contacts**, which will prevent emails from people in your contact list from being flagged as SPAM. Generally, you can turn this off to prevent junk email that may have been automatically forwarded by people you know from appearing in your inbox. We saw how bots can do this without a person realizing it in Chapter 10, Protecting your kids.
- **POP3 options**, which has a checkbox that indicates you'd like to be sent a daily report about SPAM that may have been received. This allows you to release or delete any mail that may have incorrectly been flagged as SPAM.
- **Virus protection activated**, which checks your incoming and outgoing mail for viruses.

Other options in the security section of your mail.com account include:

- **Whitelist**, which allows you to add email accounts and domains that should always be trusted, and never marked as SPAM.

- **Blacklist**, which allows you to add email accounts and domains that should never be trusted, and you never want to receive mail from. This is especially useful if you are being harassed by a person, getting unwanted email from a company, or know that a particular site is a problem.
- **External content**, which after being clicked, shows a page with a checkbox that allows you to prevent any content hosted on an external site (such as images) from appearing in your email. If this is activated, a link will appear in your email that allows you to show the images, and does not apply to any emails in your SPAM folder (which already keeps external content from being displayed).

GMAIL SECURITY

Gmail offers a number of features designed to protect your privacy and enhance the security of using email. After logging into Gmail, you can access your settings by clicking on the gear shaped icon in the upper right-hand corner, and then clicking settings. After doing so, you're presented with a screen with tabs along the top of the screen. Clicking **Accounts and Import** will provide you with a variety of options to maintain your account, including a section called **Change account settings**. In this section, you can click on any of the following links:

- **Change password**, where you can enter a new password, and will tell you the strength of that password.
- **Change password recovery options**, which provides the ability to set recovery options if someone hijacks your account, or your password is forgotten. We'll discuss more about this shortly.
- **Other Google Account settings**, which presents a screen of additional options to control your account preferences, and options and tools related to your privacy and security settings. Again, we'll delve deeper into this in the paragraphs that follow.

The password recovery features in Gmail allow you to set what happens when you forget your password or it appears an unauthorized person is trying to get into your account. The options on this page allow you to set the following:

- **Mobile phone**, which (after providing your phone number) will be used to send a text message. Because an unauthorized person probably wouldn't have your mobile phone, this ensures that you're the person who the account belongs to.
- **Recovery email address**, which can be used to challenge someone attempting to logon, and allows you to reset your password if you're locked out.
- **Alternate email address**, which allows you to specify a secondary way to log onto your account. This would be a different email address than your gmail.com account.
- **Security question**, which allows you to set a question and answer that will be used to establish that you're the person who should be logging in.

The *Other Google Account settings* link takes you to the My Account page at https://myaccount.google.com, where you can access settings that control your account preferences, personal information and privacy (which we'll discuss further in chapter: Protecting yourself on social media), and sign-in and security options. The My Account page also provides tools for doing a checkup on your security and privacy settings, and will take you step-by-step through setting many of the options we're about to discuss.

If you click on the **Signing in to Google** link, you're given a number of options we've already discussed, including the ability to change your password, provide a recovery email address, provide a phone number to recover your account, and set a secret question. You're also given an option in the *Password and sign-in* method section to use 2-Step Verification.

When 2-Step Verification is used, you would log onto Gmail as you normally would, but after entering your password, a code is sent via text, voice call, or the Google mobile app. This feature becomes especially important if you use untrusted computers or devices to access your mail, such as public computers. You must then enter this code to access your mail. To set up Google's 2-Step Verification, follow these steps:

1. After logging into Gmail, go to https://myaccount.google.com.
2. Click on **Signing in to Google**.
3. Click on 2-Step Verification.
4. Click Start setup.
5. When the *Set up your phone* page appears, enter your phone number.
6. If you want Google to send you a text message with a code, click the **Text message (SMS)** option. If you want a voice call, then click the **Voice Call** option.
7. Click **Send code**.
8. When you receive the code, enter it in the box on the *Verify you phone* page, and then click **Verify**.
9. When the *Verification codes on this computer* screen appears, check the **Trust this computer** checkbox if you're using a trusted computer (such as your home computer). In doing so, you might still be able to access your account without a code.
10. Click Next.
11. When the *Turn on 2-step verification* screen appears, click **Confirm**.

The next link on the My Account page is the **Device activity & notifications link**, which provides important information about how your account is being accessed. Here, you'll find information on security events (such as password changes, modifications to your account, and so on), and devices that have recently been used to access the account. It shows the current device you're using to access your account, as well as any other computers or mobile devices that were previously used. You should regularly review this section to determine if someone else is accessing your account. If something seems amiss, you can click the **Secure your account** link to change your password, review settings, and add or change recovery information that we discussed earlier. If you don't think you'll regularly visit the page to monitor this (as is the case with most people), you should click the **Manage Settings** link under *Security alerts settings*. In doing so, you can set whether you'll receive an email and/or text message when there is a security risk (such as someone trying to access your account) or other account activity (such as when security settings are changed).

The final link is **Connected apps & sites**. As we saw in Chapter 1, What is cyber safety?, various apps on your mobile device or sites may connect to your Gmail account. By clicking the **Manage Apps** link on this page, you'll be able to view which apps have access, and what they have access to (inclusive to such things as your mail, calendar, contacts, or basic account info). If there's an app you no longer use, you would click on the **Remove** button beside the app's name to complete revoke its access. The page also provides a *Saved Passwords* section, where you can manage passwords saved with Google Smart Lock, which we discussed in Chapter 2, Before connecting to the Internet.

At the bottom of this section, you'll see an option to **Allow less secure apps**, which should be turned off. If an app uses less secure technology to sign-on, it can leave your Google account vulnerable, so by default this option is turned off.

NOTE

Other Ways of Checking Gmail Security and Privacy

You can also access your security settings by going to https://myaccount.google.com/security, and your privacy settings at https://myaccount.google.com/privacy. These sites will present you with the same options that we previously discussed related to security and privacy.

ENCRYPTION

There may be times when you need to send an email that's secure, ensuring that no one other than the person it's intended for reads it. There are a number of options available for encrypting messages, some of which require installing software like add-ons or extensions to your browser, while others are simple and straightforward.

Infoencrypt (www.infoencrypt.com) is an easy to use site, in which you type a message in a box on the web page, and provide and confirm a password. After clicking the **Encrypt** button, the page reloads and the message in the box is encrypted. For example, if you were to enter a phrase like "This is encrypted" and used the password *test*, it would return something like what follows:

```
-----BEGIN INFOENCRYPT.COM MESSAGE-----
Encryption-Info: null
Key-Info: null
Decrypt-URL: https://www.infoencrypt.com
ugb9B5G9FkB+Zot1mTsPpM/
Vn6RkBXF82ARPrgKizOqKnzU5Rg43Ct64wzzkfPNnRyEguhEd1yUP
XuZ7LPkFqJgIbTMNSE+EN++tpor4Q/OphGZ/OjW2ICss4Mwj6VJw
-----END INFOENCRYPT.COM MESSAGE-----
```

The message itself is meaningless, unless the recipient uses the correct password to decrypt it. You would copy and paste the contents of the box and email it to the intended recipient, secure in the knowledge that no one else can read it.

When the recipient receives it, they would click a link that takes them to Infoencrypt's website, where he or she copies and pastes the email message into the box, and enters and confirms the password you provided separately. After clicking **Decrypt**, the message is then revealed.

Another tool you can use to encrypt email sent through Gmail is a Google Chrome extension. By visiting Chrome's Web store at https://chrome.google.com/webstore/, you can search for "Secure Mail for Gmail" and find the Secure Streak Gmail extension. Alternatively, you can also type the nightmarishly long URL https://chrome. google.com/webstore/detail/secure-mail-for-gmail-by/jngdnjdobadbdemillgljnnb-pomnfokn and go directly to it. By clicking **Add to Chrome**, and then clicking **Add Extension** when the dialog appears, it will install in the browser.

Once the tool is installed, you can then logon to Gmail (www.gmail.com) and you'll see a new red button with a padlock icon beside the *Compose* button. Clicking the padlock icon will open a new message dialog. After composing the email, you'd then click the **Send Encrypted** button.

After you click the button to send your encrypted email, a new message will appear asking you to enter a password and provide a secret hint. The hint should be something that only the recipient would know the answer to, thereby revealing what to enter as a password. After filling this out, click the **Encrypt and Send** button.

The message that the recipient receives will be encrypted. If they receive it on a standard email client, it will include a link to install the Secure Streak Gmail Extension. If they already have the extension, they will see a link to decrypt the email, and when clicking it will be asked to enter a password and see your hint. After providing the password, the message is decrypted.

SUMMARY

Because email is such a widely used method of communication, it's important that you set any security and privacy settings to provide the most protection. In this chapter we discussed a number of settings that could leave you vulnerable to attacks, and when you should be wary of emails you receive. Now that you have a good understanding of this, we'll move on in Chapter 5, Cybercrime, to some of the common scams and problems you may encounter through email, other messages, and sites you visit.

Cybercrime

5

INFORMATION IN THIS CHAPTER

- What Is a Cybercriminal?
- Identity Theft
- Social Engineering
- Hacking
- Scams

Sometimes when people use the Internet, they have a false sense of security. You're sitting in your home, comfortable and enjoying the time you're spending surfing the Web. You assume no one can physically harm you through a computer screen, so any sense of danger doesn't even register in our minds. Some computers already have security programs installed, and keeping the default settings is probably good enough. After all, you have to trust the people who made those programs right? Besides, if anything happens, it will probably happen to someone else.

It's easy to lull yourself into a false sense of safety. While you should feel comfortable using the Internet, you should also be wary. After all, anything that could happen to someone else could happen to you.

WHAT IS A CYBERCRIMINAL?

A *cybercriminal* is a person who conducts some form of illegal activity using computers or other digital technology such as the Internet. The criminal may use computer expertise, knowledge of human behavior, and a variety of tools and services to achieve his or her goal. The kinds of crimes a cybercriminal may be involved in can include hacking, identity theft, online scams and fraud, creating and disseminating malware, or attacks on computer systems and sites. The core factor of what makes a crime a cybercrime is that it's directed at a computer or other devices and/or these technologies are used to commit the crime.

Cybercrime is prevalent because the Internet has become a major part of people's lives. In 2014, the FBI's Internet Crime Complaint Center (IC3) reported they received 269,422 complaints from people with an adjusted dollar loss of $800,492,0731 (Internet Crime Complaint Center, 2014). These numbers of course

The Basics of Cyber Safety. DOI: http://dx.doi.org/10.1016/B978-0-12-416650-9.00005-X

only reflect reported crimes, and not the numerous others who fall victim but never report it because they're too embarrassed or for other reasons.

HOW CRIMINALS CHOOSE THEIR TARGETS

The way that cybercriminals choose a target depends on their motivation. As we'll see later in this chapter, hackers will attack systems for a wide variety of reasons, ranging from altruistic intentions, personal glory, revenge, espionage, and/or financial gain. As we'll see in this chapter, the major reasons online crimes are committed are for money, sex, or power.

Cybercriminals often don't choose a particular person. The victim may be selected because they responded to an ad or email, or came in contact with the criminal through some other means. Perhaps you chatted with the wrong person, visited a site and inadvertently downloaded malware, or crossed the path of the criminal in some other way. In this scenario they didn't choose you personally, and didn't care if it was you or someone else who'd be the victim.

Criminals are drawn to where their targets are. If a pedophile wants to meet a child, it makes sense that he or she would be drawn to a site that caters to children. Similarly, if you wanted to get people's credit card numbers, you might hack a site where people enter that information. Just as you or your children are drawn to a site for a particular service or functionality, a cybercriminal will follow because it has the data or people they're looking for.

In some cases, a target is selected for very specific reasons. If you had a past relationship with someone, they might upload inappropriate picture to a site. They may stalk you online, bully you, threaten or coerce you in some way. In the same way, a company may be directly targeted because they are an inviting target, or the cybercriminal had a particular ax to grind, such as being a disgruntled employee or seeking revenge for some reason. As you can see from this, a cybercriminal isn't always the creepy nerd living in a creepy apartment that's often depicted in TV and movies. They very well may be someone you know and would never expect.

IDENTITY THEFT

Identity theft is the act of stealing a living or deceased person's identity, and using their information for the purposes of fraud. By impersonating another person, you can conceal your own identity, and use their credit history to acquire new sources of revenue, use services under their name, or use it for other personal gain. Once an identity thief has enough of your information, they can use it in a variety of ways:

- Credit card or bank/financial fraud.
- Telephone or utility fraud.
- Rent a house or apply for a mortgage.
- Obtain government documents (i.e., driver's license, apply for government benefits).

- Obtain a job using your national identification number (e.g., Social Security number). This might be done to bypass illegal immigration constraints, so they can work illegally.
- Get medical services, causing illnesses and injuries that you never had to be associated with in your medical record, and possibly accruing medical bills under your name. If insurance is used, it could also affect the available benefits remaining.
- Provide identification in your name during an arrest, leading to your name being associated with a crime, and possibly a warrant issued for your arrest.

The people who steal the identity of others can be any age or gender, as seen in the 2015 arrest of 72-year-old Cathryn Parker who was living under at least 74 different aliases and stole 7 people's identities (Serna, 2015). Most of the people she targeted were production crew members working in Hollywood, and used other people's information to lease a house, pay utilities, and acquire credit cards. She also had a previous mail fraud conviction in Hawaii for using a Jenny Craig Corp. travel account to buy plane tickets, which she then resold for $500 apiece.

Identity theft has been linked to organized crime, petty criminals who have the opportunity to use your information for personal gain, and could even been committed by a friend, family member, or someone else you know. In a survey conducted by the Federal Trade Commission (FTC), it was found that 16% of victims had a personal relationship with the thief, with 6% of the thieves being family members or relatives, 8% being friends, neighbors or in-house employees, and 2% being a coworker (Federal Trade Commission, 2007). Being most people don't know who stole their identity, these numbers probably underrepresent the number of people known to victims who have stolen their identity.

CONTROLLING THE INFORMATION YOU PROVIDE

To steal someone's identity, you need to acquire information that can be used to access a person's accounts, obtain documents, and complete applications that can be made in that person's name. The key details an identity thief will look for include:

- Full name
- Date of birth
- National identity numbers, such as a Social Security number or Social Insurance Number
- Government document numbers, inclusive to your driver's license and passport numbers
- Physical Addresses, such as where you live
- Usernames, passwords, and personal identification numbers (PIN)
- Financial account numbers, such as bank account numbers, and the numbers, expiry dates, and last three digits printed on the signature panel of your credit cards
- A copy of your signature
- Information that's commonly used for security questions, such as your mother's maiden name

The information an identity thief needs can be acquired in a variety of ways. A thief could look at social media accounts to find your full name, and links to the accounts of your friends and family, and posts wishing you a happy birthday will reveal your birthdate and often how old you are. Online resumes can provide information on past and present employers, and possibly your address and phone number. If you have a blog (especially one used as an online diary or journal), you may have published a goldmine of personal details. As we've seen in other chapters of this book, to block a potential thief from viewing these details, you want to manage what facets of your life are publicly accessible using privacy settings on an app or site, and avoid posting personally revealing or sensitive information online.

Once a person has enough details about you, they may use it to access your online accounts. For example, if your email address appears on a social media site, a thief could go to the email site and click a *Forgot Password* link, which might present a security question asking for your mother's maiden name, your hometown, or the name of your pet, which has already been gathered from previous investigation. Once they gain access to the account, they can read emails from sites you have accounts with, see monthly statements emailed to you, view your contacts, and see other information that may be useful. If they choose to try and gain access to a financial account (such as one accessed through a credit card or banking site), they might transfer funds or use the account numbers to make unauthorized charges.

Protecting yourself online can seem daunting, but it isn't hopeless. As we discussed in previous chapters, using strong passwords, nonstandard security questions and answers, and two-factor authentication whenever possible helps to prevent potential hackers from easily accessing your accounts. Limiting what information is available online, by being careful what you post, and not filling out any optional fields on accounts and forms will also limit what a hacker is able to see if he or she gains access.

You should also control what information people are able to acquire through physical means. If someone in your home or workplace can get a hold of your purse or wallet, they could quickly steal the information from there. If they're not locked or secure, any national identity cards, passports, or other documents in your home could be stolen by someone working or visiting your home. Chances are you'd never notice they were gone until you needed them, giving a thief considerable time to use the information.

A key to controlling information is to look at it as an asset. While we've been rightly trained to look at financial account numbers as being worthy of protection, you should look at other details of your life as valuable. Having the right combination of details would enable them to apply for new cards, steal your identity, or forge a new one using your information.

CHILD IDENTITY THEFT

Children are a common target of identity theft. Unlike adults, they have clean credit reports, and because they have no reason to check monthly statements or credit rating, the theft of their identity can go unnoticed for years. It isn't until later in life when they apply for student loans or a credit card, try and rent an apartment, or do any of the other things we take for granted in starting adult life that the problem is actually discovered. Reports have found that 10.7% of children have had their Social Security number used by someone else, and credit reports fail to detect 99% of child identity theft cases (May, 2012).

A child's identity can easily be stolen by someone who acquires their national identity number, such as a Social Security number. Once they have this, the thief can use a new birthdate so the identity doesn't appear as a minor, apply for other forms of identification, open new lines of credit, and qualify for government and medical benefits. When the child turns 18, his or her name and Social Security number is now associated a poor credit history and an older identity.

Using a credit monitoring service can help in identifying whether your child's identity has been stolen. Experian (www.experian.com) has a service called Family Secure (www.familysecure.com), which (for a fee) will monitor your child's personal information to determine if they have a credit file. With the information on file, if someone attempts to use their information to apply for credit, a lender is notified that the credit report requested is associated with a minor. Another free service, in which AllClearID has partnered with TransUnion (www.transunion.com) is called ChildScan (https://www.allclearid.com/personal/services/monitoring-services/), which scans databases for your child's Social Security number. If an instance of fraud is found, you can then have it investigated and have the child's stolen identity repaired.

An effective way to protect your child's identity is to freeze their credit. In doing so, creditors won't have access to their credit report, and will generally decline opening a new account. The catch 22 of this is that credit reporting agencies traditionally don't have a report on a person until they or someone else applies for credit in their name. To remedy the problem, 19 states have enacted legislation that allows a parent or guardian to have a credit record created and frozen for a child. Equifax (www.equifax.com) allows you to put a freeze on your child's records in all 50 states.

SOCIAL ENGINEERING

One of the easiest ways to gather information about you involves trickery. *Social engineering* is the practice of using various techniques to get people to reveal sensitive or personal information. By understanding how people act and react, a person influences others into performing actions or revealing confidential details. Using manipulation, technological means, or documents you've made accessible, the person is able to gather facts about you or another target. If done right, you won't realize you've given away information to the wrong person until it's too late, if at all.

There are many techniques that can be used to coax or convince a person to willingly give up information. A common method is called *pretexting*, in which you create a scenario that will persuade a person to perform some action or reveal the information you want. To give you an idea of how this might work, consider these situations:

- You might receive a call at work from someone claiming to be in the IT department, who says there's a problem with your network account. After some discussion, they ask for your username and password.

- Someone claiming to be with the police, FBI, or other law enforcement call you, a family member, friend, or neighbor, and say that your name came up in an investigation. They wonder if it's an identity confusion, and want some personal information to clear things up.
- Someone saying they're from the bank, a credit card company, or Internal Revenue Service (IRS) calls you and asks you to confirm some information to prove they're talking to the right person. They ask for bank account numbers, Social Security number, access codes, or other financial details.

The reason people are easily manipulated into giving away information is because they're convinced it's in their best interest to do so, or because they believe they're helping in some way. If the person claims to be in some position of authority, the target believes they have the right to know this information. After all, we're trained to answer and work with authority figures, and not question them.

Another way social engineering is used to gather sensitive details is through the use of surveys. Perhaps there's an enticement of some reward, the person conducting the survey is personable, or you want to help the person out by answering a few questions. Regardless of the reason, the results can often be surprising.

When InfoSecurity Europe (www.infosecurityeurope.com) conducted their second annual survey, they asked office workers at Waterloo Station in London, England, a series of questions with the reward of receiving a cheap pen. The questions included asking people to reveal their password, which 90% of those questions did. Of those questioned, 75% disclosed their password when asked "What is your password?" and 15% gave their password after some additional questions, such as asking the category their password fell into. Applying some social engineering tricks, a CEO of a company initially refused to compromise security and give up his password, but later said it was his daughter's name. When asked what his daughter's name was, he replied without thinking, thereby giving up his password.

While most people in this survey gave their password when asked, a social engineer will often structure the questions so it doesn't seem like you're revealing anything important. You may be in a chat room or conversation, and asked seemingly innocuous questions or drawn into a conversation where you reveal more as your trust in the person builds. The information can also be drawn out of you in ways you wouldn't consider. For example, you may have seen questions posted on Facebook notes or in email, where you're asked to share things that wouldn't normally come up in conversation so others can learn more about you. They may seem funny or silly, but if you searched Google for "Facebook notes questions," some of the types of questions include:

- What is your favorite color?
- What is your real name?
- What city were you born in?
- What is the name of your favorite pet?

While these may not seem important, especially when mixed in with fifty or a hundred other questions, you'll notice that these are also common security questions used if you need to reset a password. Even if a social engineer didn't send you the questions, they may be able to read ones you've answered previously by looking at your previous posts or Notes section.

Protecting yourself from social engineering requires being aware of the potential security risks, and taking steps to minimize them. In addition to the various tips we've discussed in relation to specific kinds of interactions (e.g., chat rooms and email) here are some additional tips:

- Be mindful of the information you post on the Internet, and realize it could be visible to strangers. If you're talking with someone you don't know in real life (i.e., Facebook friends, people in chat, those who call you), be wary of them. After all, they're still a stranger, even though they may have built up some trust.
- Question (and ask yourself) why someone is asking for the information. If you don't feel comfortable answering, then don't.
- Never reveal personal, financial, or other sensitive information over the phone or Internet. If it's in person, make sure it's in a secure location, such as the offices of your bank.
- Realize that anyone in an IT department won't request information like usernames and passwords over the phone or in an email.
- If a caller asks for confidential information, ask for their contact information, and then verify that it's real. Don't trust the phone number they give you, as it may be false. Use the phone book, dial information, or use the company's website (if you're familiar with it) to get the correct phone number, and have them redirect you to that person's extension. If they claim to be from a financial institution, you could call the number on your monthly statement.

TECHNOLOGY AND SOCIAL ENGINEERING

Different communication methods are used by social engineers to find and target a victim, including the mail, phone, email, instant messaging, and other Web-based technologies. Since the early days of the Internet, various ploys have been used to get credit card numbers and other personal details. Some would use it to setup fake accounts with Internet Service Providers, so that they could exchange pirated software, while others used the information to access other people's accounts, commit fraud, or other crimes. As the years progressed, using the Web has become a mainstay for cybercriminals to find and interact with potential targets.

Phishing is a common process in which cybercriminals try and fool you into revealing login credentials, financial details, and/or other sensitive information that can be later used to commit fraud or access accounts. The attacker will send messages that appear to come from an official source, such as a bank, credit card company, auction site, social media site, or another popular site that can be used to lure victims. Because it appears to come from a trusted source, and may include the logo of the company it's posing as, you're more likely to believe it's legitimate. If the site contains a link, clicking it may download malware or take you to a bogus website where you'll be asked to enter personal, financial, and other sensitive information.

The term *phish* is a homonym for "fish," as in *you have to cast a big net to catch a few fish*, which also describes how it works. A scammer will send out unsolicited email (SPAM), text messages, or other forms of communication in bulk. While many people will dismiss the message, a few will respond to it. There are some variations phishing, including:

- *Spear phishing*, where an individual or group of people in the same company or department are the focus of an attack. Because it addresses a specific person or group, it may have information related to them, and even appear to be coming from another area of the organization (such as Accounting or the IT department); there is a great likelihood for recipients to open and respond to it.
- *Clone phishing*, where a previously sent email that's legitimate is copied and resent, with alterations made (such as a link to a bogus site and a malware attachment). Because the original email is known to be real, and the cloned one has the same content but perhaps claims to be an updated or resent version of the original, people will believe it to be real and likely to open it.
- *Whaling*, where management and senior executives are targeted in an attack. An email may appear to be customer complaint, legal document, subpoena, or other messages that are likely to be opened by the recipient.

Many of the things mentioned above are sent in emails with either links to other sites or attachments that they want you to open. The sites that may be included in links within the message can be quite elaborate in mimicking a legitimate site. A *copycat site* may have a similar URL to the real company's site, and the person running it may have even used website tools to promote the site in search engine results, so it appears to be the real company when you do a search. Even government sites have been copied, asking fees for services that are free to citizens, and requesting payment for licenses, passports, and other items at an excessive price. Another indication that it's a copycat site may be that they request you provide information on an insecure site (i.e., not using HTTPS).

Even though the copycat site appears the same at face value, you should try and pay attention to any errors or odd things about the site. If you're visiting a site that's familiar to you, it may be obvious that there have been changes. Perhaps the logo is outdated, the URL is different, or the quality of the site doesn't seem to match the company's professional image. Even if it's your first visit, you may notice spelling and grammar mistakes, even to the point that it seems created by someone who speaks English as a second language or used Google Translate to generate the text. If it seems wrong, don't trust the site.

SUSPICIOUS EMAILS AND SPAM

As we mentioned, *SPAM* is a term used to describe unsolicited email or messages that are sent to groups of people. The person sending the message is referred to as a *spammer*. The email may contain advertising, and simply be an annoying marketing tactic, or could be used by scammers and hackers to find potential victims.

A spammer may also post on various sites, or implement software known as a *spambot*. The spambot may be designed to gather email addresses from sources on the Internet so that email can be sent to those people, or create new accounts to send email or post messages on a site. A spambot could also be used to search the Internet for comment sections, guestbooks, wikis, or other forums so it can post a message. You may have seen these and thought it was an actual person claiming they made huge amounts of money working from home, or providing a link to a video sharing, dating, or pornography site.

SPAM is used for a variety of purposes. It's often used to promote substandard or fraudulent products and services, such as those making outlandish claims that appeal to human desires. It might promise sure-fire ways of seducing women or losing weight. In purchasing the offer, you'll generally find it doesn't work as promised. As we've discussed, it's also used as a communication method for social engineering ploys. The message may contain links to bogus sites that automatically download malware, a site where you're fooled into providing login credentials or personal and financial information, or contain attachments that are virus infected or install malware.

To get a potential victim to a bogus site, malware may be used to modify your computer. *Pharming* is the process of being redirected from a legitimate site to one that may be used for phishing information. As we explained in Chapter 1, What is cyber safety?, when you type a URL into the address bar of your browser, it's translated by a DNS server into an IP address. This information may be saved on your computer in a DNS cache, so the next time you go to the site your computer can resolve the name from previously stored information, rather than having to contact the DNS server again. Unfortunately, if this information is poisoned in some way, like a virus or other malware, you could be redirected to a different IP address, where you'll be presented with a site that looks like the one you meant to visit, but is designed to fool you into providing sensitive information.

To avoid the problems of SPAM, it's important not to open unexpected or suspicious emails, and don't click any links within them. As we discussed in Chapter 4, Email safety and security, using the SPAM filters on an email client or site will help detect and remove any known or suspected SPAM messages, so they're sent to a Junk folder rather than appearing in your Inbox.

BAITING

Baiting is a tactic in which a social engineer will entice you with something that you with something that's difficult to resist or intrigues you, so you ultimately perform an action that the cybercriminals wants you to take. Visiting a site, you might be offered free music and movie downloads on the condition you provide your login credentials for a certain site. Even if you're not required to give any information, clicking the link may download a file containing a Trojan virus, or pop open another browser to a site that automatically downloads malware.

Baiting isn't always done online. A common way to bait someone is to leave a USB flash drive where someone is likely to find it, such as at a bus stop, restaurant, or parking lot. If targeting a particular company, it might be left it by an employee entrance or the smoking area where they take breaks. When a person finds the USB, they may be curious about what it contains, especially if it's labeled as "Employee salaries" or some other intriguing topic. The person may go back to their desk and plug it into their computer, only to find they've installed a hacking tool or some other form of malware. Even if the employee turns the USB in to the IT department it still poses a risk because security may try and open it to find who it belongs to. If the IT department does this, the user may have administrative privileges, meaning the hacker's tool or malware has full permissions and wider access to the network. By trying to be helpful, the person may have compromised his or her own account, or infected the network.

HACKING

Hacking is a term that's come to refer to the act of breaking into a computer system. Originally, the term *hacker* referred to anyone who was a computer enthusiast, and would "hack" away at a keyboard, programming or working on the computer in some other way. A *cracker* on the other hand was someone who would attempt to crack the security of a system, crack passwords, or perform other actions to gain access. For ease of understanding, we'll use the terms interchangeably throughout the book.

Unlike what's shown in the movies, there is no cookie cutter image or motivation behind modern day hackers. There are good and bad hackers, who fall into several distinctive groups:

- **White hats**, who are professional security experts hired by companies, and attempt to penetrate a network to identify problems that can be fixed. After debugging and testing the existing system, they will submit a report showing where the network is vulnerable, and make suggestions for improvement.
- **Gray hats**, who are individuals having ethical standards that may be altruistic and/or malicious. While a white hat hacker obtains permission from a vendor to find and exploit vulnerabilities, a gray hat may tell the vender that a vulnerability exists but will only provide additional information for a fee or publicize how it can be exploited. Gray hats are also associated with activists who may attack a target believing it's for altruistic purposes.
- **Black hats**, who are what most people tend to think of as hackers, who compromise accounts and systems for malicious purposes and/or personal gain. These are individuals who crack passwords, gain unauthorized access, and may cause disruptions and damage to systems. When a black hat discovers a vulnerability or ways to exploit a system, he or she will generally keep it to himself or herself or share it with other hackers.

As you can see, the reason someone will hack a system or account varies. Some will try to flex their intellectual skills, and try to see if they're smart enough to find and bypass security measures. Others may focus on a target for a specific purpose. *Hacktivists* are hackers who rationalize going after a company or person because they believe they're doing some good, seeking revenge, or righting some wrong. In this case, the target and purpose is clear, and often publicized to make everyone know the reason. If hackers disapprove of a particular business or government agency, they may attempt to disrupt service so that clients are unable to access their website, or the company is unable to do business.

In the age we live in, hacking is done primarily for the purpose of financial gain or espionage. The goal is profit and information, whether it be personal or on behalf of a client. A company may hire hackers to acquire the corporate secrets of their competition, and government agencies will gather intelligence on other countries or its own citizens. In these cases, the hacker may focus on acquiring specific information about the target, such as looking at the stability of a government, a new product that is being developed, or corporate financial records.

A hacker may focus his or her attack on gaining entry to customer databases. Depending on the company targeted, the information compromised in a data breach could involve personal, financial, medical, or other sensitive records. A hacker may access a company's database to acquire usernames and passwords, credit card numbers, or other details that could be used for extortion, identity theft, fraud, or shared and sold online, where others can then use the data to commit other crimes. Some of the more serious data breaches in recent years include (Collins, 2015):

- eBay, in which 145 million records were stolen, including the login credentials, email addresses, and physical addresses of active users.
- Target, in which 110 million records were stolen in 2013, including credit card numbers of customers.
- Home Depot, in which 109 million records were stolen, including credit card numbers and email addresses of customers.
- JPMorgan, in which 83 million records were stolen in 2014, including email addresses and physical addresses.
- Anthem, in which upwards of 80 million records were stolen over a course of several weeks in December 2014, including names, birthdates, Social Security numbers, health care ID numbers, income data, email addresses, and physical addresses (Anthem, 2015).
- Premera Blue Cross, in which 11 million records were stolen in 2015, including bank accounts, birthdates, Social Security numbers, claims data, and clinical information (Finkle, 2015).

HIJACKING/HACKED ACCOUNTS

When you hear of hacking, much of what's reported in the media focuses on instances where organizations have had service disrupted, or major data breaches where records have been stolen. This can give the false assumption that hackers only focus on larger targets. While many attacks are on larger targets, hackers, identity thieves, and other cybercriminals may also set their sights on individuals.

One reason an individual's account may be hacked is to access details that aren't public, and only available to friends or the account owner. In 2014, 12% of all complaints the FBI's Internet Crime Complaint Center (www.ic3.gov) received were somehow related to social media, and in many cases these instances involved gathering information on the person through a compromised account or social engineering (Internet Crime Complaint Center, 2014).

Hacking an account is done to acquire access, but if the person uses the account to impersonate the owner, it's referred to as *hijacking*. The attacker has the ability to view your settings, contacts, calendar, and other details that are accessible through the compromised account. If an email or social media account is linked to other sites, they can then logon as you to use various other online services. By posing as you, he or she can also communicate with your contacts to gather more information, or ask them for money or help with an illegal or bogus activity. They may even go through a process of making posts, sending emails, and sharing information to ruin your reputation.

Spammers and other cybercriminals may hijack an account to post messages as you. In doing so, there is a better chance of getting others you know to follow a link, sign up for a service, purchase a product, or enter information into a site designed to acquire login credentials, or personal and financial information. Hijacking the account may be done by guessing your password, using cracking tools, or social engineering tactics to gain access. They may also use malicious software or hide code in a link or page you visit. For example, you might click on a post, and it is then shared by you. In doing so, a spammer is able make it seem that you're endorsing the site, so that your friends and followers will also click the link.

Someone using social engineering may pose as you to gain the trust of others you know. If you don't already have a social media account, it would appear that you just joined the site, so people wouldn't think much about adding you as a friend or following you. If you're already a member, they could make it seem that you've ditched your old account in favor of a new one. Once you're added as a friend, the bogus user posing as someone you know could see any posts and personal information that you haven't made public.

On Facebook, you're not allowed to create a fake account and pretend to be someone else. If you find an account where someone is impersonating you or someone else, you can simply go to the person's profile page, click the button with three dots ··· , and then click **Report**. When the form appears, fill it out to report the account as impersonating someone else.

If you don't have a Facebook account and want to report something, you can go to www.facebook.com/help/, click **Report Something** in the left pane, click **Don't Have an Account?** in the left pane, and then click on the **How do I report a fake account that's pretending to be me if I don't have a Facebook account?** link. When the section expands, click the link to file a report, and file a report.

DEFACED SITES

Another reason that hackers will try and access a website is to deface it, as an online version of vandalism. Just as any other vandal would spray-paint on a wall, a hacker will often deface a site for "fun," as part of a larger attack, or as a form of protest by hacktivists. They may change graphics, or modify text, or even sign their work by adding an alias that identifies them. The attack might bring attention to an issue being protested, embarrass a targeted organization, and can have a negative effect on a company's business. As a visible sign that the site was hacked, existing clients and potential customers are shown that the site is insecure. To see examples of various defaced sites, you can visit Zone-h (www.zone-h.org), click **Archive**, and then click on the mirror link beside an entry to see what the site looked like after being defaced.

COMMON METHODS

While movies and TV shows tend to show a person sitting at a computer and miraculously penetrating a network with a few keystrokes, hacking often involves research, skill sets, the right tools, and time. This isn't to say that there aren't times when opportunity presents itself: a computer with no security might be on an open Wi-Fi network, the wrong permissions applied to a folder allow everyone access, or mistakes in a seemingly secure site allow entrance to areas that are supposed to be reserved for members. While such things happen, most times you'll need to discover what's available, what's vulnerable, and find the best way to get in and out without being detected.

Reconnaissance is the first step a hacker will take, where they try to gather as much information as possible about a target. Often, a hacker will begin with *passive reconnaissance*, which doesn't involve direct interaction, is harder to detect, and doesn't involve using tools that touch the target's site, network, or computers. Some of the ways you might do passive reconnaissance include:

- Search engines, which may reveal documents with the names of a Virtual Private Network (VPN) the company uses, vendor documentation mentioning that the target is a client using certain products (routers, software, etc.). In doing this, you may get information on the company's remote access, and see cache pages that allow you to stay passive.
- Job advertisements, which can reveal contact information, requirements to know certain software or equipment that may have vulnerabilities that can be exploited, and so on.
- LinkedIn and other sites where employees have identified their involvement with a target.
- Whois sites (like www.who.is) that provide the names of servers, IP address ranges, the names of administrators, email addresses, and so on.
- Wayback Machine (www.archive.org) to see past versions of a website, allowing you to review the target's site, see contact information for employees, and even content that may have deemed a security risk and removed from the current site.

Once you've learned what you can do without touching a site or network, a hacker will move onto *active reconnaissance*, which involve interaction with a target and could be traceable. For example, a hacker may call or talk to employees, visit their website, or other actions in which they touch the network as a normal user. After gathering everything you can on a company, its infrastructure, personnel, and other details that can help you gain access, you should have a good idea of the company's structure and network, and ready to move onto other steps:

- **Scanning**, where you try and identify what hosts are live and their purpose on a network. The hacker might use the PING command to see what servers are running, or use port scanning software to find weaknesses like open ports or ways to bypass firewalls. In doing so, he or she may throttle the scan so its slow pings and scans hide in the normal network traffic, and isn't easily detectable.
- **Service Enumeration**, where you identify the services running on a server, and determine any vulnerabilities they might have.
- **Assess Vulnerabilities**, where you identify vulnerabilities in an app, site, or network. You might use a vulnerability database, knowledge bases, and a vulnerability scanner like OpenVAS (www.openvas.org) to scan a system and provide a report.
- **Exploit Vulnerability**, where you either find an existing exploit or develop a new one that can take advantage of vulnerabilities you've discovered.

At this point, the hacker is finally at a stage where he or she can use the gathered information to attempt breaking into a system or site. The method used will depend on the skill level of the hacker, and what's easiest and makes the most sense to achieve their goals. For example, if they can get a username and password for an FTP site from a list or through social engineering, they might logon as an authentic user, and then modify or upload web pages so the content is different. If they've accessed an administrator account, they have full control of the server or system. If not, they may try to exploit vulnerabilities they've found to elevate their privileges to this level.

A hacker's goal may be to roam the folders and file structure of a server, hoping to find documents and data sources that make their expedition fruitful, but they may not even need to go this far. If a Web developer has poorly coded an application, an administrator hasn't set permissions properly, and/or security is ineffective, a hacker might be able to do what he or she wants using forms that accept user input or URLs that accept parameters.

Depending what the hacker hoped to achieve, he or she may leave a site so it appears untouched. Any evidence of what was done is cleaned up, permissions are reset, and log files are deleted. The hacker may install a rootkit (which we discuss later) or other malware; he or she may create fake accounts or backdoors that will allow him or her future access. By the end of it, administrators and users may be fooled into believing nothing's happened, and they're safe.

Despite the appearance, a hacker might modify links to spread malware or redirect users to a site they control. *Click jacking* is a method of adding a hyperlink to clickable content. You might visit a page, and a popup window appears that you try and close by clicking an "X" button. Because the link's been modified, clicking it may actually download a Trojan Horse, transfer money from an account on the site you're visiting, send you to another site to gather information from you, or some other action you didn't expect.

A variation on clickjacking is *likejacking*, where you'll see a post or status update on Facebook.

Facebook is a common venue for clickjacking, where it often takes the form of likejacking. A post or status update may promise a video or have an intriguing or scandalous draw, such as saying "OMG This GUY Went A Little To Far WITH His Revenge On His EX Girlfriend." When you click on it, you might be asked to like or share the post before you've even seen it, presented with a fake CAPTCHA or a link that asks you to take a test to prove you're human. However, these aren't actually challenges to prove you're not a robot. Links and buttons on the page will run code to share or like the posts, distributing the spam to others viewing your posts. These scam posts are often used to gather user information, and may redirect you to other spam, phishing, or other malicious websites.

While hacking a site may seem covert, many hackers will post information about it on the Internet. Details of the hack, samples of data, or links to a complete dump of the database may appear on sites like Pastebin (www.pastebin.com), allowing others to view and download the data. Other sources of finding hacked data include Internet Relay chat, tweets about new dumps on Pastebin through Dump Monitor (@ dumpmon), or Twitter accounts belonging to a person or group responsible for the data breach. This shares the information with other cybercriminals, who may then use the data to commit other crimes.

Doxing is another practice of sharing information acquired through hacking and other means. *Dox* is a homonym for docs (i.e., documents) and involves uploading sensitive documents or a dossier of information onto the Internet. For example, in March 2013, the personal and financial information of numerous celebrities were posted on a site called Expose.su. Some of the victims included FBI Director Robert Mueller, Kim Kardashian, Hillary Clinton, Mel Gibson, Ashton Kutcher, and others. Web pages on the site displayed such information as their full names, birthdates, Social Security numbers, current and previous addresses, phone numbers, and copies of a credit report. It was found that while some details on the site were false, other information was accurate.

Groups

While hackers may work alone, there are informal and organized communities of hackers who work together and share information. Those involved include elite hackers with programming and database skills, *script kiddies* who use other people's scripts and instructions because they lack the expertise to do it themselves, and those who fall in between who are developing their skills and evolving into a more sophisticated threat. For those involved, it may provide support, a sense of belonging, and a way for new hackers to find mentorship.

While members of a group may know each other, other groups like *Anonymous* have no central leader and many members may only know each other through online interactions. These groups may use message boards, Twitter, and other forums to share resources and information. In joining together, a group of hackers will coordinate efforts so that they understand their target(s), type of attack, and timing of what events are to occur. This allows them to engage one or more targets effectively in large campaigns or operations (*ops*).

Inside jobs

Not every attack originates from an outside source. Private data becoming public, unauthorized access being given, and other threats can be caused by malicious or careless users in an organization. According to a report from Intel, 43% of data loss was attributed to those inside an organization; half of which was intentional, while the other half was accidental (Intel Security, 2015).

The simple fact is that in any organization mistakes happen. A person may send confidential information to the wrong person or erroneously post classified information on a public site. For example, in December 2015, a configuration error resulted in 140,000 records on a Southern New Hampshire University database being exposed to the public (Ragan, 2016). Other types of accidental loss may involve situations where a computer, laptop, or other device or storage media is discarded or lost. Such an incident occurred in November 2015, when staff at the Indiana University Health Arnett Hospital realized an unencrypted flash drive was missing. Spreadsheets on the drive contained information on 29,000 patients, including their names, birthdates, phone numbers, and medical information like diagnoses and treating physicians (Indiana University Health, 2015).

Where insider threats are particularly dangerous is when a breach occurs because of a malicious user. While a lost USB drive may never be found and an exposed database may never be discovered, someone has a reason for stealing information. As we discussed in Chapter 1, What is cyber safety?, when Edward Snowden had access to top secret documents, he took it for the purpose of leaking it online. A cybercriminal might acquire a position to have access to data, while a disgruntled employee may see an opportunity to sell it or leak it.

Even though no one has ever attacked a site or system, the results of an accidental or malicious data breach can be the same. It can damage confidence in an organization, resulting in a loss of business, and threatens the confidentiality and privacy of customers. Sixty-eight percent of data breaches were serious enough that the company public disclosure was required or had a negative financial impact on the business (Intel Security, 2015). Regardless of how the information gets out there, the damage is done and the cost can be high.

Low tech

Some of the best methods to get a person's password are the low-tech ones. As we saw when discussing social engineering, it's often easier to simply get a person to give you what you want. In addition to the methods we've discussed, there are a number of other tactics that can give a cybercriminal access to what they want.

Shoulder surfing involves looking over someone's shoulder to see what they're typing. If you have a clear view, and a good memory, you can watch them type and then use what you've seen to gain access. If someone can see your PIN as you use an ATM or a debit/credit card payment machine, all they need is your card. For situations like entering a code for a rented locker, unlocking the screen on a phone or tablet, or other single-factor authentication, or typing in a username and password, they only need the PIN or password. To avoid becoming a victim, ensure that any usernames and passwords are shielded as you type them.

Modern technology has made it more difficult defending yourself against shoulder surfing. While you should be wary of anyone behind you or nearby, who may be watching what you're doing on a keyboard or screen, you probably won't notice someone watching you over a closed circuit security camera or watching from a distance with binoculars. Therefore, even though no one is in sight, don't assume no one is watching.

Another useful tactic is *dumpster diving*, in which a person simply goes through your trash trying to get a hold of telling information. If it's a business' garbage, they may find printed maps of the network infrastructure, billing records, manuals, or employee names. This could be useful for social engineering, or (if someone threw out a sticky note with a password) hacking. If it's your home garbage, they may find preapproved credit cards, a bill with account numbers, or other information to steal your identity. To avoid being a victim, you should shred any documents with sensitive or personal information, as well as ID, and financial cards.

If a hacker wanted access to the building so they could have direct access to employees, computers, and other devices, they might *tailgate* someone who works there. *Tailgating* involves following a person into a restricted area. The person may say that they forgot their keycard at their desk and fumble with a number of things to appear as if they're having trouble finding their door card. If it was cold or raining, they might simply scurry inside behind you, complaining about the weather. Since people often want to be helpful, and don't commonly challenge others if they appear confident and as if they belong there, tailgating is a simple and effective way of gaining entry.

Once a person is in a restricted area, he or she may have better access to a company's information and network. While the Wi-Fi and network wall sockets in a public area may be limited, a hacker may find fewer restrictions plugging their laptop into a free wall socket in an office. The hacker may also see confidential documents on desks, usernames, and passwords that someone's written on a sticky note and attached to a monitor or under a keyboard. They can also ask if they might use someone's laptop or computer for a moment to check something, giving them the ability to install a program they'll use to hack the system remotely. By giving people the benefit of a doubt, you've helped them in their attack.

TOOLS

There are a variety of tools a hacker may use to gain access, disrupt service, or damage systems. In many cases, a hacker may use the same ones an IT professional would use to analyze network problems and other issues. There are also tools that are specifically designed for the purpose of cracking security and causing problems.

BOTNETS AND ROOTKITS

Rootkits are tools that may be installed on a computer to give a person elevated privileges to a system and/or to install other software. The rootkit may be installed automatically by hiding it in other software you've downloaded, as a Trojan horse, or installed manually once a hacker's gained access to your system. Once installed, it may create a backdoor that gives a hacker remote access to your computer, install other malware, or install *bots* (small programs designed to perform a specific task).

Bots aren't always malicious, as seen by *spiders* or *crawlers* that are used by search engines to access websites and gather information about what content is on a site. Unfortunately, the ones that aren't innocuous may be designed to access accounts, or determine what downloads are on a site so malware can be created that's disguised as programs that site offers. Another kind of bot is a *spambot*, which gathers valid email addresses, so mailing lists can be created to send SPAM. Bots are particularly dangerous when they're deployed to large collections of computers, called *botnets*. Once a computer is infected, the bot can lay dormant until an attacker chooses to activate them. At this point, the attacker has control of your computer (now called a *zombie*) and all the other computers in the botnet (also called a *zombie army*). The attacker can send a signal to have these computers distribute viruses, or send messages to a particular server in a coordinated attack called a *Distributed Denial of Service* attack. Because the server gets so many messages from the zombie army, it can't serve legitimate requests to provide a web page or send-and-receive emails. By flooding the targeted server with traffic, the websites and services it provides become inaccessible and the server may crash.

Password cracking

Despite improvements in authenticating a user, passwords are still a common method of determining if a person or process is supposed have access. While someone may try and crack your password manually by guessing and/or using social engineering tactics, there are also tools that will automatically try combinations of letters, numbers, special characters, dictionary words, check for patterns, and other methods to determine the password. Even if a password is encrypted, it doesn't mean that it can't be cracked. A brute force cracking tool may try millions of combinations per second until the hacker gives up or the password is finally discovered.

Password cracking tools are often associated with hacking an account on a site, app, or computer, but there are also ones designed to crack the encryption keys used on Wi-Fi networks. Some of the password-cracking tools that may be used include:

- John the Ripper (www.openwall.com/john/)
- Cain and Able (www.oxid.it/cain.html)
- AirCrack (www.aircrack-ng.org)

Because the tool goes through a calculated method of guessing passwords, the time it takes to crack a password varies. The strength of the password, whether encryption is used, and whether there is a limited number of attempts before the account is locked out are all variables in this. In August 2014, Apple's cloud services called iCloud was hacked, resulting in almost 500 private images of celebrities, including those with nudity be stolen. The accounts were accessed using a combination of spear phishing and brute force attacks, and Apple later patched a vulnerability that allowed unlimited attempts to guess usernames and passwords (VoVPN, 2015). Such a vulnerability isn't unique. When AppBugs (www.appbugs.co) randomly tested 100 popular apps, they found that 53 of them allowed unlimited logon attempts, meaning a hacker could try over and over again to guess the password without being locked out (AppBugs, 2015).

Another way to get someone's password is to use recovery tools. In using recovery tools, you're able to do such things as see the passwords saved on a person's computer, such as those used in email clients and ones saved in the browser, as well as view other information and restore data that may have been deleted.

Keylogger

Keyloggers are programs that record what you type, logging each keystroke. Some provide the ability to record mouse clicks, what programs you're using, and may even take screenshots at regular intervals. They can be installed manually or automatically without your knowledge, such as by inserting a flash drive into a USB slot or through a rootkit. Once it's on your computer, someone can discreetly monitor everything you're doing. The keylogger may save the recorded keystrokes on your machine (such as to a local or external drive, or flash drive), to a remote location (such as sending it to an FTP site), or emailed.

As seen in the Fig. 5.1 (www.blazingtools.com/bpk.html), Perfect Keylogger provides an easy-to-use interface that allows you to navigate through different dates. Once you've selected a particular date in question, you can then choose to see the text someone typed on their keyboard, chats, websites they visited, and screenshots of their activity. If you're using it to monitor someone, it also includes useful date and time stamps to show when the person did something.

As we'll see in Chapter 10, Protecting your kids, and Chapter 13, keyloggers can be useful in situations where you want to monitor someone's activity, such as when your child is using the Internet. However, in the hands of a cybercriminal, it can be a vital resource in seeing the usernames and passwords someone typed, the sites those credentials are used for, and other data that may be used for identity theft, blackmail, fraud, and countless other crimes.

REALIZING ANY SITE COULD BE HACKED

Regardless of how diligent you are in securing your own computer and devices, data can reside on systems that you rely on others to protect. Being careful of the kinds of information you provide is important, and certainly minimizes the risk, but despite your efforts you do need to accept that some things are out of your control. There is no guarantee that a site won't be hacked, because any site or system could be.

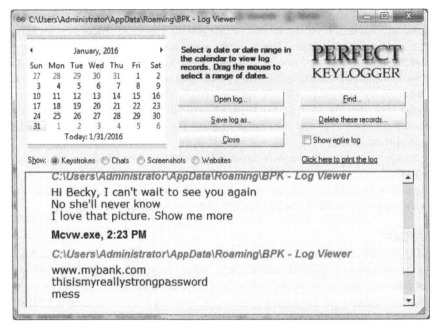

FIGURE 5.1

Perfect keylogger.

Without a doubt, the most sensitive data you own is stored by the government, but even their systems aren't impenetrable. In May 2015, the IRS discovered it was hacked through a "Get Transcript" Web application on their site. It resulted in 330,000 taxpayer accounts being accessed (Phillips, 2015). In June 2015, a separate hacking incident resulted in one of the largest breaches of government data. When the United States Office of Personnel Management was hacked, 21.5 million records were stolen. Most of the data belonged to those who'd been subjected to government background checks, and consisted of personally identifiable information like Social Security numbers, birthdates, places of birth, addresses, financial histories, and even fingerprints (Hirschfeld Davis, 2015). Since there's no way to avoid filing income tax returns or getting background checks for employment and volunteer work, there's no way of avoiding your information being in such systems.

Because any site could potentially be hacked, it doesn't mean that a hacked site should be considered off limits and never used again. Once a site or system's compromised, you should look at how the business, agency, or organization has handled the breach:

- Did they admit the breach occurred, admit any fault, and accept responsibility? Customers should be notified and told what data may have been accessed.

- Are they transparent? They should provide details of how it happened, what they've done to mitigate the problem, and what they're doing to prevent it from happening again.
- What are they doing for you? They should provide solutions for affected customers and educate them so they understand steps to take. For example, when the IRS was breached, they offered free credit monitoring to those whose accounts were breached.
- Are they providing updates? While it's important to notify customers, and they may have released a press statement about the data breach, it's important to provide updated information. When Anthem was hacked in 2014, they setup a site at www.anthemfacts.com to keep customers informed and understand what help was available.

Until you have some certainty that their systems are secure, don't use the site or enter any additional information. If they provide a service you need, contact them and ask about alternatives. For example, if it's your insurance company, ask if there are alternate ways of submitting your claim. Once they've taken every possible step to fix the problem, and updated or upgraded their security, you can decide whether the site is worth visiting again.

PROTECTING YOURSELF

While you have no control over whether a site is secure, or whether a Web developer has properly coded and sanitized user input, there is protection on the user end. As we've discussed in this and previous chapters, you can protect yourself by:

- Not clicking on unfamiliar links, such as those sent to you in email, which may download malware or take you to phishing sites.
- Using encrypted connections, such as those using HTTPS to transfer data across the Internet, avoiding unencrypted Wi-Fi, and using the strongest possible encryption on your home network.
- Running a firewall to protect the machine from hacking attempts.
- Updating antivirus/malware software. Such security can block hacking and phishing attempts, prevent the download of malware, and remove malware as it's detected.
- Keep your computer and other devices updated, so they can't be harmed by known exploits.

Using up-to-date browsers also provides better security when using the Internet. Modern browsers will make use of *whitelists* of trusted sites and *blacklists* of sites that are known or suspected of being used for phishing or other malicious purposes. For example, on Chrome, you can do the following to turn on safe browsing:

1. Click on the **Settings** icon in the upper right-hand corner
2. Click on **Show advanced settings**
3. Ensure the **Protect you and your device from dangerous sites** checkbox is checked. If not, click on it so it appears checked.

Once turned on, if you try to browse to a site that's known to be dangerous, you'll instead be presented with a screen that warns you that the site contains malware, is suspected of phishing, or may be otherwise harmful. With this turned on, you'll also receive download warnings, such as when Chrome blocks you from downloaded a virus infected or otherwise unwanted file.

Firefox also blocks harmful sites and attempts to install browser add-ons. Once you visit a site, it will see if it's on a blacklist of sites to be avoided. To ensure this protection is turned on:

1. Click on the **Settings** icon in the upper right-hand corner
2. Click on **Options**
3. When the *Options* dialog box appears, click on the **Security** icon at the top
4. Ensure the following checkboxes are checked. If not, click on the checkbox so it appears checked:
   a. Warn me when sites try to install add-ons
   b. Block reported attack sites
   c. Block reported web forgeries

Similarly, Internet Explorer 8 and higher provide a *SmartScreen Filter*. When turned on, Internet Explorer will check a site you visit and files you attempt to download against a list of reported sites and programs that are known to be unsafe. It will also analyze pages you visit to see if it has characteristics that are suspicious, such as those used for phishing. If you do try and visit such as a site, you'll see a page showing you've been blocked. To turn on the SmartScreen Filter:

1. Click on the **Tools** menu
2. Select *SmartScreen Filter*, and then click **Turn on SmartScreen Filter**

An added measure of security to protect you from cross-site scripting, clickjacking, and force the browser to use HTTPS is NoScript Security Suite (www.noscript.net). NoScript is a Firefox extension that blocks JavaScript, Java, Flash, Silverlight, and other plugins that can be potentially harmful. Unless you've added the site to NoScript's whitelist, the active content on a site is blocked.

Portable tools

Part of dealing with problems is being prepared before they happen. That's why you need to have antivirus/antimalware installed to remove any malicious programs before they're installed, and regularly backup devices before there's a need to restore the data. In a situation where malware a rootkit or other malware has slipped past the antimalware installed on a machine, you may need to use additional tools and find it useful to use portable ones that can be installed on a flash drive. When your antivirus wasn't able to fend off a particularly new and nasty infection, these can help. Some of the tools available include:

- Sophos Anti-Rootkit (www.sophos.com/en-us/products/free-tools/sophos-anti-rootkit.aspx)

- Malwarebytes Anti-Rootkit (www.malwarebytes.org/antirootkit)
- ClamWin Portable (portableapps.com/apps/security/clamwin_portable)
- VIPRE Rescue (www.vipreantivirus.com/support.aspx)
- Spybot-Search & Destroy Portable (www.portableapps.com/apps/security/spybot_portable)

SCAMS

A *scam* is a scheme that's intended to defraud or trick you, generally as a dishonest attempt to obtain money or something else of value. As we discussed earlier in this chapter, a person or group may send out unsolicited messages through email, instant messages, chat rooms, letters in the mail, phone calls, and other methods of communication that allow them to make contact with a potential target. While we'll discuss a number of different scams throughout this book, as you go through them, you'll find elements that help you recognize them as swindles and cons.

ADVANCED FEE SCAMS

While scams may use the latest technologies, they're often based on much older methods of conning people out of their money. An old scam that goes back to the 16th century is the Spanish Prisoner, which originally involved gaining a person's confidence and telling them that they or someone else was wealthy and being held prisoner. By raising a ransom, the wealthy person could then be released, and would reward his or her benefactor(s) with a generous reward. In some cases, there was an added bonus of promising the prisoner's daughter would marry the benefactor, meaning that you would now be a member of a family with wealth and status. Once you've paid, the con artist would either disappear or ask for more money, continuing on until you had nothing more to give or refused to pay.

Over the centuries, the scam has been adapted and incorporated methods of reaching a wider audience. In the 19th century, letters postmarked from Spain would promise rewards for raising money to release a wealthy prisoner, or assure you a cut of the money if you raised funds to pay, or bribe a court official to release baggage containing hundreds of thousands of dollars. Today, scammers will send bulk email or hijack a social media account to appear as someone you know, all to entice you into wiring money as an advance fee that will result in a higher return. It may say that you've won a lottery in another country, and need to pay taxes and fees. Others might promise a share of the money in an overseas bank account containing millions of dollars, if only you can help pay the fees to have it released.

Rather than originating in Spain, the scammer may be (or claim to be) from anywhere in the world. Because a number of the scam emails will mention a Nigerian prince, or claim a connection to Nigeria or another West African country, the scam is often referred to as a "Nigerian 419 scam." As we'll see in this and other chapters, there are a number of variations to scams involving an advanced fee.

INTIMIDATION AND EXTORTION

Not every scam is an exercise in duping someone, so they're fooled into giving into a person's wishes. Intimidation and extortion scams are designed to frighten and/or coerce a person into giving into a scammer's demands. The FBI's 2014 Internet Crime Report notes that these kinds of scams have resulted in people suffering a total loss of $16,346,239, with men and women over 60 suffering the greatest losses (Internet Crime Complaint Center, 2014).

Payday loans or cash advances are ways to get a quick loan at a high interest rate, and so common that scammers will use these to get money from you. You may receive emails saying that a loan you have is delinquent, and you need to pay it immediately. The person may say they're with the loan company or even claim that they're from a collection agency, and unless you pay it now your credit rating will be ruined, you'll face additional penalties, you may be sued, or might even go to jail. The scammer may begin harassing you at work, and even attempt to intimidate you by threatening physical violence.

This scam may occur after the criminal has acquired personal or financial information about you. By reciting your national identification number (such as a Social Insurance Number), bank account numbers, or other information, they may seem legitimate.

Another scam that's been seen on the Internet involves an email being sent to a person, informing them that the sender was hired to kill them or a loved one, or knows someone who's been hired. The professed hit man offers to call off the hit, providing they're paid a sum of money, and may even provide a tape showing who hired them to kill the email recipient. If the money isn't paid, the hit will go as originally planned (Donovan, 2012).

If you receive any threats or attempts to extort money, you should contact law enforcement immediately. Even though you might recognize one of these scams, any threat to your safety should be taken seriously and reported.

GETTING SOMETHING FOR NOTHING

When you're dealing with offers on the Internet, it's important to remember the rule that if something seems too good to be true, it probably is. There are plenty of scams, hoaxes, and sales pitches that try and coax you into parting with your money by trying to convince you that you're getting a better deal than you really are. Unfortunately, you'll generally find that promises are hollow and that free offer or bit of good luck was a costly lesson in not taking people at their word.

Free offers and downloads

When a business has a new product, they may try to coax customers into buying it by offering free samples. It works because people are able to try something their unsure of without it costing them anything. If it isn't offered by a company you know and trust, you should be wary of the offer. Scammers will use the promise of something free as bait for their scams.

Scammers may make their money by hiding costs in the agreement, or using the offer as a phishing tool to get you to provide personal information and a credit card number. For example, a site may offer a tea that will help you lose weight, and have glowing testimonials that are peppered over different sites to make it seem legitimate. The bogus claim may offer a free trial, but charge you for additional monthly deliveries or sneak in a monthly charge for a subscription to a newsletter or a paid membership to a support website. While the initial offer sounded risk free, the fine print in the agreement may show you're agreeing to more than you bargained for. As we'll discuss in Chapter 9, Beyond technology—dealing with people, if the free offer is for something to ingest or medical, you may also find that you're putting your health at risk.

Another scam that hides in the fine print involves free social networking games. You might take an IQ test, and at the end of it be asked for your cell phone number to get the results. By providing the phone number, you've signed up for paid services that are charged to your phone bill like ring tone downloads, jokes of the day, astrology forecasts, and so on.

You also may see offers to download free games and programs, or ones that require you to download a program to use free services (such as streaming video). Taking advantage of these offers is risky, especially if antivirus/antimalware software hasn't been setup on your computer, phone, or other devices. A costly example is smartphone apps that may install phone dialers. In 2010, a number of free games for Windows smartphones had been repackaged with malware inside, and once installed would begin to dial phone numbers to foreign countries like the South Pole and Somalia. Unfortunately, many people didn't realize they were victims until getting their phone bill.

Contests and sweepstakes

There are a number of scams involving the chance to win big. Some sites will sell courses that promise high chances of winning a lottery using a secret system. While it makes more sense that they would spend their time using their own system to make money winning the lottery, as opposed to being an online huckster, many people still fall for the scam and buy systems that don't work.

Scammers will also try and get people to buy lottery tickets, giving you the opportunity to purchase a chance for a big windfall. Many times, they may take your payment, but you'll never receive a ticket. You may also receive telephone solicitations or direct mail offering to buy a ticket for a foreign lottery, which is actually illegal under US law and prohibits the sale or purchase of lottery tickets by phone or mail. In some countries, such as Canada, it's illegal to advertise, sell tickets, or even participate in a foreign lottery, meaning any ticket you purchased would be invalid and punishable by law.

As we saw earlier in this chapter, advanced fee scams are common, requiring people to pay a fee to receive a larger amount of money. A version of this scam involves receiving notification that you've won the jackpot in another country, but you need to pay taxes and fees to receive your prize. The scammer may ask you to pay the taxes up front, or send you a check for your "winnings" and ask you to wire the taxes and fees back. As with other wire transfer scams, you'll find that the check is fake, and you're responsible for any money you've sent or spent. The cost of this scam can be quite high. Over a 6-month period between June 1, 2014, and December 31, 2014, the Internet Crime Complaint Center found that 2194 victims had lost $8,026,189 to this type of scam (Internet Crime Complaint Center, 2014).

When you receive notification of any winnings, be skeptical. The fact that you never bought a ticket for the foreign lottery should be your first clue. Any taxes or fees could have been deducted before your check was sent, and they're insisting the money is transferred should be another red flag.

If you do purchase a ticket for a foreign lottery, you may also find that you're suddenly getting more offers. Just as telemarketers use shared lists of numbers, those involved in scams may share or sell your number to others involved in bogus ticket sales and investment offers. By saying "no" to the first offer, you can avoid being targeted by other scammers.

ONLINE CHARITIES

When someone is hurting, most people want to help. They feel empathy toward those in need, associating those affected with people in their own life. If you were the victim of a disaster, impoverished, or ill, you would want a cure or someone to help. Unfortunately, con artists have long been taking advantage of people's desires to give what they can.

Fake charities often start up after a tragedy. A publicized disaster will urge you to give to victims, or a celebrity may die and you'll see emails or posts urging fans to give to the person's favorite charities. They may ask you to send it quickly as a wire transfer, or include personal and credit card or banking information. Unfortunately, the money never reaches the victims, and the scammer may make additional charges to your credit card or transfer money from your bank account.

The theft from such cons can range from petty to astounding. You may see people asking for donations of money, clothing, and other items on social networking sites, which they keep for themselves. On the other end of the spectrum are bogus charities that can be highly organized, and make use of their own websites, crowdsourcing sites to raise money for projects, and other funding platforms. For example, in May 2015, the FTC and law enforcement from every state charged four fake charities. Operators of the charity took more than $187 million dollars in donations to help cancer patients, but kept the overwhelming majority of the money for themselves (Federal Trade Commission, 2015).

You can identify some fake charities by asking yourself and them some questions. If a person is asking to help for a "friend" in need, why aren't they referring their friend to a food bank, government services, or established charities? When disasters happen, new charities suddenly pop up, but you should ask yourself: Would a new charity even have the resources and infrastructure to get what's needed to disaster victims? You should also ask them for:

- Detailed information about the charity, such as their name, address, and phone number.
- Registered charity number, which you should then confirm online.
- How donations are processed. Avoid ones that ask for case, money wired to them, or offer to send a courier to get the money immediately.
- Ask for time to think about it and do research. If they have high pressure, need the money now, and don't provide contact information to give the donation later, it's likely a scam.
- If the request is for a local organization (such as police and fire departments), contact the community group they're representing.

By donating to established charities, there's a greater likelihood that your money or other donations will reach an affected area and its people, and not pocketed by a scam artist. States and countries will often have a registry search, such as through the IRS Exempt Organizations Select Check Tool (https://apps.irs.gov/app/eos/), Canada Revenue Agency (www.cra-arc.gc.ca/chrts-gvng/lstngs/menu-eng.html), and England and Wales (www.gov.uk/find-charity-information). You can also check if a charity is trustworthy by researching them on the following sites:

- Better Business Bureau (www.bbb.org/charity)
- Charity Navigator (www.charitynavigator.org)
- Charity Watch (www.charitywatch.org)
- GuideStar (www.guidestar.org)

TAX SCAMS

Another common scam involves a person receiving an email from a person who claims to be a government employee or high-ranking official. For example, it may claim that you owe taxes or a fine and unless you make immediate payment, you could be subject to additional penalties or even jail. This can be a frightening situation, motivating you to simply pay the fine or back taxes, and move on. In paying it, you may be required to provide additional personal information, which can be used for identity theft. You may also get a follow-up call requesting additional payments, such as for covering interest or penalties that have accumulated.

Since government agencies don't send unsolicited email, you should ignore any emails you receive. If you receive a call from someone claiming to be with the government, get their information, and then use the phone book to call the actual agency they claim to be with. By contacting the agency directly, and not using contact information they provide, you'll ensure that you're talking to the right people rather than a potential scammer claiming to be someone they're not.

RANSOMWARE AND SCAREWARE

Ransomware is a malicious program that takes control of your computer, under the threat that it won't be released until a fee or ransom is paid. Once installed, the malware may prevent you from using the keyboard, stop certain apps from running, and block the desktop so you can't access the taskbar or run additional programs. It may even hijack the camera to display a photo or video of you using the computer, making the presentation more intimidating. Worse yet, some forms may encrypt files on your hard disk, which may be difficult or impossible to decrypt without the encryption key.

To coerce you into paying and think twice about contacting the police, the ransomware may have fake messages that show it originated from an official source, and claim that child pornography was found on your machine and/or the lockdown is a consequence of "illegal cyber activity." To free the computer, you'll need to pay a "fine." It may have the name(s) and logo(s) of federal or state/provincial police, or some other law enforcement or government agency. To make it more effective, versions will target machines in certain geographic areas, so that an American computer shows it's from the FBI while a computer in Canada will state it originates from the Canadian Association of Chiefs of Police and Ministry of Public Safety. If you see this, don't worry. When you consider tampering with your computer is illegal, you'll soon realize that this couldn't be the case.

Scareware is another type of malware that frightens the user into visiting a malware infested site, install programs, or buy bogus software. You might visit a site and see a pop-up that appears to be a warning from an antivirus program. In clicking the pop-up, you're redirected to another site that infects your computer with malware, or informs you that you need to buy bogus antivirus software or install programs to "fix" the problem. Because the warning is designed to frighten the person, the hope is that they'll react without thinking.

If you do get a message trying to frighten you into performing an action, think twice. In looking at the warning, you may see that it doesn't look like the message box you'd normally see if a virus were detected, or refers to an antivirus program you've never used. Remember that legitimate antivirus and antimalware vendors won't detect software, and then try and peddle their product to remove it. Don't click on the warning. Instead, open Task Manager on your Windows computer, and use it to close the browser. When reopening the browser, don't click on the link or button to Restore Previous Session.

Whatever you do, don't follow the instructions in the ransomware or scareware. You don't want to send any money, phone a number it provides, or click on any links. If you're able to run programs, run the antimalware software on your computer and try to remove it that way. If you can't start the program, you might be able to run the antimalware after starting the computer in safe mode, by restarting and pressing F8, and/or use a portable tool installed on a flash drive (as we mentioned earlier). As we discussed in Chapter 3, Software problems and solutions, you might also try restoring your system to a point previous to when it was infected.

SUMMARY

The scams, tricks, and tactics of cybercriminals vary and adapt to changes in technology and people. As we've seen, old schemes may be dusted off and updated in an attempt to get your money, personal information, and other data. Protecting your computer and devices with the right tools, and being aware of how cybercriminals work, you're less likely to fall for their tricks and better able to deal with them when a problem occurs.

REFERENCES

Anthem, 2015, August 8. *How to access & sign up for identity theft repair & credit monitoring services*. Retrieved January 8, 2016, from Anthem Facts: www.anthemfacts.com.

AppBugs, 2015, August 12. *Password brute force vulnerabilities*. Retrieved January 31, 2016, from AppBugs: https://appbugs.co/html/bugs_category.php?c=password_bruteforce.

Collins, K., 2015, March 18. *A Quick guide to the worst corporate hack attacks*. Retrieved January 8, 2016, from Bloomberg: http://www.bloomberg.com/graphics/2014-data-breaches/.

Donovan, K., 2012, March 27. *FBI warns of extortion/hitman scam*. Retrieved October 20, 2015, from Federal Bureau of Investigation: https://www.fbi.gov/anchorage/press-releases/2013/fbi-warns-of-extortion-hitman-scam.

Federal Trade Commission, 2007, November 27. *FTC releases survey of identity theft in the U.S. study shows 8.3 million victims in 2005*. Retrieved November 15, 2015, from Federal Trade Commission: https://www.ftc.gov/news-events/press-releases/2007/11/ftc-releases-survey-identity-theft-usstudy-shows-83-million.

Federal Trade Commission, 2015, May 19. *FTC All 50 States and D.c. charge Four Cancer Charities with Bilking over $187 million from consumers*. Retrieved July 12, 2016. https://www.ftc.gov/news-events/press-releases/2015/05/ftc-all-50-states-dc-charge-four-cancer-charities-bilking-over.

Finkle, J., 2015, May 17. *Premera blue cross breached, medical information exposed*. Retrieved January 8, 2016, from Reuters: http://www.reuters.com/article/us-cyberattack-premera-idUSKBN0MD2FF20150318.

Hirschfeld Davis, J., 2015, July 9. *Hacking of government computers exposed 21.5 million people*. Retrieved December 15, 2015, from New York Times: http://www.nytimes.com/2015/07/10/us/office-of-personnel-management-hackers-got-data-of-millions.html.

Indiana University Health., 2015, December 31. *Notice to patients of lost portable storage device*. Retrieved January 28, 2016, from Indiana University Health: http://iuhealth.org/newsroom/detail/notice-to-patients-of-lost-portable-storage-device/.

InfoSecurity Europe 2nd Annual Survey, 2013. Retrieved April 28, 2016 from: https://www.advisen.com/pdf_files/2013Cyber_Risk_Management_Survey_Report.pdf.

Intel Security, 2015. *Grand theft data*. Retrieved January 28, 2016, from Intel Security-McAfee: http://www.mcafee.com/us/resources/reports/rp-data-exfiltration.pdf.

Internet Crime Complaint Center, 2014. *2014 Internet crime report*. Retrieved October 31, 2015, from Federal Bureau of Investigations: https://www.fbi.gov/news/news_blog/2014-ic3-annual-report.

May, J., 2012. *Child identity theft report 2012*. AllClear ID.

Phillips, K., 2015, August 21. *Taxpayers sue IRS for illegal account access in data breach*. Retrieved December 15, 2015, from Forbes: http://www.forbes.com/sites#/sites/kellyphillipserb/2015/08/21/taxpayers-sue-irs-for-illegal-account-access-in-data-breach/.

Ragan, S., 2016, January 6. *SNHU still investigating database leak exposing over 140,000 records*. Retrieved January 28, 2016, from CSO: http://www.csoonline.com/article/3019278/security/snhu-still-investigating-database-leak-exposing-over-140-000-records.html.

Serna, J., 2015, April 17. *Woman had 74 aliases, stole Hollywood film workers' IDs, police say*. Retrieved November 20, 2015, from Los Angeles Times: http://www.latimes.com/local/lanow/la-me-ln-woman-aliases-identity-theft-20150417-story.html.

VoVPN, 2015, May 20. *Online security—Hollywood hit by "Celebgate."* Retrieved January 31, 2016, from VoVPN: https://vovpn.com/blog/internet-security-blog/online-security-hollywood-hit-by-celebgate.html.

Protecting yourself on social media

6

INFORMATION IN THIS CHAPTER

- What Is Social Media?
- Securing Social Media
- Securing Facebook
- Securing Twitter
- Securing YouTube

While sites have traditionally been one-sided, in that a person creating a web page conveys information, social media allows people to create their own content, interact with others, and be exposed to different kinds of threats. While there are various settings available to protect your privacy and security, all-too-often people will accept the default settings and not even look at what settings have been preconfigured for them. In this chapter, we'll discuss settings on popular social media sites, and how you can change these settings to best protect yourself.

WHAT IS SOCIAL MEDIA?

Social media is a term that refers to sites, apps, and tools that are used to create user-generated content. People using social media create, share, collaborate and exchange information, photos, video, and other content. While social media itself is a broad term, it can be broken down into different categories, inclusive to:

- **Bookmarking**, in which people create, organize, and tag links to make them easy to share. These would be sites such as Delicious (www.delicious.com) or StumbleUpon (www.stumbleupon.com).
- **Forums and Blog Comments**, where people can write posts and interact with others in forums that tend to focus on a particular question or topic.
- **Media Sharing**, in which people upload and share photos or videos. These would include sites like YouTube (www.youtube.com), Flickr (www.flickr.com), and Instagram (www.instagram.com).
- **Microblogging**, which allows you to post short messages that others can subscribe to, such as seen with Twitter (www.twitter.com).

The Basics of Cyber Safety. DOI: http://dx.doi.org/10.1016/B978-0-12-416650-9.00006-1

- **Social networking**, where people can make connections to others with similar interests, goals, or relationships. There may be professional networks like LinkedIn (www.linkedin.com) or personal ones like Facebook (www.facebook.com).
- **Social News**, where people can write news items or share links to external articles. Other users can then vote to choose the most popular ones. Examples of these sites include Reddit (www.reddit.com) and Digg (www.digg.com).

SECURING SOCIAL MEDIA

If you think that changing the security and privacy settings on a social media site is difficult, you wouldn't be alone. According to a 2012 study, 48% of people using social media reported some difficulty managing the privacy controls on sites they used (Madden, 2012). Interestingly enough, those who were college graduates were significantly more likely to experience difficulty than those with lower education. While taking the step to properly configure your account may seem intimidating or confusing, you'll find it easier once you learn how to configure the best possible settings, and understand how they'll protect you.

Security should be on your mind from the time you log in to the time you log out of a site. When you first logon, the site may have a checkbox to *Keep Me Logged In* or *Remember Me*. By checking the box, a cookie is stored on your computer, which is used to automatically log you on the next time the browser's opened. While this may be convenient, anyone else who uses the computer and opens the browser would also automatically be logged in to your account. To prevent unauthorized logins this way, you should never check this checkbox on shared, insecure, or public computers. To ensure that you're properly logged off, you should sign out of any site you use when you're done.

Because so many use social media sites, it attracts a wide variety of people, including those seeking to learn more information about you, such as criminals looking for potential victims. To avoid problems, you should do the following:

- Never provide personal, sensitive, or embarrassing information on a profile or in posts. The information you post could also be used by identity thieves, stalkers, and other cybercriminals. It can be seen by employers or teachers and have an impact on your career.
- Be aware of what others are posting about you, and the photos you're tagged in. If you see personal details, embarrassing posts, or information about your activities, ask them to untag your or edit their post.
- Don't use identifying information in the usernames or email addresses you use. Having a name like *michaelcross* may seem convenient, but it also reveals who you are. You should also setup a new email account to register with the site, and receive email from it. If you stop using the site, you can simply stop using the email. In creating these accounts, you should also use strong passwords and change them regularly.

- Don't be pressured into doing things you don't want. Your peers on these sites may convince you to do things you're not comfortable with, or you may see large numbers of people participating in online campaigns or challenges. If you don't want to do something, don't.
- Don't post information about when you're on vacation or attending an event. This includes turning off location features that show where you are, and not using sites that allow you to check-in to a location. If you show you're not at home, it advertises to burglars, stalkers, and other criminals that your house is an easy break-in.

USING THE INFORMATION YOU LEARN ON ONE SITE TO SECURE OTHERS

It would be impossible to provide detailed steps to secure the accounts of every social media site on the Internet. In this chapter, we'll discuss settings on some of the most popular ones, inclusive to Facebook, Twitter, and YouTube. In Chapter 7, Finding a job online, we'll also tell you about settings in your LinkedIn account. In looking how to configure these accounts, remember that other social media accounts you have would also have settings, and many of them will be similar to other sites. By using the knowledge you gain from adjusting settings on one site, you'll generally be able to make educated changes to the privacy and security settings on others.

MONITORING ACTIVITY

An easy way to see if someone has gained unauthorized access to your account is to simply view its activity. If you see any unfamiliar posts or changes, it may indicate that someone has hacked or hijacked the account. Having said this, a heavy social media user may have difficulty keeping track of the browsers and devices they've used to logon and what they've done online. Fortunately, sites may provide features that allow you to quickly review your online activity.

On Facebook, your account can be monitored using the *Activity Log*, which is an easy-to-use listing of what you've done, as well as any posts you were included in. After going to your homepage, click on the **View Activity Log** button that's located on your cover photo. When the *Activity Log* page appears, you'll see a list of recent activities. You can scroll down to see posts you made, what you liked, comments you've made and other items, and also filter the list using controls in the left pane of the page. For example, to only see posts you've made, click on the **Your Posts** link, or if you'd prefer seeing your comments, click on the **Comments** link.

While you have control over your own posts, you should pay particular attention to posts others have mentioned you in. On the Activity Log page, click on the **Posts You're Tagged In** link to see any textual posts where your name was mentioned and photos that others have tagged you in. You should always review such content to see whether you're being associated in a way you want to be portrayed online.

While the Activity Log is an important tool, it's not the only method of monitoring your activity. It's important to know when someone logs on, so you can determine if an unauthorized person is using your account. In Facebook, you can configure your settings to notify you when someone logs on and where they were located. This is done on the *Security Settings* page, which is accessed by clicking on the downward arrow in Facebook's top navigation bar, clicking **Settings**, and then clicking the **Security** link in the left pane of the page.

As seen in Fig. 6.1, the *Security Settings* page has a **Login Alerts** section, where you can set whether you'll receive notifications when someone logs in from a new device or browser. By clicking on the **Edit** link, the section expands to reveal additional options. Once clicked, you'll see a *Notifications* section where you can click on an option to either **Get notifications** or **Don't get notifications**, and an *Email* section that allows you to specify whether or not you'll be alerted via email when someone logs in. If you click the option to get notifications but don't have them sent to your email address, information about the login attempt will appear in Facebook Notifications, which can be viewed by clicking the world-shaped icon on Facebook's top navigation bar.

The *Security Settings* page also has a *Where You're Logged In* section, which allows you to see where you (and possibly others) were when logging into Facebook. As seen in Fig. 6.1, when you click on this you'll see your current location at the top, and the device and browser used to logon. Below this, you'll see a list of previous locations, devices, and browsers used to login. If you haven't configured Facebook to send notifications of when people login from a new device or browser, you should review this section regularly. If you see an unfamiliar location in the list, then click

FIGURE 6.1

Where you're logged In in Facebook.

the **End Activity** link to the right of that entry to log them off. To logoff every device or browser that's been used to login to your account, click on the **End All Activity** link beside your current location.

NOTE

Your Location May Not Be Your Location

When you view the locations where logins have occurred, don't be surprised if the location isn't exact. If your ISP isn't in your area, the location information may show the city and state or province they're in rather than your own. If you're unsure, play it safe and click on the **End All Activity** link to terminate any sessions. After you log back in, you can check *Where You're Logged In* again, and see what your location is showing as.

On Twitter, you can also monitor the activity related to your account, and see if someone logged in from an unknown device. To view this information:

1. Click on the **Profile and Settings** button, which is located to the left of the Tweet button, in the upper right-hand corner of the page. Once the dropdown menu appears, you would then click **Settings**.
2. On the left-hand side menu, click **Your Twitter data**.
3. Review the information in the *Account History* section, which tells you when your account was created, and allows you to view and edit your Twitter handle, email, and phone number.
4. In the *Device history* section, review the devices you've used to access Twitter.
5. In the *Login history* section, review the apps and sites that have been used to access your account. If you see an app that is no longer used or seems suspicious, click on the **Apps** link in the left pane of the page, find the app in the list, and click the **Revoke Access** button beside that app's name.

SECURING FACEBOOK

Facebook (www.facebook.com) is a social networking site, where people can connect and interact with others, share photos, play games, and join networks of people with similar interests. According to the Pew Research Center, as of September 2014, 71% of the adults who are online use Facebook (Pew Research Center, 2014). In terms of social networking as a whole, they also found that 72% of men and 76% of women use social networking sites. This is a jump from their May 2013, which found 74% of women and 62% of men used this type of social media. Of those who use the sites, 40% of them access the sites on a mobile phone, and 28% do so daily.

Although Facebook is extremely popular, it has had a reputation for not respecting privacy. Prior to 2014, any posts you made were Public by default, allowing anyone to view your posts, photos, and other information unless you changed your privacy and security settings. Although this is no longer the case with new accounts created on the social networking giant, anyone who already had an account and hadn't reviewed and changed the settings retained the previous defaults. Even if you had made changes, Facebook adds new features and settings, which may be missed if you don't regularly review and change your settings.

GENERAL

The *General* settings page in Facebook is primarily used to configure basic information about your account. When you click on the downward arrow in the upper right-hand corner of the top navigation bar and click **Settings**, it's the default page where you'll find the following settings:

- **Name**, where you can change how your name appears.
- **Username**, where you can set your public username, which is the same as your Timeline address.
- **Email**, which allows you to add and remove email addresses and mobile numbers, set whether to use your Facebook email, and configure whether friends will see your email when they download a copy of their Facebook data.
- **Password**, where you can change your password.
- **Networks**, which allows you to have your primary network appearing beside your name.
- **Temperature**, which you can change from Fahrenheit to Celsius.

By clicking the **Edit** link beside any of these settings, the area will expand to show additional options. For example, if you clicked the link beside Name, you would see boxes where you can change your first, middle, and last names. You can change your name once every 60 days, and any friends you've added will see that change immediately. Modifying your name can be useful if you've gotten married and taken a spouse's name, divorced, and reverted to a maiden name, or want to change your name so that others won't be able to search and find you easily. While convenient, you should also realize that others may change their name to conceal themselves, such as when someone you don't like wants you to add them as a friend. You can also click the **Add other names** link and be taken to the *About* page of your profile (which we'll discuss later in this chapter), where you can add any nicknames, aliases, birth names, and so on.

The *Username* section allows you to set the name used for your Timeline address. Rather than people going to an obscure URL, when you enter a username, people will be able to type www.facebook.com/<*username*> into their browser and go directly to your profile page.

The *Email* section allows you to set primary and additional email addresses, as well as a mobile number. If you add a mobile number and don't set privacy on it (as we'll discuss later in this chapter), it will appear to others in the About section of your profile. The section also has a checkbox to use your Facebook email, which is the Username you set in the previously discussed setting with the Facebook domain (e.g., username@facebook.com). If you check this option, any emails sent to it are forwarded to your primary email address.

The other option in the Email section that you want to leave unchecked is the **Allow friends to include my email address in Download your information**. The *Download your information* option, and how you can use it to download a copy of content on your Facebook account, inclusive to information you'd see in your timeline and other data. When this archive is downloaded, it also includes information about people added as friends. To avoid your email address from appearing in another person's download, you should leave this checkbox unchecked. After all, if their account was hacked, and the hacker downloaded an archive of the account, you wouldn't want the unauthorized user to have your email address.

The *Password* section informs you of the last time you changed your password. Clicking **Edit**, the section will expand, showing boxes where you would enter your current password, a new password and another box to confirm it. Once you click **Save Changes**, your password is immediately changed. As we discussed in Chapter 2, Before connecting to the Internet, you should always use a strong password to protect your account and change it on a recurring basis. Also, if you believe someone other than yourself has logged into your account, you should end their activity (as we discussed earlier), and then change your password.

SECURITY

As we saw earlier in this chapter, the *Security Settings* page has a number of features that allow you to monitor your activity and disconnect other devices and computers that are logged in. It also has features related to logins, passwords, and other setting to control access to your account. After going into Settings, you would access this page by clicking **Security** on the left-hand navigation of the page and see the following options:

- **Login Alerts**, where you can configure Facebook to send you notifications when someone logs in from a new device or browser, which we discussed earlier in this chapter when we talked about monitoring activity.
- **Login Approvals**, which sets a requirement that a security code is needed to login to your account. If you or someone else is using a browser that hasn't been used to login to Facebook, the security code is required.
- **Code Generator**, which is used to enable the code generator in the Facebook mobile app. If you've enabled Login Approvals, the mobile app can be used to generate security codes and reset your password.
- **App Passwords**, which allows you to set special passwords for Facebook apps, so they don't login using your Facebook account.
- **Trusted Contacts**, which is used to select friends who can help you access your Facebook account if you're locked out.
- **Your Browsers and Apps**, where you can review and remove devices and browsers that you've confirmed as trusted, so you aren't notified about logins or require a security code to login.
- **Where You're Logged In**, which shows where you're logged into Facebook. We discussed this option earlier, when we talked about monitoring activity.

- **Legacy Contact**, where you can control what happens to your account and who has control of managing it if you pass away.
- **Deactivate Your Account**, which allows you to disable your account temporarily. We'll discuss this feature in more detail in Chapter 11.

The Login Approvals feature is useful in preventing unauthorized access to your account. Once set, anyone who logs in from a browser or device that isn't listed in the *Your Browsers and Apps* list will require a security code to login. To activate it, you'll need to have a mobile number associated with your account. You would then click **Edit** beside *Login Approvals*, click the **Require a security code to access my account from unknown browsers** checkbox so it appears checked, and then click the **Save Changes** button.

The Code Generator is part of the Login Approvals process. A code is required to login to Facebook from new browsers or devices when Login Approvals is enabled, so the Code Generator is used. It works with the Facebook app on Android and iOS devices, where a new security code is created every 30 seconds. Once you have a code, you would then login to Facebook with your password, and then enter the security code as a second method of authentication. Once you've clicked **Enable** in the section on your Facebook page, you would do the following:

1. After opening the Facebook apps installed on your iPhone, iPad, or Android device, tap the Settings icon (depicted as three horizontal bars).
2. Scroll down and tap **Code Generator**. A code will be generated that you would use to login to Facebook.

The *App Passwords* section is used to generate passwords that can be used to log onto an app. Rather than using your Facebook password, you can generate a unique password that you'd use to login to Facebook the first time you use it. If Login Approvals are turned on, you wouldn't need to wait to receive a code to use an app password. To use this feature:

1. Click on the **Edit** button beside *App Passwords*.
2. Click **Generate app passwords**, and when prompted, click the **Generate App Passwords** button.
3. Type in the name of the app you want to approve and then click **Generate Password**.
4. When the password is presented, use the password in the password field of the app, and then click **Finish**.

Once you've created the password for an app, the app's name will appear in the App Passwords section. To remove an app from the list, click the **Remove link** beside the app's name, and then click **Save Changes**.

If you ever have a problem logging into Facebook, you can get a security code from friends you've previously added to the *Trusted Contacts* section. You would then use the codes to login. To avoid potential problems, you should choose people who are able to confirm your identity prior to giving out a code. To add a trusted contact, you would do the following:

1. In the *Trusted Contacts* section, click **Edit**.
2. Click **Choose trusted contacts**, and when prompted, click the **Choose Trusted Contacts** button.
3. When prompted, type the names of three to five friends, and select the ones you want from the list that appears. Click **Confirm**.

PRIVACY

The *Privacy Settings and Tools* page is where you would configure who is able to see your posts, and control who can contact you or look you up. You can access this page by clicking on the downward arrow in the top navigation bar, clicking **Settings**, and then clicking **Privacy** in the left-hand navigation. Once done, you'll be presented with a page similar to what's shown in Fig. 6.2.

The Privacy page is broken into three sections, the first of which is titled *Who can see my stuff?*, where you can review and set who will be able to see past and future posts. The settings in this section consist of:

- **Who can see your future posts?**, where you can set who will be the default audience that will be able to see any posts you make. You should have this set to **Friends**, or (as we'll discuss later in this chapter) a specific list. If you want to set a post to being visible to everyone, then you should modify the audience of that particular post, as we'll discuss later in this chapter.
- **Review all the posts and things you're tagged in**, which provides a link to **Use Activity Log**. Clicking this link will open the Activity Log we discussed earlier,

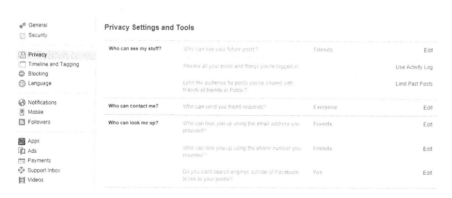

FIGURE 6.2

Privacy settings and tools.

showing the *Timeline Review*, where you can see any posts, photos, and so on that you've been tagged in.

- **Limit the audience for posts you've shared with friends of friends or Public**, which will change all of your past posts to only being visible to Friends. If you've never set the default audience for future posts, are unsure of what you've posted Public, and/or have had most or all of your posts posted publically, then you should click the **Limit Past Posts** link on this setting, and then click the **Limit Old Posts** button. After limiting past posts, make sure you set the proper audience level for future posts as we just discussed.

The *Who can contact me?* section contains only one setting to control who can send you friend requests. By default, it is set to **Everyone**. If you wanted to vet requests, so that only people who share a mutual friend with you can make a request, you could reset this to **Friends of Friend**. However, keep in mind that just because someone else added the person as a friend, this doesn't mean that they're necessarily safe and shouldn't be treated as a stranger.

The final section is *Who can look me up?*, where you have some control over search results. The settings in this section are:

- **Who can look you up using the email address you provided?** If people don't have access to see an email address you provided, people within the group you specify will be able to use it to look for you. The options are *Everyone*, *Friends of Friend*, and *Friends*. Since you probably don't want strangers and other people finding you by a search for your email address, set it to the most restrictive option of **Friends**.
- **Who can look you up using the phone number you provided?** If people don't have access to see a phone number you provided, only those who fall into the group you specify will be able to search for you using that number. The options are *Everyone*, *Friends of Friend*, and *Friends*. Since your phone number may be easily obtained using a phone book, resume, or some other document you've given out, it's recommended that you set this to the most restrictive option of **Friends**.
- **Do you want search engines outside of Facebook to link to your profile?** If enabled, search engines like Google, Bing, and so forth may link to your profile and show its contents in search results. To prevent people from seeing your profile in search results, click on the **Allow search engines outside of Facebook to link to your profile** checkbox so it appears unchecked.

Privacy shortcuts

The *Privacy Settings and Tools* page isn't the only place where you can configure settings related to privacy. By clicking the *Privacy Shortcuts* icon (depicted as a padlock) on Facebook's top navigation screen, you're presented with a number of settings that we just discussed, as well as others mentioned in other chapters. Here, you can control who can see your stuff, who can contact you, and also block people (as we'll discuss in chapter, Beyond technology—dealing with people).

A useful item on this menu is the *View As* feature, which allows you to view your page as others see it. It's accessible in several ways. First, you can go to your profile page, click the button with three dots that's on your cover photo, and then click **View As**. The other way is by clicking on the Privacy Shortcuts icon, clicking **Who can see my stuff?** and then clicking **View As**. You can also access it from the *Timeline and Tagging Settings* page, which we'll discuss later. Once clicked, you'll be redirected to your Timeline, and see it as someone would with no access to your page (i.e., Public). To view it as if you were someone else (such as your mother or boss), you would do the following after clicking View As:

1. Click **View as Specific Person**.
2. In the box that appears, begin typing the person's name, and then select the Facebook account that appears in the list. The Timeline will change to show what that person sees.
3. Now that you're viewing as that person, click on the tabs in your profile to reveal additional information about you, and see what's visible.

Another option on the Privacy Shortcuts menu is the *Privacy Checkup*. Once clicked, a new window will open, taking you step-by-step through the process of configuring your privacy settings. Even though this is an easy to use tool, you should continue to check the Security and Privacy settings we've discussed to ensure everything has been configured as you expect.

Know your audience

When you update your status, post a photo or other content, you can click on the audience selector tool beside the Post button and control who can see that post. As seen in Fig. 6.3, when you click on the button you have the option of that post only

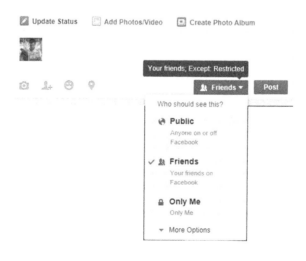

FIGURE 6.3

Audiences in Facebook.

being visible to the Public, Friends, Only Me, or other lists (which we'll discuss later in this chapter).

Once you've selected a particular audience, the tool will remember it and use that setting for future posts unless you change it. In other words, if you posted something and decided it should be Public, the next post you make will also be Public. This can be particularly awkward if you've posted an embarrassing photo, or a rant that doesn't portray you in the best light. If you're switching audiences, be careful of what you select and ensure that you haven't given greater access than desired.

TIMELINE AND TAGGING

The *Timeline and Tagging Settings* controls who can add and view content on your Timeline, as well as content others have tagged you in. The features allow you to regulate what people post and associate with you, preventing others from publishing content that may be embarrassing.

As seen in Fig. 6.4, the *Who can add things to my timeline?* section has two features. When you click the **Edit** link beside *Who can post on your timeline?*, you have the option of allowing either *Friends* or *Only Me* to post on your timeline. If you're concerned about what others may post, select **Only Me**. The other option here is *Review posts friends tag you in before they appear on your timeline?*, which can be either enabled or disabled. It's recommended that you set this to **Enabled**, so that you can look at what someone's posted so you can either approve or reject it prior to others seeing it.

The second section is ***Who can see things on my timeline?*** The first option allows you to view your Timeline as the public or a specific person would, which we discussed earlier. The second option ***Who can see posts you've been tagged in on your timeline?*** allows you to control who will see posts others have tagged you in.

	Timeline and Tagging Settings			
⚙ General 🛡 Security				
🔒 Privacy 🕐 **Timeline and Tagging** ⊘ Blocking 🌐 Language	**Who can add things to my timeline?**	Who can post on your timeline?	Friends	Edit
		Review posts friends tag you in before they appear on your timeline?	On	Edit
🔔 Notifications 📱 Mobile 📡 Followers	**Who can see things on my timeline?**	Review what other people see on your timeline		View As
		Who can see posts you've been tagged in on your timeline?	Custom	Edit
		Who can see what others post on your timeline?	Custom	Edit
📦 Apps 📄 Ads 🗂 Payments 📧 Support Inbox 🎞 Videos	**How can I manage tags people add and tagging suggestions?**	Review tags people add to your own posts before the tags appear on Facebook?	On	Edit
		When you're tagged in a post, who do you want to add to the audience if they aren't already in it?	Custom	Edit
		Who sees tag suggestions when photos that look like you are uploaded? (this is not yet available to you)	Unavailable	

FIGURE 6.4

Timeline and tagging settings.

By clicking on the dropdown, you'll be able to select specific groups or lists that will have access to this content. The final option is *Who can see what others post on your timeline?*, which controls access to posts others have made. As with the previous option, you can click on a dropdown and select a specific list of people who will be able to view this content.

The final section on the Timeline and Tagging Settings page is ***How can I manage tags people add and tagging suggestions?*** The first option allows you to ***Review tags people add to your own posts before the tags appear on Facebook?***, which can be either enabled or disabled. You should **Enable** this so that you can check whether someone has tagged another person in a photo or post that may be inappropriate or embarrassing, before others on Facebook can see it. The second option in this section allows you to control ***When you're tagged in a post, who do you want to add to the audience if they aren't already in it?*** In using this option, you can add people from a list so they can see the post if they don't already have access.

LISTS

When you add a friend, you may think that you're limited to only allowing them access to everything you've posted. However, you can add them to lists to organize them into different groups, and control how much of their posts you see in your news feed, and what appears in theirs. The different lists available include:

- **Close friends**, which will prioritize their posts so you'll see more of them in your newsfeed, and get notified when they make a post.
- **Acquaintances**, which will cause fewer of their posts to appear in your newsfeed. When you post, you can exclude these people from seeing your posts by clicking *Friends except acquaintances* in the audience selector.
- **Restricted**, which limits the person to only seeing public posts and those they're tagged in.

Alternatively, you can also create new lists to keep track of why people are your friends, and organize them accordingly. To illustrate how this might be used, consider how you should never add someone as a friend that you don't know. However, many people do, and sometimes it seems necessary. You'll play a game, and one of the requirements to continue may be that you need a certain number of "neighbors" or allies to continue. If none of your friends are playing that game, you might go on the app's page and tell people to add you. In doing so, they'll make a friend request, and you can add them as an ally. Unfortunately, you've just added a stranger, and given them access to what you and possibly your friends and family are posting, as well as access to additional information appearing on your profile. Even if you stop playing the game later, you might forget that these people have been added. To keep track of them, you might create a new list named after that game, and add them to this list and the Restricted list. Now those people can only see your public posts, and if you leave the game, you can just unfriend anyone in that games list.

To add a person to a list, go to your profile page, and click the **Friends** link on the navigation bar below your cover photo. When the list of friends appears, do the following:

1. Click the button beside their name that says **Friends**, and then either click *Close Friends*, *Acquaintances*, or **Add to Another List**.
2. If you clicked *Add to Another List*, the dropdown will appear allowing you to select another list to add them to.

When you accept or send a friend request, you can also add them to lists. In doing so, the person automatically gets the level of access you've set, without them being notified.

ABOUT

One of the biggest threats to your privacy is the information you reveal to others. The *About* section of your profile is where you tell people about yourself, inclusive to contact information, your interests, and other facts about yourself. You can access this page by going to your profile, and clicking on **About** under your cover photo.

What you add to the About section can be considerably more than you want revealed. In fact, it can be a virtual treasure trove of details, useful to identity thieves, stalkers, bullies, and other unwanted or criminal elements. In this section, you can enter such things as:

- Contact information, such as your address, city, neighborhood and zip code, phone numbers, email, and other social media accounts you use.
- Professional information, inclusive to where you work and went to school, and skills.
- Personal information, such as who you're married to or in a relationship with, family members, current and previous places you've lived, your birthdate, other names (such as nicknames or maiden names), gender, religious and political views, and other details and life events.

There are also sections that show your likes, ex: sports, books, TV shows, movies, music, and places you've checked in. In looking at this information, you might find they reveal words or phrases you've used in a password, or answers to common questions that you'd answer to gain access to an account after forgetting your password. If you've ever forgotten your password and been asked a security question like the high school you attended or your favorite thing, the answer could be readily available on your Facebook profile. Even the more difficult security questions may be answered by visiting a couple of profiles. If you wanted to get into someone's account and the security question asked for their mother's maiden name, you could probably find who their mother listed as a friend, and by visiting her page see the maiden name.

Some information on your profile could also bias people against you. There are those who might take issue with the religious or political views you've mentioned in your profile. As we'll see in the Chapter 7, Finding a job online, if a potential employer saw your birthdate, they could discriminate against you because of your age. Even if such action is illegal, you would never know that they saw something on your profile that was detrimental to your being hired.

Other information you put in the About section is blatantly risky. Under no circumstances should you enter any information that would allow a stranger to contact you. Despite this, you may come across those who've entered an address, mobile phone number, or other contact information and not adjusted the settings to restrict just anyone from viewing it.

To see how you can restrict access to information in the About section, let's look at the field that shows your birthdate, which you provided when you first signed up to Facebook:

1. On your profile page, click on the **About** tab under your cover picture.
2. In the left navigation of the *About* section, click on the **Contact and Basic Info** link.
3. Under Basic Information, hover your mouse over the year of your birth, and then click the **Edit** link when it appears.
4. Click on the audience dropdown to the right of the entry, and then select who will be able to see it. Since its sensitive information, select **Only Me**.
5. Click **Save Changes**.

Now that you've changed access to one piece of information, review what's on your profile and repeat the process. Look at any answers with a discernible eye, questioning the benefit of having it even appear on your profile. In some cases, such as a business page, you may want the company's address and phone number. For a personal account, it's dangerous having such details online, and you should restrict access or remove these facts completely.

SECURING TWITTER

Twitter (www.twitter.com) is a microblogging site in which people can write 140 character messages called *tweets*. If you've never used Twitter, you'll find it uses a unique terminology in describing what's done and who uses it. The person sending the tweet is called a *tweeter*. The tweets themselves can include attachments, and be shared by others as a *retweet*. If people have particular interest in the content you're providing from your account, they can follow you and see them as they come out. They can also like or favorite a tweet, showing their approval of it.

If you don't already have a Twitter account, chances are you know someone who does. According to the Pew Research Center, as of September 2014, 23% of the adults who are online use Twitter (Pew Research Center, 2014). As we'll see in Chapter 10, Protecting your kids, it is also a popular social media site used by children and teens.

With the ability to send out a quick message, and no way to edit it afterwards, you can imagine that a large number of people have gotten themselves into trouble using this site or the mobile app. In November 2014, comedian Roseanne Barr tweeted

"Got in a tussle w bill cosby. U shoyld see that mfer" with a photo of her swollen face after getting a chemical peel. Although she deleted the tweet shortly afterwards, the backlash from those who had seen and retweeted it was severe. The moral is *think before you tweet*.

Other instances of tweeting gone wrong is seen when hashtags are used. A *hashtag* is a word with the # symbol in front of it. When included in a tweet, it acts like a link, where people can click on it and see others in conversation who also used the hashtag. In 2012, McDonalds decided to start a Twitter campaign using the hashtag #McDStories, which allowed people to share their memories and favorite stories of the restaurant. After all, who doesn't have a nice memory of getting a Happy Meal with their parents? Unfortunately for McDonalds, the hashtag became a bashtag, and people began sharing horror stories of eating the food, working for the company, and snarky comments and jokes.

As you can see by these examples, the level of control you have over your tweets is limited compared to other social media sites like Facebook. You can't edit what you've tweeted, so you need to get your point across the first time. While you can delete a tweet, there is no guarantee that someone hasn't quoted or retweeted it, so that a copy still exists. You also can't control the responses of other people, or what they may say when you use hashtags to share your point with a greater number of people. As we've seen, hashtags can take on a life of their own, and not in a way that you expected.

SECURITY

Twitter provides a number of settings related to privacy and security. After logging into your account, you can click on the **Profile and Settings** button (which uses an icon of your profile picture) in the upper right-hand corner, and then click **Settings**. Once this is done, you're presented with a page of account settings, which has navigation on the left side of the screen to configure different features. As the steps below show, clicking on the **Security and Privacy** link provides options to control how you login, how to recover your password, and whether to verify login requests.

Once you click the *Login verification* checkbox, when you try and login to Twitter from a mobile device, you'll also receive an email or SMS text message with a six-digit login code. To gain access, you need to have both the code and your password.

If you use Twitter for iOS and don't have login verification turned on, you can configure Twitter to allow logging with either a password or a code. After entering an incorrect password on an iOS device, Twitter would then send you a temporary code to your email or as an SMS text message, which you could then enter to gain access to your account. Of course, this provides an obvious hole in keeping your account secure. If your phone was lost or stolen, and the person who had it tried to login using Twitter, they would simply need to use the code sent to that phone to login.

To access the security settings in Twitter, you would do the following:

1. Click on the **Profile and Settings** button, which is located to the left of the Tweet button, in the upper right-hand corner of the page. Once the dropdown menu appears, you would then click **Settings**.

2. On the left-hand side menu, click **Security and privacy**.
3. Click on the **Verify login requests** checkbox in the *Login verification* section so it appears checked. Click **Okay, send me a message** when prompted, and then click **Yes** when you receive the code. If you haven't added a phone number that Twitter can use to notify you about a login attempt, you'll need to click on the **add a phone** link and provide a number before you can configure the setting to verify login requests.
4. In the *Password reset* section, click on the **Require personal information to reset my password** checkbox so it appears checked. Once checked, you'll need to provide the email address or phone number associated with your account before you can request a password reset.
5. In the *Log in with code* section, click the **Always require a password to login to my account** checkbox so it appears checked.
6. Click the **Save changes** button.

PRIVACY

Many people don't really associate privacy with Twitter, as it's commonly used to make public comments that anyone can see. Whether you want to shout your opinions to the world or a select few, Twitter does gives you options over how much of your life is exposed. When you scroll down on the *Security and privacy* screen, you'll see a number of privacy settings you can change to meet your personal needs.

By default, when you open a Twitter account, any of the tweets you make are public. For most people, allowing anyone to see what they've tweeted is what's expected, but you can change the settings so that the tweets are protected, and can only be seen by those you've approved. This is useful when you only want to communicate with your friends, within a company, or with a select group of people. If you switch your account so that tweets are protected, any of your previous public tweets won't appear in searches and will only be visible to you and those you've given access. However, this isn't entirely instantaneous. Old tweets may still appear in search engines until Twitter's been crawled and results have been updated, and (of course) any screenshots people have taken of your previous tweets will still be out there.

Other settings in this section will also determine how much is revealed about where you are, and how easy it is for others to find you or see content about you. The *Discoverability* setting determines whether people can find you by your email address, or if they'll only find you by the handle you give them. The *Photo tagging* setting will control if anyone can tag you in a photo, if only the people who follow you, or no one can tag you in photos. Also, the *Location* controls whether your location will appear in tweets, while other settings determine what's revealed to third parties and whether Twitter will retain information on sites you've visited.

To have greater control over the content on Twitter, you should make a number of changes to the privacy settings. On the *Security and privacy* page, these changes would include:

1. In the *Photo tagging* section, click on the **Do not allow anyone to tag me in photos**.

2. If you only want certain people to see your tweets, click on the **Protect my tweets** checkbox in Tweet privacy so that it appears checked. Click on the **Delete all location information** button to remove any existing location information in past tweets. If you click this button, it may take upwards of 30 minutes before it disappears from previous tweets.

3. In the *Tweet location* section, ensure that the **Add a location to my tweets** checkbox is unchecked. This will prevent Twitter from storing your location, and locations from appearing in the tweets you make.

4. In the *Discoverability* section, ensure the **Let others find me by my email address** checkbox is unchecked.

5. In the *Personalization* section, ensure the **Tailor Twitter based on my recent website visits** checkbox is unchecked. If its checked, Twitter will store information on the sites and web pages you've visited for up to 10 days. While Twitter may use this to provide relevant suggestions on who to follow, you may not want them to know what you're doing on the Internet, so its suggested you uncheck this box.

6. Similarly, you may be concerned that Twitter will match your account to information shared with ad partners, inclusive to information that's browser-related, identifies your mobile device, and so on. If so, you should uncheck the **Tailor ads based on information shared by ad partners** checkbox in the *Promoted content* section.

7. Finally, in the *Direct Messages* section, you should uncheck the **Receive Direct Messages from anyone** checkbox. This will prevent people you don't follow or who don't follow you from sending you Direct Messages.

8. Click the **Save changes** button.

PASSWORDS

As we saw in Chapter 2, Before connecting to the Internet, a strong password is an important first line of defense, especially when it comes to the sites you visit. In Twitter, you can modify your password by doing the following:

1. As we saw earlier, click on the **Profile and Settings** button, and then click **Settings**.

2. On the left-hand side menu, click **Password**.

3. In the **Current password** box, type your current password. If you've forgotten it, click the *Forgot your password?* link.

4. Type the new password in the **New password** box, and then retype it in the **Verify password** box.

5. Click **Save changes**.

SECURING YOUTUBE

YouTube (www.youtube.com) is a media sharing site where people can view, create, and share videos online. Even if you don't have an account, you can still visit the site and watch streaming content. Once you register an account with YouTube, you're then able to create a channel and upload your own videos.

The desire to create videos and post them online isn't unique. According to the Pew Research Center, as of August 2012, 46% of the adults who are online post original photos and videos, and 41% repost or share them on other sites (Pew Research Center, 2014). According to YouTube, there are over a billion users, with more people watching videos on their site than on any American cable network and 80% of the views coming from outside the United States (YouTube, n.d.).

The content you'll see on YouTube varies, as the creators of the videos are diverse. You'll find complete or segments of movies and TV shows from networks and major production companies, instructional and entertainment videos created by adults, and even content created by children. These videos can also be shared on other sites like Facebook, increasing their exposure to a wider audience.

CREATOR STUDIO

Once you've signed into YouTube with a Google account, you're prompted to create a channel, where you can create playlists and upload videos. You maintain and configure your settings through *Creator Studio*, where you'll find a variety of tools and features. After clicking on the icon with your profile picture in the upper right-hand corner, you then click the **Creator Studio** button. There are categories of options related to your channel in the left navigation bar of the screen, inclusive to:

- **Dashboard**, which gives you a high-level view of your channel and its popularity. You'll find analytics of how many people have viewed videos and the length of time they watched them, a list of videos, tips, and comments.
- **Video Manager**, where you can organize and update videos.
- **Live Streaming**, which allows you to stream a video live on YouTube.
- **Community**, where you can view and respond to comments, read messages, view subscribers, and change settings on how YouTube will handle comments to videos.
- **Channel**, which is where most of the settings affecting your channel are found.
- **Analytics**, where you can view greater details about views, likes, and watch time of your videos. It also provides information on the geographic location of viewers, their gender, and where they're watching your videos.
- **Create**, which is where you can edit the audio and video content you've uploaded to your channel.

Community

When you click on the **Community** link, you'll see additional links to view comments, private messages, subscribers, videos you've been credited in, and options for closed captions. By clicking **Comments**, you'll see all the comments people have made. Clicking the trash can icon to the right of a comment will delete it, while clicking the flag icon will present the following options:

- **Report spam or abuse**, which reports the comment to YouTube.
- **Hide this user's comments on this channel**, which prevents any comments from the user from appearing.
- **Always approve comments from this user**, which will allow the user's comments to appear automatically if you've configured the channel to hold comments from appearing until they've been reviewed.

When you create your own content, you should not only be concerned with your own protection, but also that of those viewing what you've created. Clicking the **Community Settings** link in the *Community* category on the left navigation allows you to configure settings relating to approving and hiding commenters and other creators, and configure default settings.

The top of the *Community Settings* section consists of *Automated Filters* settings. The top two sections provide a list of approved and hidden users. *Approved Users* are those that you've flagged as always being allowed to have their comments appear on your channel or videos. *Hidden Users* are those that won't have comments appear to others, such as those from trolls (someone that posts rude, abusive, or disparaging comments), bullies, or other unwanted users.

The *Blacklist* section is where you type in words that will be used to indicate a comment is inappropriate for your channel. For example, if you entered the word "crap," and some troll wrote a comment that "this video is crap," YouTube would flag the comment so it needs to be reviewed. Any live chats with these words would be blocked. If you have a child with a YouTube channel, you should handle the settings yourself. After all, it makes no sense protecting them from offensive words if they're going to see them anyway in the blacklist.

The *Default Settings* allow you to control the behavior of comments and credits that appear on your channel. If you're concerned about trolls and other unwanted people from making nasty or derogatory comments, you should set these so that either comments aren't allowed or they're held for review so that others can't see them without your approval. The options in this section are:

- Comments on your new videos, where you can set YouTube to *Allow all comments* (in which comments will appear immediately), *Hold all comments for review* (which causes all comments to be hidden until you approve them), and *Disable comments* (which prevents anyone from posting comments).
- Comments on your channel, which also has the options of *Allow all comments*, *Hold all comments for review*, and *Disable comments*.
- Creator credits on your channel, where you have the options to *Allow all creator credits* or *Hold all creator credits for review*.

Channel

When you click on the **Channel** link, it will expand to show a number of categories including options for *Upload defaults*, where you can set default options for any videos you upload. The Privacy dropdown on the page allows you to set whether a new video is **Private** (which can only be seen by you and the users you select) or **Public** (which is available for anyone to see).

The *Comments and Ratings* section is another important setting, especially if you have a child who has a channel.

Another important default setting is in the *Comments and Ratings* section. If the *Allow Comments* checkbox is set, you can then choose whether **All** or **Approved** viewers can post comments on a video. If the *Users can view ratings for this video* checkbox is checked, they can also view the ratings on a particular video.

Blocking and reporting

You can deal with problem users on YouTube by going to their channel page, and then clicking on the *About* tab. On the page, you'll see a flag-shaped icon, which when clicked on allows you to **Block User**, **Report channel art**, **Report channel icon**, or **Report User**. If you choose *Block User*, the user will be unable to comment on videos or send messages to you.

Restricted mode

If the video is potentially offensive, you need to affirm that you're over 18 years of age before you can watch it. In addition, you can also set YouTube so that content you may find objectionable or don't want family members to see is filtered out. At the bottom of any YouTube page you'll see the **Restricted Mode** button, indicating whether it's turned on or off. Clicking it, you can then click an option to turn it **On** or **Off**.

SUMMARY

In this chapter we discussed settings on a number of the most popular social media sites. These not only control the default behavior or your activity, but can also be used to protect your privacy and reduce the chance of unauthorized users gaining access to your account, or problem users causing issues for you with their comments and posts. Now that you've seen the options available to you on Facebook, Twitter, and YouTube, let's move on to Chapter 7, Finding a job online, where we'll discuss settings on YouTube and ways you can protect yourself looking for work online.

REFERENCES

Madden, M., 2012, February 24. *Privacy management on social media sites*. Retrieved November 20, 2015, from Pew Internet Center: http://www.pewinternet.org/2012/02/24/privacy-management-on-social-media-sites/.

Pew Research Center, 2014. *Social networking fact sheet*. Retrieved November 20, 2015, from Pew Research Center: http://www.pewinternet.org/fact-sheets/social-networking-fact-sheet/.

YouTube, n.d. *Statistics*. Retrieved November 23, 2015, from YouTube: https://www.youtube.com/yt/press/statistics.html.

Finding a job online

INFORMATION IN THIS CHAPTER

- Looking for Work Online
- Online Resumes
- Work-at-Home Scams
- Securing LinkedIn

Even if you don't have much money and are looking for work online, you're not immune to criminals looking to prey on others. In this chapter, we'll discuss ways to spot fake job offers, and common scams that focus on those looking for work. We'll also discuss what information should be included in an online resume, and what details you want to avoid revealing online.

LOOKING FOR WORK ONLINE

The Internet has changed the way we hunt for jobs. While you'll still find employment ads in a local newspaper's classified section, an employment site's search engine could show relevant results from a database of hundreds of thousands of jobs. Many businesses will only post vacant positions online, saving themselves the cost of paying for ads in multiple papers. If you have an online resume, then you may have employers hunting for you to fill a position.

If you've never looked for work online, it may seem strange at first. Job search sites can offer a considerable amount of resources. You can use search features to look for jobs in a specific geographic area, use keywords to find a specific job title, or even look for jobs with a specific company or industry. Some will provide tips on creating resumes and cover letters, or allow you to post your resume on their site to apply for positions quicker or allow employers to search for talent. Some of the popular job search sites include:

- Monster (www.monster.com)
- CareerBuilder (www.careerbuilder.com)
- Workopolis (www.workopolis.com)

The Basics of Cyber Safety. DOI: http://dx.doi.org/10.1016/B978-0-12-416650-9.00007-3

In addition to sites where employers can post a job or search for new potential hires, there are also sites that help in a search. Some sites like Indeed (www.indeed.com) and Simply Hired (www.simplyhired.com) show aggregated job search result. By using such a search engine, content is displayed from other job boards, online newspapers, recruiting sites, career pages of companies, and other sources. You'll also find job boards that target positions in certain industries, those sponsored by the government to help people seeking work, and smaller employment agencies.

While some services are free, job search sites may ask you to sign-up for an account or pay for premium services. For example, LinkedIn (www.linkedin.com) offers a premium account with such features as being able to compare your education and skills to other applicants, the ability to filter jobs by estimated salary, and other features not available with a normal account. Before paying for services or even creating an account, you should research the site you're using and see what it's offering. If it offers services you don't need or are available for free elsewhere, you might be better off saving your money. As with any site, you should check their privacy policies to see what information is collected, how it's used, and whether it's shared.

When you're looking for a job, you don't want to miss opportunities. It's important to let people know that you're seeking employment, and social media can be useful in that regard. A post that your friends and family can see will let them know that you're looking for work, and they may have heard about something that's right up your alley. A public post may be tempting and expand the number of people who might tell you about a potential job, but it can also expose you to people who want to take advantage of your need for work.

Rather than finding vacant job positions, you want to increase your chances of getting a job. According to Jobvite (www.jobvite.com), you have a better chance of getting a job if you're referred by an existing employee. Using data drawn from their customers, they found that 39.9% of hires came from employee referrals, and that these successful candidates were hired 55% faster than those hired through a career site (Jobvite, 2016). Using professional social networks like LinkedIn, you can add contacts and build a network of colleagues within your field, and these contacts may be able to refer you to their employer.

FRAUDULENT JOB POSTS

If you look at enough job posts, you're bound to find ones that are sketchy or fraudulent. You'll often see job postings that are too good to be true (and generally are), saying they offer a large salary but require no experience or skills. If an offered salary seems questionable, you can see what the average salary for that position is by using sites like Salary.com (www.salary.com), Indeed (www.indeed.com/salary), or Monster (http://monsterca.salary.com/). Other signs that a post may be fraudulent include:

- Contact information lacks relevant information, such as the business' address, corporate website, and/or email addresses that use free Web mail services like Gmail (https://mail.google.com) instead of a corporate email address.

- The post contains fake details, such as referring to facilities that don't exist, incorrect locations, or other mistakes that may raise red flags that it isn't a legitimate job offer.
- Information is unprofessional, containing spelling and grammar mistakes.
- They request a fee for applying, or ask that you pay for training.
- The post redirects you to a site where you're required to enter personal information before seeing the post.
- They request personal information (like your birthdate, mother's maiden name, etc.).

There are many reasons why someone might post a fraudulent job offer, but it isn't to hire you. Cybercriminals will use it as a lure to get others to reveal information for the purposes of identity theft, while others will try to scam you into paying for services or training materials. If they want to meet you in person, such as under the guise of an interview, it could even be for the purposes of robbery, rape, or even murder. In 2013, Richard Beasley was convicted and given the death sentence for the murder of three men, and attempted murder of a fourth, who he met by posting fake job ads on Craigslist (www.craigslist.com) (Rosin, 2013). The possibility of getting a job is never worth your safety. If a job advertisement or interview invitation doesn't seem right, don't trust it.

RESEARCH THE COMPANY

How you react to a job offer often reflects the situation you're in. If you already have a job, you'll look at the offer logically, and might take a few extra steps to see if the offer is legitimate and a good fit for you. If you need a job, it's easy to get a feeling of desperation and jump on any offer that comes along. However, just as a company considers you as a candidate, you need to consider whether that company is worth working for.

If you visit a company's website, you'll discover a lot about them, which can be useful during interviews and deciding if they're someone you want to work for. However, any corporate site will only show information the company wants to reveal, and not what they're like to work for. Also, not all businesses have websites, so you may find nothing. To gain a better understanding, look at what their past and present employees have to say about working there by using employer review sites like:

- Glassdoor (www.glassdoor.com)
- TheJobCrowd (www.thejobcrowd.com)
- RateMyEmployer (www.ratemyemployer.com)

Researching the company will also reveal whether it's legitimate or a scam. If you don't see the company on a review site, it doesn't necessarily mean it doesn't exist. Take the time to check whether they're referenced on other sites related to the industry, and see what appears in the results of a search on Google (www.google.com) or Bing (www.bing.com). You may find blog entries or other results reporting misconduct, scams, or find that it has the qualities you're looking for in an employer.

You should also check the Better Business Bureau (www.bbb.org), as this may not only show that it's an actual business, but how they're rated, what complaints are against them, and how the company deals with complaints.

There are a number of tools that can be used to research a person, which you can also use to see if a business appears legitimate. If a job post has a phone number, you can verify whether it belongs to a business by doing a reverse lookup on sites like Whitepages (www.whitepages.com) or by giving them a call. If a posting has a business address (not just a P.O. Box), you can enter it into Google Maps (https://maps.google.com) to see if it exists, and even use their Street View to see what their business location looks like and whether it seems appropriate for that kind of company.

Social media and bogus companies

Social media is a common tool for business, and many companies have a presence on Facebook, Twitter, and other platforms. In researching a company, you may find accounts on many of the major sites. In looking at them, you should be careful about the account's legitimacy. An account may have been created with a real company's name and logo, but is actually a scammer posing as a genuine business.

Fake job offers and opportunities are common scams that are used to try and get you to provide personal and financial information, or pay money for nonexistent services or fees. A scammer may use social media, email, and websites to disseminate bogus job opportunities or disguise themselves as a real company. By making the account, page, or message appear legitimate using a real company's name, logo, and other information, it has a better chance of fooling you. With social media however, a fraudulent opportunity may be shared by a friend, making it seem more authentic.

Before believing a social media account is legitimate, look for elements that seem strange. If it's a larger company and there are a small number of followers, such as a few hundred, it's a strong indication that it's bogus. You can also visit a known company's official site, and generally find links to their Twitter, Facebook, and other social media accounts. If the links on their website take you to a different account, you'll know the account you were previously looking at is fake.

RECRUITERS

A *recruiter* is someone whose job is to fill vacant positions in an organization. There are *internal recruiters*, who work in-house for a company and scout new talent, and external recruiters (also referred to as *headhunters*), who work for staffing agencies that are hired to fill job openings. These recruiters are not hired by those seeking a job but are paid by employers, and generally don't have any decision-making power on who's hired. If you're asked to pay a fee to get a job, it's a scam.

As with any potential employer, don't automatically believe the promises offered by a recruiting service. A headhunter may overplay what they can do for you, or say they have more vacancies than they really have. They also don't know you or understand what would be the best fit for you in a company, so you will need to work with them to understand what you want in a job so they can match you with an opening.

A bad recruiter is looking for a warm body to fill a seat, but a good one is looking for the best candidate. While a good recruiter will work with you, don't assume their role is that of a career counselor. They are part of the hiring process, and represent the employer. Even though they might be friendly, they're not your buddy, and you shouldn't assume they represent you or are on your side.

When dealing with recruiters, you should take the steps to research them, just as you would a potential employer. In doing so, you'll generally find that an internal recruiter works out of the same facilities as the business, and has an email address with the company's domain name. An external recruiter will work for a firm outside the company but should be using a professional email address and not a free email service. If the recruiter and firm they work for has a bad track record, or reviews indicating it's a scam appear, don't deal with them. Just as job seekers use the Internet to look for open positions many recruiters now use the Internet to find good candidates for jobs. You may get emails or other correspondence from recruiters. Before you open those emails or any attachments they may send double check to make sure they are from a legitimate organization.

BACKGROUND AND CREDIT CHECKS

Depending on the job, you may be required to have a criminal background check or credit check. For example, if you're applying for a job with a position of responsibility, such as with the government or working with vulnerable persons like children or the elderly, an employer will want to know if you've ever been arrested. Similarly, if you're going to work at a bank or with money, the employer may want to do a credit check to see if you have financial problems. While it's a legitimate request, you should never be asked this prior to being hired. These checks are asked as a contingency of employment, meaning that you've got the job so long as you pass the credit or background check.

A common scam involves a potential employer, recruiter, or job board sending an email offering you a job. It may say you're the perfect candidate, and request personal and financial information to do a background and/or credit check. It may also request you go to a website to enter the necessary information, which is really a phishing site. The point of requesting this information isn't to get you a job, but to get information needed to steal your identity or commit other frauds.

INTERVIEWS

Just as you should take precautions when meeting any stranger or person new in your life, you should be careful about meeting someone for an interview. Researching the company will give you a good idea of whether it's legitimate, but what about the interview location and interviewer? Before meeting the person(s), you should determine whether the location for the interview is the same facility listed as a business address. If it isn't, check it on Google Maps again or drive by before the interview to see if it seems a fitting place. If the venue is isolated or remote, appears derelict or with little human traffic, and/or the people around the facility make you uncomfortable, you may want to think twice. In addition:

- Never meet at their home. If they don't have a formal business venue, try and meet at a neutral location or public place.
- Try and schedule the interview during the day.
- If you're asked to continue the interview over dinner and/or drinks, decline.
- If offered a ride (such as being picked or driven home), decline.

You should always let someone know when you're going to the interview, where it is, and when you're expecting to be back. Agreeing to call a friend before and after the meeting will ensure someone knows when you went in, and that you're safe afterwards. Another alternative is to have someone with you. While they obviously can't sit in the interview with you, or join you in the waiting room before the interview starts, a friend could always wait in the lobby downstairs, a nearby coffee shop, or outside in the car. If at any time your instincts tell you something isn't right, trust them. It's better to miss an opportunity than risk your safety.

ONLINE RESUMES

An *online resume* is a resume that is available on a website. Just like a paper resume, it outlines your education, skills and past employment, and is used to show potential employers that you'd be a good candidate for their team. The online resume may be a web page, or created as part of your profile on a job board or professional social networking site like LinkedIn. While it's tempting to reveal a lot of information so you don't miss an opportunity, an online resume can also be a useful tool for identity thieves hoping to get details that can be used to apply for credit and loans under your name.

There is some information you never want to reveal on any kind of resume (paper or digital) or in an interview. While you may be asked for sensitive information after you're hired for tax purposes, background checks, insurance coverage, or direct deposits of your paycheck, they don't need to know this information before the hiring process has begun:

- National identity number (i.e., Social Security or Social Insurance Number)
- Driver's license number
- Passport number
- Age, birthdate, and marital status
- Banking or other financial information

With an online resume, you also want to avoid giving out personal information that would normally appear on a paper resume. Unlike a traditional resume, which you have some control over who reads it, a resume that's publically accessible can be read by anyone. If you're really concerned about giving out your address or phone number, consider getting a P.O. Box and using that as a means of contacting you. Also, don't include the street addresses of employers, as you don't want to be contacted by strangers at work, or any references, as you don't want your friends, family, and colleagues put at risk. If someone's interested in hiring you, they'll ask you to submit a traditional resume or come in for an interview, where you can provide the necessary details. While safety is important you want to be sure to include enough information that the employer can see you'll be beneficial to their organization.

If a recruiter or potential employer has seen your online resume, they can connect with you by sending a direct message through the job board, or contact you via email. The email account you use should be one you've created for job search purposes. Not only will this hide your personal email address, but help you keep track of job offers and interactions with potential employers who are interested in learning more about you. Once they have contacted you, you then have the information you need to research them, and can decide whether to send them a traditional resume or apply online.

ONLINE APPLICATIONS

Many companies will have a section of their website where you can submit a resume and/or apply for a job online. Take steps to research the site first before you use it, and make sure it isn't a phishing site as we discussed in Chapter 5, Cybercrime. If you're applying to an organization that's well known and reputable, they should have made efforts to keep your data secure. Even if you believe the site is trustworthy, take a few moments to ensure:

- The address bar of your browser shows you're connecting over HTTPS, so that data is sent encrypted.
- The URL is correct, and uses the correct domain name (e.g., google.com and not google.phish.com).
- The site has a privacy policy, and contact information that includes a physical address.

Remember that even though the online application is in a different format than your resume, and may ask additional questions related to their hiring process, you should still never provide sensitive or financial information like a national identification number, or pay a fee. If they're asking you to pay money, or give up information that can be useful to an identity thief, it's an automatic indication that something's wrong.

CLEAN UP YOUR DIGITAL PRESENCE

During the hiring process, some employers will be looking at your social media accounts. By looking at what you've posted, there is a good chance they'll see photos and posts that reveal your age, race, marital status, whether you have children, or other details the employer shouldn't have access to. If they decided not to hire you, it could lead to a complaint or lawsuit arguing that they decimated against you on the basis of what was found.

The Internet is a source of information that many potential employers and recruiters may use to prescreen you or do a background check. They may check your social media accounts, and look at the photos you've posted, comments you've made, and things you've shared. This isn't a violation of privacy, because any content they look at is public and easily seen by anyone. As we saw in Chapter 6, Protecting yourself on social media, if you don't want everyone seeing what you've done, it's important to change your settings so that sensitive or embarrassing information isn't public.

If you're asked to provide your usernames and passwords during an interview, don't. You should never reveal your usernames and passwords on any resume, application, or during an interview. Depending on where you live, it may be illegal for the employer to ask this. Many states have legislation preventing current or prospective employers and schools from asking for your Facebook or other social media passwords. According to the National Conference of State Legislatures, since 2012, 23 states have enacted laws preventing employers from requesting this information, and fourteen have enacted laws that apply to educational institutions (National Conference of State Legislatures, 2016). If your state doesn't provide this protection, you should ask yourself whether the job is worth giving up your privacy.

On the chance an employer sees the content on your social media accounts, you should be concerned over what they find. An off-color joke, photo showing you doing drugs or drinking too much at a party, or other activities that might raise a red flag should all be removed from the public eye. There are many cases where people have been fired over what appears on a social media account; whether it was seen by an employer, or reported to them by someone's "friend" on an account. Regardless of how fair it is, remember that such content reflects on your reputation, and can impact your status and standing as a representative (or potential employee) of an organization.

WORK-AT-HOME SCAMS

Not all opportunities on the Internet come in the form of nine-to-five jobs. You may find work-at-home or contract positions that offer you the chance to do the job remotely from home. While there are legitimate work-at-home positions, there are also a wide variety of scams that dupe people into paying money or responsible for expenses.

A scammer may create a site to register, post an ad on online classifieds or in newspapers, or send bulk email offering the job. When you apply, it may ask that you pay to register, buy a directory of companies who may be potential customers or employers, or ask that you pay for a recruitment kit that provides you with all the tools and information needed to do the job. Unfortunately, after paying the fee, you're never offered any work.

Mystery shoppers are people hired by a company or market research firm to act as customers and evaluate the store and its employees. The secret shopper poses as a patron of the store, and collects information on how the staff performs, prices, displays, quality of service, and other factors the business is interested in gathering data about. As a reward for reporting on your experience, you're reimbursed for expenses, keep the product or service purchased, and may receive payment as well. While it's a legitimate job, scammers often use it to defraud people seeking employment.

A common scam involves being hired and told that you'll be evaluating a cash office like Western Union (www.westernunion.com) or MoneyGram (www.money-gram.com). They send you a cashier's check or money order, and you're told to cash it. You're to keep a portion of the money as payment, and wire the rest to someone in another state, province, or country. You later find that the check or money order you cashed is counterfeit, and you're responsible for paying it back to the bank.

The easiest way to spot a fraudulent job is to first remember that the company should pay you, you shouldn't pay them. If they ask for money, assume the worst. To find reputable firms that hire secret shoppers, you can do a research yourself by searching reviews about the company. As we discuss in Chapter 8, Protecting your reputation, be careful of positive reviews as they may be posted by the scammer. Another way to find reputable companies is to visit the Mystery Shopping Providers Association website and use their Service Provider Search (www.mspa-na.org/search) to find companies that provide these types of assignments in your area.

SECURING LINKEDIN

LinkedIn (www.linkedin.com) is a professional social networking site that allows you to connect with others in your field, post your qualifications in a profile, search job opportunities, and access news and information related to your occupation. Employers and recruiters use LinkedIn as a resource for finding new talent and market their company, and you can see when these and other users have viewed your profile. According to the Pew Research Center, as of September 2014, 28% of the adults who are online use LinkedIn (Pew Research Center, 2014).

TWO-STEP VERIFICATION

As with any social media site, you should review your settings to ensure they're configured in a way that best protects your privacy and security. To start, you should use two-step verification to prevent unauthorized users from accessing your account. Once turned on, it will log you out of LinkedIn anywhere you're currently logged in. After this, if someone tries to logon from a new computer or device (i.e., one that's never been used to sign-in to LinkedIn before), a code is sent to your phone, which must be entered the first time you sign-in. Once this is done, the site remembers that you've used that computer or device, and won't require the code when you login with it. To turn on two-step verification:

1. After logging into LinkedIn, click on the **Account & Settings** menu (which uses your profile picture as an icon) on the rightmost side of the top navigation bar, and then click the **Privacy & Settings** menu item.

2. In the left navigation, click the **Account** tab, and then click **Manage security settings**.

3. When the *Security Settings* screen appears, click **Turn On**.
4. Enter your cell phone number, and then click **Send Code**.
5. When you receive a text message with the code, enter the code into the box (where you're signing in). Click **Verify**, and then click **Done**.

HISTORY

Even with two-step verification turned on, you should regularly check where you've logged onto LinkedIn, as this may show you that someone's logged on from a machine you've previously used. At the top of the *Privacy and Settings* page, there are two links that can be clicked to view activity:

- **See where you're signed in**, which will display where you're currently logged in, inclusive to how many sessions are open, when the account was last accessed, the browser used, and the IP address. To sign out of other sessions you can click the **Sign out of all these sessions** link, or to sign out of a particular session click the **Sign out** link beside a particular entry.
- **View purchase history**, which shows purchases you've made on LinkedIn. You can filter to show the last 3 months of activity, year to date, or a custom date range. This will help you identify any suspicious purchases made with your account.

PRIVACY CONTROLS

As seen in Fig. 7.1, the *Privacy Controls* section of the *Profile* tab gives you access to a dozen options that determine what is shared or displayed to others. In going through these settings, you can limit who can access your profile, see certain items on it, follow your updates, and other information.

FIGURE 7.1

Profile tab on LinkedIn.

The first option allows you to control whether news items found with LinkedIn's *Mentioned in the News* feature are shared with the contacts you've added to your network. If you're getting bad press or concerned about what might appear to others, you can turn this off by clicking on the **Turn on/off your news mention broadcasts** link. When the window appears, click on the **Yes! Let them know** checkbox so it appears unchecked, and then click **Save Changes**.

The **Choose whether or not to share your profile edits** setting is used to control whether others are notified when you change your profile, make recommendations, or follow companies. If you already have a job and are concerned about your employer seeing who you're suddenly following or changes that indicate you're seeking another job, or simply don't want everyone seeing every minor change you've made to your profile, you should turn this off. To do this, click on this link, and when the window appears, uncheck the box and click **Save Changes**. If you have significant changes or news you want others to know about, you can then turn it back on, make the changes, and then turn it off again.

In LinkedIn, your activity feed shows such information as who you're following, groups you've joined, and other actions you've taken. Since your activity feed is visible to your network by default, you may want to make it more private by clicking the **Select who can see your activity feed** link, select **Only You** from the dropdown box, and then clicking **Save Changes**.

When you look at someone's profile, the person will be able to see that you've visited. If you want to limit or prevent others from seeing you've viewed their profile, you can click the **Select what others see when you've viewed their profile** link, which presents you with options shown in Fig. 7.2. If you want your name, headline, photo, and other location shown, then select the first option. Semiprivate will only show information like your industry and title, while the final option will keep your information private. If you choose either of these options, it will erase the history

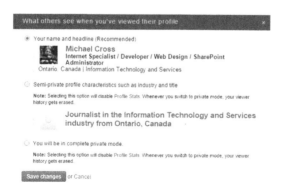

FIGURE 7.2

What others see when you've viewed their profile.

showing who viewed your profile. Therefore, you should view your profile to see who viewed prior to going semiprivate or private.

While many people believe that everyone can see your connections on LinkedIn, the fact is that first-degree connections (people you've invited or have invited you as a connection) can only see your other first-degree connections. If you want to make it more private, you can set it so that your connections can't see other contacts you've made by clicking the **Select who can see your connections** link, and when the window appears, select **Only you** from the dropdown list, and then click **Save Changes**.

By default, anyone with an account on LinkedIn can connect with you using your phone number. If someone uploads their contacts to LinkedIn, the site will discover you based on your phone number, and suggested as a connection. To limit who can discover your account in this way, you should click the **Manage how people who have your phone number can connect with you** link, and then decide on an option other than the *All LinkedIn members*. If you choose **People in my 1st-degree network**, only those you've invited or invited you as a connection will be able to discover you, while choosing **People in my 1st-degree and 2nd-degree network** will allow your connection's contact to also discover you. Once you've made the selection, click **Save Changes**.

SECURING YOUR PROFILE

Your profile contains relevant information about you as a professional, job history, education, skills and other details that can help you get a job and connect with others in your field. This information is important to your profile, as it's used when potential employers search LinkedIn for potential candidates. This doesn't mean you should be indiscriminate and reveal more details than you want others to see. Even though you have control over who you add as a connection, you should still limit what's visible.

As we discussed earlier in this chapter, an online resume doesn't contain everything you'd include in a traditional resume, and the contents of a LinkedIn profile is no different. When adding a new job or school to your profile, you have the option to provide a location. You should never include street addresses, but only give a geographic location like a city or region. Similarly, information on you personally should not reveal where you live.

When adding a description to a job, school, or other achievements, review what you've added to see if there's anything you wouldn't want a stranger to see. You don't want to include a student number in the details about a school you attended, financial information, or other details that could be useful to steal your identity.

By default, LinkedIn makes all of the information in your profile visible to everyone, meaning that someone on a search engine could find you in a search and see everything. To limit what's public, you need to do the following:

1. Click on the **Account & Settings** menu (which uses your profile picture as an icon), and then click the **Privacy & Settings** menu item.

2. In the left navigation, click the **Profile** tab, and then click **Edit your public profile**.
3. On the right-hand side of your profile, you'll see a section entitled **Customize Your Public Profile**. Under this, you have the option to **Make my public profile visible to no one**, which will prevent any information from appearing in search results on Google, Bing, and other search engines. If you want to limit what's visible to the public, select **Make my public profile visible to everyone**, and continue with the following steps.
4. To have your picture, name, title, location and industry, skills, and your websites visible to the public, ensure that the **Picture**, **Headline**, **Websites**, and **Skills** checkboxes are all checked. This will make a minimal amount of information available publicly.
5. In the checkboxes below, identify what information you want to make available to the public, and check those boxes.
6. Once you're comfortable with the information available, click the **Save** button.

SUMMARY

No one can argue that finding work is difficult, and while looking for work online can be a benefit, it can also be a complex and arduous task. It's important to understand what details should be shared and at what time in the hiring process you should reveal information. In this chapter, we've discussed a number of topics that should help make that clearer, and make sure your experience in seeking work is a safe and secure one.

REFERENCES

Jobvite, 2016. *Jobvite index*. Retrieved February 10, 2016, from Jobvite: http://www.jobvite.com/resources/jobvite-index/.

National Conference of State Legislatures, 2016, January 29. *State laws about social media privacy*. Retrieved February 14, 2016, from National Conference of State Legislatures: http://www.ncsl.org/research/telecommunications-and-information-technology/state-laws-prohibiting-access-to-social-media-usernames-and-passwords.aspx.

Pew Research Center, 2014. *Social networking fact sheet*. Retrieved November 20, 2015, from Pew Research Center: http://www.pewinternet.org/fact-sheets/social-networking-fact-sheet/.

Rosin, H., 2013, September. *Murder by craigslist*. Retrieved January 20, 2016, from The Atlantic: http://www.theatlantic.com/magazine/archive/2013/09/advertisement-for-murder/309435/.

Protecting your reputation

8

INFORMATION IN THIS CHAPTER

- Think Twice, Post Once
- The Real World and Cyberspace
- What to Do After a Security Breach
- Digital Legacies

FINDING YOURSELF

If you've been using the Internet for any length of time, you've probably been asked whether you've ever Googled yourself. What you're really being asked is whether you've ever typed your name into a search engine, like Google, to see what you'll find. Alternate names for searching yourself that aren't company-specific are *ego-surfing* or *vanity searching*.

So is egosurfing truly a sign of vanity? Not if you're doing it for the right reasons. In a 2013 survey, Pew Internet found that 58% of men and 54% of women used search engines to search their own name, and see what's online about them. By monitoring their digital footprints, people have a better understanding of their online reputation. It shows what information and photos of you are readily available and revealed to others if they were to search for you.

If you are going to do a search for yourself, you should go beyond just entering of your first and last name. By entering variations of your name, additional criteria, and different input you'll be able to narrow and expand your searches to see different results. This would include:

- In addition to searching for your name, also put your first and last name in quotes to limit the results to pages where that exact text (i.e., your full name) is used.
- Use variations of your name, such as any nick names, shortened versions of your name, maiden name, your middle name, and any applicable titles you may have (such as Dr. or Doctor) or aliases you use.
- Do an image search for yourself, as we showed you in Chapter 9, Beyond technology—dealing with people.

The Basics of Cyber Safety. DOI: http://dx.doi.org/10.1016/B978-0-12-416650-9.00008-5

- Narrow your searches by adding keywords specific to what you're looking for. If you're concerned about leaked photos, type your name and the word "leaked," or if you're concerned about some other content (such as a profile, review, and complaints), add that word to your search.
- Similarly, if you're concerned about your professional reputation, include the name of your business in the search. This will narrow the search to content where your name and business are mentioned.

When searching for yourself, you should start by opening an InPrivate browsing window in Internet Explorer (by clicking **Tools**, and then clicking **InPrivate Browsing**) or an Incognito window in Chrome (by clicking the **Settings** icon, and then clicking **New incognito window**). As we'll discuss later in this chapter, working in one of these windows prevents cookies, browsing history, and search history from being stored, and will also prevent your search results from being skewed by previous searches and other factors. This will give you a better understanding of what others see when they search for you.

In doing the search, you'll find results that apply to others who share your name, so be prepared to navigate through several pages of search results before finding ones that relate to you. It may take time, but it may also be well worth the effort.

WHAT NOT TO DO WHEN SEARCHING YOURSELF

When you look for yourself on a search engine, you should also be prepared to pull up information and photos that you don't want others to see. While it may be disconcerting, it's better to know what's out there than not see it at all.

When searching yourself online, don't limit yourself to one search engine. Many make the mistake of looking themselves up on Google, and forget that different search engines may yield different results. Search engines will use different algorithms to return search results, and (as we saw in chapter: Finding a job online) may not display certain content due to takedown notices, so you'll want to get a good understanding of what's returned on several of the more popular ones. According to Net Marketshare (www.netmarketshare.com), the most used search engines as of September 2015 are:

- Google (www.google.com)
- Baidu (www.baidu.com), a Chinese language search engine
- Bing (www.bing.com)
- Yahoo (www.yahoo.com)

Another important aspect of searching yourself is to not limit or restrict your results in any way. As mentioned throughout this book, you can set your preferences on search engines, activate parental controls on devices, configure filtering, and install software like NetNanny (www.netnanny.com) to filter out adult content. If you've blocked certain content, any photos or comments that are restricted may not appear in your results, and/or you may be unable to open the site to review what's there. Before monitoring your reputation online, ensure that you've removed any restrictions on what can be returned.

GOOGLE ALERTS

Google Alerts (www.google.com/alerts) is a site where you can specify a search term or phrase, and be notified when it appears in search results. To use it, you would enter your name, email address, business name, or anything else you're interested in into the *Create an alert about...* field. As mentioned earlier, if you want to be notified about an exact phrase, enclose the phrase in quotation marks. Once you begin typing, you'll see a field appear that allows you to enter the email address where Google will send a notification. If you click on the **Show Options** link beside it, you'll see additional options appear, similar to that shown in Fig. 8.1.

Once you've specified what Google is to look for, you then configure how often you're to be notified (i.e., daily, weekly, or as it happens), the language to use, and how many results you want. You can also narrow searches to specific sources of content, such as blogs, news, and so forth. Once you enter your email into the field at the bottom and click **Create Alert**, you'll be notified of when content matching your search criteria is found.

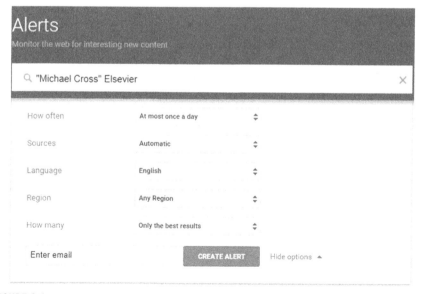

FIGURE 8.1

Google alerts.

IS THERE A PROBLEM?

When you're searching yourself online, you should also look at the sites you're using. If a site is hacked and believes your account was compromised, they will often notify you of the problem. However, you shouldn't rely on anyone to tell you if a data breach occurs. Some won't bother, or are unable to notify you since your contact information has changed since initially signing up for an account. Searching for media releases or news articles may tell you if a site you use has been hacked, and indicate your information is at risk. Another tool to view information on data breaches in the United States that have compromised personal information is the Privacy Rights Clearinghouse's Chronology of Data Breaches (www.privacyrights. org/data-breach). Using this tool, you can filter the results to see incidents where data has been compromised since 2005 in various types of organizations.

Identifying if your account has been compromised is vital to dealing with the repercussions. One way of discovering this is with *Have I been pwned* (www.haveibeen-pwned.com). As we mentioned in Chapter 5, Cybercrime, hackers may take the data acquired from a successful hack and publish it online. In doing so, anyone can now read the email address, username, and other information that was stolen. Using *Have I been pwned*, you can enter your email address into a search field, click the **pwned?** button, and see if the account was compromised in a particular attack. The results show which site was hacked, a description of the incident, and the kinds of data illegally obtained. To take a proactive approach, you should also use the feature to notify you if your account appears in future data breaches that are published online.

OTHER TOOLS

Trying to keep track of being mentioned or tagged on different sites would be an overwhelming and impossible task if you didn't take advantage of tools that will do most of the work for you. Using them you can monitor mentions of your name, business, or other terms you're interested in on social media. Some of the useful search tools include:

- IceRocket (www.icerocket.com)
- Social Mention (www.socialmention.com)
- Keotag (www.keotag.com)

You can also do a Deep Web search to find results that aren't indexed by mainstream search engines. Such a search will go beyond the static web pages commonly crawled by search engines and return results from online databases and other sources.

MAINTAINING PRIVACY

Depending on what you find out about yourself and your activities online, you may want to keep others from finding out what you do. There may be embarrassing photos you're tagged in, and some search engine results about you may show up high in the list of results. Even if your activities aren't showing online, there may be sites you visit and activities you enjoy that you simply don't want others to find out about. Fortunately, it's not impossible to hide what you've done from most people.

In Chapter 8, Protecting your reputation, we discussed ways in which you can have embarrassing photos, videos, and other content removed from sites and search engines. Unfortunately, your success rate may vary. As we discussed, search engines like Bing recommend that you contact the site owner to remove the offending content, and then it will be removed from the search engine on the next search. While true, it's not very helpful. Even if an image or article about you is removed from a site, it doesn't mean every site will be as accommodating.

One way to prevent these links from coming up at the top of search results for your name is to add fresh content that's positive. You might consider starting a blog that highlights your achievements and interests, add a LinkedIn page that shows your education and experience, and possibly consider building your own website. While any party photos and snide comments may still reside in cyberspace, the new content that portrays you in a positive light will hopefully appear higher in the results, burying the old posts and pictures further back in the results.

One of the ways that search engines determine a site's rank is by looking at the number of times other sites link to it. By creating new social media sites, and adding content and linking them together, someone searching for you will see these before the other content you're trying to hide. For example, create a Twitter account, add a link to it on your Facebook account, and then add links to each of them on your blog. If you use them frequently, the new content will also increase your ranking.

PRIVACY OF SEARCH

Major search engines don't simply process your search criteria and give you results. Your queries are stored and associated with either the IP address of your computer, or an account you're logged into. For example, if you have logged onto Google and then used their search engine, your searches can be tied to the account. By associating your computer or account with your searches, recent searches can be offered in the search box as you type, and more relevant results may be returned. Unfortunately, by recording your search criteria, the information can also be used to target advertisements to things you've searched for. As we'll see in Chapter 9, Beyond technology—dealing with people, someone with access to your Google account could view your history and see your browsing habits, which could be problematic if you're concerned about privacy.

There are search engines that don't track your queries, allowing you to search anonymously. Because the site doesn't keep any information on you, it also means that they have nothing to give to third parties. Some of the anonymous search engines include:

- DuckDuckGo (www.duckduckgo.com)
- Startpage (www.startpage.com)
- Ixquick (www.ixquick.com)

UNTAG YOURSELF

A *tag* is a type of *metadata*, which is information about a piece of information. When a photo, bookmark, or other piece of data is tagged, it helps to describe and associate it with other content. For example, when you tag a photo or other content on Facebook, you're associating it with a particular person, creating a link to their account, and posting it on their timeline. If you write a blog, you might add tags to index a post so it's categorized and can be easily found later. When a search engine crawls the site, it may use these tags to associate the content with text in the tag. In other words, if you're tagged in a photo or post, that content may show up in the results when you search for your name.

It isn't unusual to be tagged on social media sites. According to the Pew Research Center, 12% of Facebook users have tagged a friend in a photo, and 35% were tagged themselves (Pew Research Center, 2014). On Facebook, you're notified when someone tags you, so you'll be able to decide whether you want to be associated with a particular picture or post. As we saw in Chapter 6, Protecting yourself on social media, you can also use the Activity Log to view posts you're tagged in, and there are *Timeline and Tagging Settings* that control what happens when you are tagged by someone else.

Of course, not everything a person tags you in is flattering, and you may not want to be associated with a particular image or comment. In such cases, you can untag yourself by doing the following:

1. In Facebook, hover over the post you're tagged in. When a downward arrow button appears in the top right of the post, click on it.
2. Click **Remove Tag**.
3. When prompted that the tag will be removed, but the picture will still appear in feeds and searches, click **Okay**.

Another way to remove tags from photos in Facebook is to navigate to the photo you're tagged in and click on the photo so it appears larger. At the bottom of the photo, you'll see a number of options, but to untag yourself, click **Options** and then **Remove Tag**. There will be a prompt telling you that the tag will be removed; click **Okay** to confirm.

PRIVATE BROWSING

For a variety of reasons, you may not want your computer to record your Internet activity. By default, your browser will keep track of the sites you visit and even download website content (i.e., pictures) to your hard drive. This makes it easier to return to the places you like and perhaps make the pages load faster. While this functionality greatly improves your Web browsing experience, it also enables others to see what we've been doing. Private browsing features are common to all popular Web browsers and allows us to surf the Web without being concerned that others can follow our path.

When you open a private browsing session like *InPrivate Browsing* in Internet Explorer or *Incognito* in Chrome, information about your browsing will not be saved to the computer or will be only kept temporality. After you close the tab or browser, it's gone. For example:

- First party cookies or *session cookies* kept in memory will work normally. These allow you to do things like add items to a cart on a shopping site, and remember information as you move between pages.
- Third-party cookies like those used for tracking your movements between sites are blocked.
- Temporary Internet files are deleted when you close the browser.
- History on sites you visited and files you downloaded, form data, passwords, address bar, and search AutoComplete aren't stored.

If you're using Internet Explorer, you can open an *inPrivate Browsing* window by clicking **Tools**, and then clicking **inPrivate Browsing**. A new instance of the browser will open, and you'll see you're using private browsing by the word *inPrivate* beside your address bar.

To use private browsing in Chrome, you would open an *incognito* window by doing the following:

1. Click or tap the Chrome menu ≡, which is located in the upper right-hand corner of the browser.
2. Click **New incognito window** if you're using a computer, or tap **New incognito tab** if you're using an iPhone, iPad, or Android device.

Regardless of whether your computer is using inPrivate Browsing or Incognito, once you open a new private browsing window, any new tabs you open in the browser window will also be private. In other words, you don't need to start a new private browsing session for each new site you want to visit.

It's important to realize that private browsing isn't completely private, and won't mean you're anonymous on the Internet. As you surf the net, your Internet Service Provider (ISP) or employer (if you're on a network at work) may log the sites you've visited, files you've downloaded, and so on. The websites you visit may also capture your IP address, and record information about your activity, browser information, and other details of your visit. Also, if you're opening a private browsing session in Chrome on a device running iOS, like an iPhone or iPad, you should note that these devices may still store some information. Unlike the private browsing sessions in Chrome on a computer, these devices work differently, as the tabs share HTML5 storage. When you put all of this together, you can see that private browsing is better, but it isn't completely private.

Your Internet history can also be seen by someone looking at your browser. When you visit a site with a standard browser, a history is created. The sites you visit are logged, cookies are created showing the domain you visited, and files are downloaded and stored on your computer, so that the next time you visit a page it opens quicker. As we'll see in Chapter 9, Beyond technology—dealing with people, all of this may be visible to anyone using your computer. A trick to ensuring it isn't readily available to the next person using the browser is to remove traces of it. One way to do this is to use the private browsing option in your favorite Internet browser. When you use this option the information that is normally collected and stored by the places you visit on the Internet is not collected so there is no record of the sites you've visited left behind. That isn't to say that there will be no record of your Internet activity on your computer at all, but it will eliminate the possibility that someone can view your Internet activity from your browser.

Delete the history, clear the cache

In Chapter 2, Before connecting to the Internet, we discussed settings in browsers to remove and manage cookies. In the same area where you set these options, there are also settings for other types of information. For example, in Internet Explorer 11, you could control such items as:

- Temporary Internet files, which are web pages, images, and other content that are sent from a Web server and stored on your computer so that it can then be viewed in a browser.
- History, which is a list of sites you visited.
- Download History, which is a list of files you downloaded.
- Form Data, which is saved information that was entered into Web forms.
- Passwords, which are passwords that are saved by the browser, and automatically filled in when returning to a site.
- ActiveX Filtering and Tracking Protection, which are sites that are excluded from filtering.

To remove this information from your computer using Internet Explorer 11, you would do the following:

1. After opening IE, click on the gear-shaped Tools icon in the upper right-hand corner, select **Safety**, and then click **Delete browsing history**.
2. Ensure that the checkbox for items you want to remove (described in the bulleted items we just mentioned) are checked. If you want to keep the cookies and temporary Internet files for sites you've added to favorites, also click the **Preserve Favorites website data** checkbox.

If you are using a Chrome browser, you would remove information on your browser by doing the following:

1. Click on the Chrome menu , which is located in the upper right-hand corner of the browser.
2. Click **Settings**.
3. Scroll to the bottom of the page and click **Show Advanced Settings**.
4. Scroll to the *Privacy* section of the page, and click the **Clear browsing data...** button.

5. In the **Obliterate the following items from** dropdown menu, select the time limit of past data to remove. For example, to clear out everything, select *the beginning of time*.
6. Ensure the checkbox for each item you want to remove is checked, and then click **Clear browsing data**.

If you are using Firefox, you would remove information on your browser by doing the following:

1. Click on the **History** menu, and then click **Clear Recent History**.
2. In the **Time range to clear** dropdown, select the time limit of past data to remove. For example, to clear out everything, select *Everything*.
3. When the dialog box appears, click on the downward arrow button beside *Details*.
4. Ensure the item beside each item you want to delete is checked, and then click the **Clear Now** button.

Automatically clearing private data

If you never want to leave a trace of what you did online, then you probably don't want to have to manually remove your history, temporary Internet files, and other private data. Instead, it makes more sense for the information to be removed each time you close the browser. In Internet Explorer 11 this is configured by doing the following:

1. After opening IE, click on the gear-shaped Tools icon in the upper right-hand corner, and then click **Internet Options**.
2. On the General tab, in the *Browsing history* section, click the **Delete browsing history on exit** checkbox so it appears checked.
3. Click **OK**.

Firefox also allows you to have Internet information removed automatically. To configure this:

1. Click on the **Tools** menu, and then click **Options**.
2. When the *Options* dialog box appears, click on the **Privacy** icon.
3. In the *History* section, click on the dropdown menu and select *Never remember history*.
4. Click **OK**.

As we saw in Chapter 2, Before connecting to the Internet, you can set Chrome to remove cookies when you close the browser, but there aren't settings to remove everything. If you want such information saved on the browser, then you should look into using a private browser window.

Tor

As we discussed in Chapter 7, Finding a job online, using the Tor browser (www.tor-project.org), you can browse, chat, and send instant messages anonymously. Because communication between your browser and the site you're visiting are bounced across different servers, the site can't see where your request to view a page originated. Any chat or instant messaging application that uses Tor is likewise made anonymous.

Unfortunately, some activities with the Tor network can reveal your identity. For example, let's say you were downloading a movie using a torrent file-sharing application. If you setup the application to use Tor, it would still send out your IP address as it makes a direct connection to get the file. If you downloaded a document and opened it, the PDF or Microsoft Word file could contain resources that are downloaded outside of Tor, which would reveal your IP address.

Another aspect of using Tor that you should be prepared for is a decrease in performance browsing the Web. Because any requests you make go through a network of servers before reaching its destination, you'll notice that it's slower than other browsers you may have used. Unfortunately, that's the tradeoff for anonymity.

Virtual private networks

A *Virtual Private Network* or *VPN* is a private network within a public network like the Internet, and can be used to hide your identity. After logging onto a VPN, any requests to view a web page or other traffic from applications you use are passed through a proxy server. Any site you're visiting will see the IP address of the proxy server, and not the one given to you by your ISP when you first connected to the Internet. Some VPN service providers include:

- Private Internet Access (www.privateinternetaccess.com)
- TorGuard (www.torguard.net)
- CyberGhost (www.cyberghostvpn.com)

Depending on your needs, in choosing a VPN, you should check whether they log activity. If they log what you do, it's possible that a government or law enforcement agency could subpoena the logs related to your activity.

Another benefit to using a VPN is that it can make your computer appear to be located in other countries, making content that's blocked in certain countries available to access. For example, you might live in a country that heavily censors what you can view online, or want to stream a TV show that's only available to a specific region. By using an IP address associated with that certain region, your computer appears to be in that country and allows you to see the content.

Tools

As we'll see in Chapter 13, one way of others seeing what someone has done is to look through their computer. By looking at a person's history, cookies, cache, recent documents, Recycle Bin, and other data stored on the computer, you can piece together a profile of someone's browsing patterns, interests, and behaviors. Obviously, the best way for someone to hide what they've done is to delete this evidence so it isn't visible to others.

Windows provides its own tool to analyze the computer and remove unwanted files. By running *Disk Cleanup*, you can remove temporary files, empty the Recycle

Bin, and delete other files that may be slowing down your computer and reveal information about your activities. To run Disk Cleanup, you would do the following:

1. In Windows 7, click on the start button, type *Disk Cleanup*, and then click **Disk Cleanup** in the list of results. In Windows 8.1, right-click on the **Start** menu, click **Control Panel** on the context menu that appears, click **Administrative Tools**, and then double-click **Disk Cleanup**.
2. When Disk Cleanup opens, select the drive to cleanup from the dropdown list, and click **OK**.
3. On the *Disk Cleanup* tab, in the *Files to delete* list, click on the checkbox beside each type of file you want to delete, so the checkbox appears checked.
4. Click **OK**.
5. When prompted if you want to permanently delete the files, click the **Delete Files** button.

Another tool that can remove unwanted files from computers running Windows XP and higher, Apple Mac, and Android devices is *CCleaner* (www.piriform. com/ccleaner). On a computer, it will delete such information as browsing history, cookies, and temporary Internet files from major browsers, and get rid of temporary and unwanted files left by programs like Adobe Flash Player, WinZip, Microsoft Office, and others. The version for Android will delete the app cache, clipboard content, call logs, and other unwanted data. While free, there are also versions you can purchase that have additional features, such as scheduling CCleaner to run automatically.

EVEN THOUGH IT'S DELETED, IT MAY NOT BE DELETED

Generally, when someone deletes something, they assume it's gone forever. Just because you remove something, doesn't mean it's been erased from existence. If the data hasn't yet been rewritten on the computer then, using the proper tools, someone might restore the data. If you've uploaded information to the Internet or sent to someone else (e.g., in an email), it may still be lurking out there for someone to find.

Tools

When you delete files on your computer, it isn't actually gone. It may have been sent to the Recycle Bin, which you can then open, right-click on the file, and click **Restore** to return it to its previous undeleted location. Even if you delete it from there, or a program has "permanently" deleted it, it can be recovered using tools like those discussed in Chapter 9, Beyond technology—dealing with people. The reason is that when a file is deleted, the space occupied by the file is *deallocated*, which means the computer now sees it as a free space that can be overwritten. The files are still there, you just don't see them. To make these files unrecoverable, you need to wipe the free disk space so your deleted file is overwritten with new data.

There are a number of tools you can use to wipe a drive, including free ones and those native to your operating system. Windows includes a tool called *Cipher* that is

FIGURE 8.2

CCleaner drive wiper.

used to encrypt/decrypt data, but also has the ability to overwrite deleted data. To use the tool, you would:

1. Open a command prompt by clicking **Start**, typing **cmd**, and clicking **cmd.exe** in the list.
2. When the command prompt window opens, type *cipher /w:* followed by the drive letter and (optionally) a folder name. For example, to overwrite free space in a folder called D:\Data, you would type *cipher /w:D:\Data*. Press **Enter** on the keyboard.

As we discussed earlier, CCleaner (www.piriform.com/ccleaner) removes unwanted files, but also has features to overwrite deleted data or completely wipe a drive. As seen in Fig. 8.2, CCleaner also allows you to specify how many times the free space should be overwritten, so that any data is completely obliterated and irrecoverable. To use this tool:

1. In CCleaner, click the **Tools** icon in the left navigation bar, click **Drive Wiper**.
2. In the **Wipe** dropdown list, select *Free Space Only* to remove deleted data. If you choose the other option *Entire Drive (All data will be erased)*, everything on the drive (including data that hasn't been deleted) will be wiped.

3. In the **Security** dropdown list, choose the number of times CCleaner will overwrite space on the hard disk. The more *passes* or times it overwrites the disk, the more difficult it is to ever recover data.
4. In the **Drives** list, click on the checkbox of the drive(s) you want to overwrite.
5. Click the **Wipe** button.

Copies others may have

Even if the data has been completely erased from your machine, it may still exist elsewhere. A file may have been transferred from your phone or tablet to a computer, or copied to a USB disk. To effectively delete the data from all sources, you'll need to think about and track down where the data might be.

One source that limits your control is when data has been shared. If you emailed or texted an embarrassing image, the photo would also be on the recipient's computer, phone, or device. Unless you had access to their devices or accounts, you'd probably have to ask them to delete it, and then trust they did so. Unfortunately, if they forwarded it to someone else, multiple copies may exist.

If the data you want removed from existence has been uploaded to social media or other websites, the likelihood of others having it increases. An embarrassing picture may have been downloaded, so even if it's removed from the site, someone still has a copy to view offline. By viewing an image online, a copy may reside in a person's temporary Internet files directory. By looking though these cached files, the person could retrieve a copy of the file.

Assuming you've been careful to keep your files offline and not share them with others, a deleted file could still exist in backups. If you regularly backup your computer and other devices (which you should), deleting a file wouldn't affect the copy stored in backup files. If you or someone else restored these files, it could still be recovered. To erase those files from existence, you'd need to create a new backup (without the deleted data), and then delete any previous backups.

Online storage

To protect data, you need to control where it resides. If you store data in the Cloud, there's an added measure of complexity. *Cloud storage* (also often referred to as *online storage*) is a service that allows you to store data on a server belonging to a third party and accessed over the Internet. You might use a service to back up the contents of your phone, tablet, or computer, or use it to store and share important documents, photos, music, or other files. Some Cloud services also provide syncing, so that you can offload files and settings from your computer to servers, making them accessible between other computers you log into. Some popular cloud storage solutions include:

- iCloud (www.icloud.com)
- OneDrive (http://onedrive.live.com)
- Dropbox (www.dropbox.com)

Depending on the service and whether it supports synchronizing between devices, your data may exist in different locations. For example, a file might only be stored on an Internet server, or a copy may be on your computer and an Internet server. When using OneDrive, your files are stored online, but a copy of the file also resides on your computer. If you modify a document or file on your computer, the updated file is uploaded to the Cloud, so that the same version now resides on both file systems. If you're not connected to the Internet, the next time you go online, OneDrive will sync the files and update the online version with an updated one on your computer.

While a Cloud storage service should encrypt data as its transmitted and stored, and have security measures in place to protect it from attack or disasters, this isn't always the case. There are many providers, and not all of them are equal. While every provider will claim your data is secure and their business is stable, an unreliable or unstable company may lack the resources or experience to live up to their promises. If the company goes bankrupt or has a disaster, your data could be lost.

You should also be aware that as data is stored in different locations, it increases the surface area for possible attacks. Not only could data be recovered from the computers and devices used to access files in Cloud storage, a hacker or malware could potentially access the data as it moves over multiple networks, and is replicated across different servers in a data center. Even though you see your data on the Cloud, you wouldn't know if it's been replicated to hard disks or servers that are being disposed, at risk of unauthorized access, or viewed by people within the company who have been compromised or corrupt.

If you're unsure of your settings or how Cloud storage works, you might even be surprised that your files are being backed up or synced to the Cloud. When Microsoft added OneDrive (then called SkyDrive) it automatically synced the PC and Internet server. Similarly, in checking the default settings on your phone, or settings for certain security apps, you may find that it's automatically set to sync and backup files to a Cloud service. To control what's sent to the Cloud, you should check the settings on your computer and devices, and any apps that may provide online storage. For example:

- On an iOS device, such as an iPhone or iPad, you would tap **Settings**, tap **iCloud**, and then tap on the iCloud features you don't want to use so they appear disabled. These include iCloud Drive, Photos, Mail, and Contacts.
- On a Mac, you would click the Apple menu, click **System Preferences**, click **iCloud**, and then deselect features you don't want to use.
- If you use iCloud on a Windows machine, you would open the iCloud for Windows program, and then deselect features you don't want.

You should also determine how the service provider handles deleted files. Rather than erasing a deleted file, it may be hidden or reside in a Trash or Recycle Bin. For example, in DropBox, you can click on a trash-shaped icon to view deleted files. To permanently delete them, you need to right-click on a deleted file that appears in gray, and then click **Permanently delete** from the menu that appears.

Just because you don't see it, doesn't mean it's not there

If you're not going to use a site or email account ever again, it's wise to download what you want and then delete the account. However, just as a deleted file may exist on a hard disk after deletion, the data from a deactivated account may still reside on a site's servers. It may take time for the deletion process to complete, not all data may be removed, or the account may simply be hidden or unusable with all the details you've provided retained in a database.

Sites commonly give you the ability to deactivate your account, but this isn't always automatic. For example, on Twitter, once you've deactivated your account, it isn't permanently deleted until 30 days after you've requested it. During that time, you can simply logon to reactivate it. Similarly, when you delete your account on Facebook, removal of the content isn't immediate. Even though others won't be able to see or search for your account, it may take up to 90 days for everything to be deleted, and even then some data may still reside in their databases. In addition, the messages others have from you won't be removed, and continue to exist after the account is permanently deleted.

Just because you don't see it, doesn't mean it's removed from a site. Ashley Madison (www.ashleymadison.com) offers a paid delete feature for $19 that removes a customer's profile, but when they were hacked in 2015, it was found that some details were not removed from their databases, including their gender, date of birth, and GPS coordinates (BBC News, 2015). While the company maintained the hard delete worked, and a significant amount of information appearing in the hacked data appeared to be removed, they offered the feature free to users after the data breach.

In removing accounts from sites, you need to read the policies and details about what is actually removed, and when removal occurs. You also need to be aware that even if the account is removed, certain data may still exist in log files and backups of the site's data, and other users may have downloaded or reposted photos or other content you wanted to get rid of.

THINK TWICE, POST ONCE

The easiest way to avoid having something embarrassing online is not to post it at all. Before posting a comment or photo, think of how an employer, loved one, or others of influence might view it. You should also review anything that you've previously posted, as anyone truly interested in you and your online identity won't simply review the latest posts. Just imagine how an old photo of someone doing drugs or drinking in college, acting sexual, or making a controversial comment will appear to a stranger or someone who's just getting to know the person. What seemed okay to share when you were younger, angry, or intoxicated could be incredibly embarrassing and damaging later in life, so it's wise to go back and review what you did in the past.

A good rule of thumb is not to post or upload anything on the Internet that you wouldn't feel comfortable putting on a billboard. By taking a few moments to review what you've written or the photo you're uploading, you can avoid possible backlash and embarrassment when and if others see it.

OVERSHARING

A common mistake that people make online is oversharing, in which people reveal too much information or say things they probably should have kept private. You've probably seen people do it in real life, where they say something embarrassing, blurt out something that they later regret, or give way too many personal details about something. While you may be able to do damage control if it's a verbal exchange, it becomes difficult if you've posted it for the whole world to see.

Many times, oversharing occurs when someone is anxious about something in their life, and they need someone to talk to. They'll go online, vent about something that angers or saddens them, and then get into a back-and-forth online conversation, giving more and more details about what's going on. They may even say something embarrassing in an attempt to impress a person, and have it backfire. Whether it's because you want to let off steam, or you're attempting to make a connection with another person, you should try to selfregulate what you say online. Remember that any posts, messages, or other digital exchanges create an online record of what you said and felt at the time.

Oversharing can also be dangerous. As we discussed throughout this book, the bits of information you provide can be compiled by someone interested in stealing your identity, password, or be used to cyberstalk you. In looking at the posts you've previously made, or looking back over a chat log with a particular person, you may have mentioned your spouse's name, the names of your children, where you or they work and go to school, and other facts that provide a telling story about your real life. You may have even posted that you're going away on vacation during a specific week, where you're staying, and other details about a trip that excites you. However, this can also be read as a declaration of when your house will be empty and easily burgled.

There is no technology that can regulate the things you say online, so you need to learn how to do this yourself. Be aware of what you're saying. If you look over the posts and comments you've made, what you've chatted with others about, and other sources of what you've said, you may identify mistakes you're commonly making where too much is revealed. While you may be able to edit and remove some of these posts, the important thing is to gain awareness, so that oversharing becomes less of a habit.

THE REAL WORLD AND CYBERSPACE

When you think of cybersafety, it's easy to forget that your activities can flow from the virtual world to the real world. You may order something online, but the shipment may come to your door, along with bills or statements that reveal personal or financial information. That person you met online may make an effort to show up at work or your home, and that job offer you saw on an employment site will probably require meeting someone for an interview. Unfortunately, things don't always go as intended. Cybercriminals don't always stay in cyberspace.

NOT EVERYTHING IS INTERNET BASED

Not every piece of information a criminal can get is obtained from a computer. You should also take steps to protect printouts, forms, and other physical documentation that might be used to steal your passwords or identity. Some of the steps you can take include:

- Keeping a minimal amount of ID and credit cards on your person.
- Not authorizing others to use your card.
- Keep national identification numbers (i.e., Social Security Number), passports, or other identification you don't normally use in a secure location, such as a safe or locked away so it isn't easily accessible.
- If asked for a national identification number, try and use another piece of government ID, such as a driver's license. Never give it to a third party you don't trust, and unless they need it (such as when applying for a credit card or loan). Before giving it to them, ask what measures they take to protect the number so it's not recorded, how they securely store it on servers to protect the data from being hacked, and if it will appear on any documents mailed to you.
- Don't leave receipts at ATMs, bank windows, or trash cans at or near the bank. Don't leave receipts behind at restaurants, gas stations, grocery stores, etc. Someone may take it to obtain your account number, see your balance to determine how much is in an account. Similarly, don't leave receipts that have any credit card or account numbers printed on them in a place where others can get them.
- Don't throw out printed copies of income tax returns, or any receipts that may have been used with them.

When you no longer need documents containing personal or sensitive information, make sure you shred them. Shredders are inexpensive, and many include the ability to shred plastic cards and CDs\DVDs. If you have an expired credit or bank card, make sure these are shredded, so no one can use them as ID, or attempt to get new ones. Since CDs and DVDs may have been used to save copies of important documents, backups, or other data, you should destroy these with a shredder as well.

While identity thieves will focus on using your ID and personal information to pose as you, other criminals may try to use the information you have to gain access to online accounts. As we discussed in Chapter 5, Cybercrime, *dumpster diving* is a simple way to get information about you that they want by going through your trash. Maybe you wrote down a username or password, had a note with a coworker's name, a bill with account information, or a printed map of computer names. In throwing them out, someone could retrieve them and read a telling tale of your habits, interests, colleagues, and accounts. Remember that one person's trash is another's treasure.

Telephone and mail scams

Cybercriminals don't just use websites and email to get you to fall for a scam. Many will try and reach a wider market of potential victims by incorporating direct mail or telephone solicitors to dupe more people. The bogus offer, opportunity, or plea in your mailbox or offered to you over the phone may seem legitimate, but it could be a variation of scams we've discussed in other chapters.

Regardless of whether the mail is sent electronically or as a printed letter, you should treat it with suspicion. If a letter or parcel is mailed to you, you should look over the packaging as well as the contents for signs that should make you wary. It might claim to be from a friend or relative but you don't remember them, or come from a foreign country you have no connection with. You might also notice that there are spelling mistakes, restrictive markings (such as saying its confidential or time sensitive), or the address is to a title or just the address and doesn't have any personal markings.

In looking at the mail, you may find that the letter or parcel doesn't have a return address or uses a fictitious one, which you can check using a search engine by looking up the sender. Of course, even if the return address is a real one, it doesn't mean it's legitimate. For example, a fraudster might do a mass mailing using your address as the return address. He or she wouldn't care about the letters that didn't reach a recipient and was returned to you, as they would only care about people who fell for their scam. If you did get such mail returned to you, you should contact the postal service and report it.

Similarly, if you get unexpected calls over the phone, you shouldn't automatically take them at their word. As we discussed in Chapter 5, Cybercrime, you should ask yourself and them:

- Who is calling and why? If they're a legitimate solicitor, they'll tell you.
- Why do they need your information if you've done business with them? If they're asking for any personal or financial information, it's a sign they don't know you. Don't "confirm" account information, as they may not have it to begin with.
- Why is there a rush? If they don't give you time to think about, there's usually a reason (and not one that benefits you). You want time to research a company, and think about what they're offering.
- If the offer is "free," why do I need to provide a credit card or pay? Any expectation to give a credit card number shows they want your account. If they need an account that could be charged, it's a purchase not a gift or prize.

As we saw in Chapter 10, Protecting your kids, there are ways to identify who is calling and block them. In doing so, you can prevent further calls from the same number. Unfortunately, if they're calling from an IP phone (a phone that transmits calls over a computer network such as the Internet) or using different numbers, you may find this difficult if almost impossible. Playing it better safe than sorry by hanging up is always your best bet. Often, the scammers and solicitors are using a system that autodials numbers, so if you hang up, they won't call back immediately.

Online "Support"

In reading your email or answering your phone, you may find yourself contacted by someone claiming to offer assistance with a computer problem. They may say they're with Microsoft and offer to install or walk you through a free Windows upgrade, or profess they're with McAfee or Symantec and say a virus has been discovered on your computer. The claim to be from a familiar company and mention a product you use lends some credibility, and aggressive sales tactics and lies may pressure you to do what they want. However, since Microsoft isn't monitoring your computer and doesn't work this way, and antivirus companies rely on their products to remove viruses, you should immediately identify it as a scam.

If you decided to follow their instructions, you'd be doing so at a great risk. The link or email attachment could install malware, or you might be given directions that would have you install a program to give the "technician" remote access to "fix" the problem. To install the software, you might need to provide personal information and make a payment (giving them your credit card number). As you've probably guessed, this can now be used to commit other frauds or steal your identity. Unfortunately, it may not end there. Once a scammer has access to your machine, they might delete important files, install malware, or do other actions that cause damage. To take another bite at the apple, they may install ransomware to get you to pay again.

The best way to deal with these offers of support is to ignore them. If you're interested in a free upgrade, check the vendor's site. If you're concerned you have a virus, run a full scan of your system. Don't ever think it's rude to hang up, especially if they're doing their best to keep you on the line and continue talking.

Do not call

Enrolling in a national Do Not Call Registry can provide some protection. Once your number is in the registry, it reduces the number of calls you'll receive from telemarketers. In the United States, you can sign up for the National Do Not Call Registry at www.donotcall.gov, while in Canada you can register at www.lnnte-dncl.gc.ca. Once enrolled, after 31 days, anyone you don't have an existing relationship with or falls into certain categories like the following should stop calling:

- Registered charities
- Political parties soliciting donations
- Newspaper subscriptions
- Market research and surveys

If you do receive a call, you can file a complaint on the site you registered with. This may lead to fines or other actions against the organization a caller's representing. Also, even though there are exemptions, you should ask to be put on the telemarketer's internal do-not-call list to prevent future calls.

Being on the Do Not Call list also provides some indicators that a caller is trying to scam you. If a caller says that they're with a company you don't do business with, and they continue or say they're with another company, it may indicate that they are a scammer. A legitimate business will thank you for their time and hang up.

Preventing mail theft

Once an identity thief has sufficient information, he or she doesn't necessarily need access to your online accounts. Having your address, they could also go to your house and take mail from your mailbox. When you think of the utility bills, monthly financial statements, preapproved credit cards, and other mail you might get in an average month, you can see how profitable stealing this information would be.

To prevent someone from stealing your mail, you should consider the placement of your mailbox, and make sure that it's visible from the house and neighbors and in a well-lit area. If a person thinking of stealing your mail can be seen doing it, they may think twice. As we discussed earlier in this chapter, if you don't want any mail that contains personal or financial information, shred it before you throw it out.

An identity thief doesn't necessarily need to go to your house to get your mail. If they apply for a change of address, they can divert your mail to another address. When they first get your mail, they could use it to steal your identity, and since any additional mail is still diverted, any additional statements for your accounts would never reach your house. If you're not receiving any mail or certain types of mail, contact the post office.

If you're going on vacation or business trip, mail piling up in a mailbox is a sure sign you're away. To prevent it from being stolen, contact the post office and have them put a hold on your mail. This won't stop fliers, free newspapers, and other unwanted mail from being delivered, so have a neighbor check each day and pick up any mail and deliveries.

To avoid getting mail, have important items sent electronically or not at all. If they have a site you can log onto to check your account, all you really need is an email saying a new statement is available. In addition to electronic statements, you should see you can use direct deposit for any checks you receive on a regular basis. If an employer deposits your paycheck in a bank account, and allows you to get other important documents like proof of income and tax statements online or picked up at the office, it will prevent anyone taking it out of your mailbox.

DELIVERY

When you shop online or order something from a catalog, it has to reach you somehow. It may be shipped by a courier, who delivers it to your home. If you're not there, they might leave a card saying they'll try again later, or you might be required to pick it up from a depot. Since policies vary between delivery companies, you might find that they've left it at your door or shoved in a mailbox, making a tempting target for anyone to simply walk over and take it, or left it with a neighbor who you may or may not trust. Even worse, the person knocking on your door might not even be a real courier, which is why you should never let a delivery person in your house. Instead, verify who they are, and check to see if they have a delivery vehicle outside and a uniform that identifies the company they're with.

You should also be wary of emails that inform you that a parcel you weren't expecting is waiting, or provides a link related to a delivery. In some cases, the link may actually redirect you to a phishing site, or download malware. In other situations, the email may be a ploy to get you to pay money, saying that it's held up at customs and a fee is required to release the package. Since customs bureaus won't send computations or assessments of taxes, duties, or other costs in email, it's likely to be a scam. If you're unsure, contact the customs bureau to confirm. In doing so, ignore any contact information provided in the email, and look up the phone number in a telephone book or search engine.

Delivering an item requires the sender to know where it's to be shipped, but you might be hesitant to give your address or credit card number to someone you've never met, such as on an auction site or some other seller you're unsure about. Before ordering, it's important to know what delivery options are available:

- Cash On Delivery, where you pay when the shipment arrives. When delivered, you might pay the post office or delivery company by cash, check, credit or debit cards. If unpaid, the item is returned to the seller.
- Direct to Store, where it isn't shipped to you, but to a brick-and-mortar store owned by the merchant. Often, this can be quicker than sending it to your home, and may be as simple as the store holding a product that's already in stock for you to pick up.
- Post Office (P.O.) Box, where it's sent to the post office or a private company (like United Parcel Service) that accepts delivery, so you can pick it up later.

When you use a P.O. Box, you have a unique address that you can use instead of your home address for orders and delivery of items, for companies that will deliver to a P.O. Box. In using one, anyone involved in a transaction doesn't necessarily need to know where you live. An added benefit to using P.O. Box is that it can help prevent someone stealing your mail, as they're secured in some way. Before renting one however, you should look how your mail is protected. Some P.O. Boxes are little more than a locked mailbox in a public lobby, while others are only accessible during normal business hours, and may be stored in an area that's only accessible to staff.

AVOIDING ONLINE RECORDS

Using a P.O. Box and shipping products directly to a store also have the benefit of limiting the information you provide online. The less information there is about you online, the less chance it will be accessed. Combined with reading a site's policies and opting out of sharing information with third parties, not giving out unnecessary details, and finding alternate methods of making purchases, you can avoid giving more information than a site really needs.

If you don't want to use a credit card or setup PayPal accounts, there are other ways to make purchases online. A retailer may have gift cards that can be used to purchase items in their store or online. Even certain online games and ecommerce sites offer gift cards that can be purchased off of a rack in your local grocery, pharmacy, or convenience store. You can pay with the card using cash, and then use a code on the card to pay for items on the online store.

You can also resort to the basics. Often, you'll hear companies complaining about how online shopping is driving them out of business, and use it as an excuse of why their stores are closing. It's difficult to argue that shopping over the computer isn't popular when you consider that 63% of Americans have made an online purchase. However, in 2014, an estimated 6.5% of retail sales in the United States came from online purchases, and by 2018 it's estimated to increase to 8.9%. Even in China, the world's largest group of online shoppers, online transactions make up only 10% of all retail purchases (eMarketer, 2014). Looking at the figures, a majority of people enjoy shopping in brick-and-mortar stores, so don't expect them to go away anytime soon.

WHAT TO DO AFTER A SECURITY BREACH

When a site or system is hacked and your data is compromised, it can be a frightening experience. Depending on how you hear about it, you may not initially know if you're even a victim, or dodged a bullet and were unaffected. You don't know what they took, who took it, what they plan to do, and whether the data's been shared with others. While you might be tempted to panic, it's wise to keep a clear head and try to minimize the damage.

The first thing you need to do is figure out whether you're affected. If you were a customer or signed up for an account, you may have done so after a breach occurred, which means your data was added after the hackers broke in. Similarly, hackers may have only accessed a subset of data, or data over a window of time. For example, if you didn't use a credit or debit card during the time the breech occurred, you wouldn't have been affected by that data breach. Even if you fall into a timeframe of using a company's site or services, it's possible that your data wasn't in the database or table the hackers accessed. As we saw earlier in this chapter, there are ways of finding out, and agencies and businesses will often notify you if your data was accessed in a breach.

If any online account is compromised, you should stop further unauthorized access. Changing the password immediately, and setting up multistep authentication on sites that provide it, will keep the hacker from getting back into the account. If the same password is used on other accounts, you should also change them with unique, strong passwords as well. If someone has accessed the one account, it's possible they may try and access others.

Once you discover whether it was stolen, you need to identify what was stolen. Not all information is valuable, or worth the concern. If someone stole your name, phone number, and address, you should realize it may already be publically available in the phone book. An email address might result in more SPAM, or could be used with a stolen reused password to gain entry into other sites. As we've discussed, some of the worst information to have stolen would include your date of birth (which can be used to verify identity), medical information, financial information, and national identification numbers.

The value of stolen data isn't necessarily calculated in dollars and cents. In 2014, hundreds of private and nude photos of celebrities were stolen when iCloud (www.icloud.com) was hacked, while the adult dating site Ashley Madison (www. ashleymadison.com) data breach revealed customer's sexual preferences and fantasies. The humiliation of having such data leaked, combined with any possible uses for blackmail, can be of greater concern than any other information taken.

You should contact authorities who can help, including to any relevant financial institutions, the site that was breached, and of course the police. Depending on the crime, local police may do the investigation, and/or forward it to federal authorities. Even if local police seem unable to do anything, they can provide an incident number that references the complaint. If your phone, tablet, or computer was stolen and/or you have insurance that covers data breaches, the insurance company may want proof it was reported to process the claim. The incident number will also provide useful information if you need to prove you were a victim of the breach, such as when there is a civil lawsuit against a company or dispute a fraudulent claim. If you had credit or debit card numbers, or other financial information stored on an affected site, make sure to contact your bank. Explaining that your account is at risk of fraud will enable them to cancel and reissue a new card and/or put an alert on the account to detect suspicious activity. Of course, online accounts aren't the only way a hacker can get your data. If your computer was hacked, you should cut off access to the computer by turning off your Wi-Fi or disconnecting the cable that connects it to your network. As with online accounts, you want to prevent someone from accessing more than they already have. Once you're sure they can't do any more damage, contact the police. Once they've indicated they don't need your computer or other device as evidence:

- Scan your device for malware, rootkits, and backdoors using antimalware software.
- Update the operating system.
- Reset passwords.
- Check email rules and filters to make sure email isn't getting redirected.
- Check all your accounts. Audit them to ensure they use strong, unique passwords, and haven't been accessed.

If you know an account was compromised, deauthorize access to any apps that use it. An app may use an account to access other sites, and a hacker may have used it to authorize other devices or services. Once you've removed their access, you can go through the steps of reauthorizing them, so they can access your account.

Monitoring your financial information is especially important after a breach, as the data someone acquires could be used to steal your identity. If financial data was possibly taken, contact your bank, credit card companies, and any other financial institutions. Check your monthly credit card and bank statements, and make routine checks of your accounts online to determine if any fraudulent activity is occurring. You should also get a free credit report from each of the three credit bureaus each year:

- Equifax (www.equifax.com)
- Experian (www.experian.com)
- TransUnion (www.transunion.com)

If there's an indication that you may be the victim of fraud, checking each year may not be enough. You should consider getting a credit report more frequently, such as every few months. By finding that someone's recently posed as you, you'll be able to deal with subsequent problems faster. In addition to manual checks of your statements and credit reports, you should also put a fraud alert on your credit report. Once this is done, if someone applies for credit, the potential creditor is informed of the alert, and can contact you to double-check that the request is legitimate. An alert can be placed on your report for 90 days, but if you're a confirmed victim of identity theft, it will last 7 years.

A security freeze can also be placed on your credit report so that it can't be pulled if someone applies for a new line of credit. As we discussed in Chapter 5, Cybercrime, freezing a child's credit can be a useful deterrent to someone attempting to steal a child's identity. For an adult, the process can present a number of difficulties, as you're more likely to apply for loans, credit cards, jobs, apartment rentals and mortgages, or other activities where a credit check is required. If you're a victim of identity theft, it's free to freeze your credit report, but there is a charge for others. Also, each time you apply for credit, you'll have to pay a service fee to lift the freeze so a potential creditor can check your report. To place a security freeze on your report, go to:

- Equifax (www.freeze.equifax.com)
- Experian (www.experian.com/consumer/security_freeze.html)
- TransUnion (www.transunion.com/credit-freeze/place-credit-freeze)

While it might be embarrassing to be a victim of a data breach, depending on the site that was hit, you should consider telling others. While those with Ashley Madison accounts might not want to be forthcoming (for obvious reasons), someone whose social media or email account was involved in a data breach should let others know. Doing so lets your friends, family, and coworkers know to be wary of odd posts or suspicious emails that appear to be from you, but are actually scams or attempts to distribute malware and/or hack them.

DIGITAL LEGACIES

While it may seem strange, your reputation doesn't end after you die. People may see the photos, posts, and tweets you've made long after you've passed away. If at first you think you don't care about this, consider that your family and friends might. If people are able to make nasty comments or post embarrassing photos that are upsetting to those mourning you, there may be no way to take them down.

In addition to your digital presence, there are also your digital assets. After you've passed away, the online accounts you have will still exist, as will any assets associated with them. You might have online-only bank accounts, investments, virtual currencies like Bitcoin, and other assets with monetary value. There are also items like music, movies, or books you've purchased that are accessible through an account like iTunes, which might be something you'd like to bequeath to an heir but overlooked.

In creating or updating a will, you should include such items in your estate, and leave clear instructions as to what should happen to them. If you want certain social media or other accounts shut down, let others know so they aren't left guessing after you're gone. If you want someone to manage them, give your executor a way to login. While your password should change regularly, include information on the location of a password list or services you use. For example, PasswordBox (www.passwordbox.com) is an identity manager software that also provides a legacy feature that allows you to specify who will be able to access the passwords if you die.

FACEBOOK MEMORIAL PAGE

Facebook (www.facebook.com) provides a feature to indicate whether you want your account deleted when you die, or name a Legacy Contact who will take care of your account. To name a friend or family member who will take on this responsibility, you can do the following:

1. After logging into Facebook, click on the downward arrow in the upper right-hand of the top navigation bar. Click **Settings**.
2. In the left navigation, click **Security**.
3. In the *Legacy Contact* section of the page, click **Edit**.
4. When the section expands, type the name of the person who will manage the account after you've died. If the account is memorialized in this way, people will be able to post on your timeline to share memories and condolences. A prompt will appear with the option to send a message letting the person know they're a legacy contact. If you click **Not Now**, they won't be notified at this time.
5. If you want your account deleted after you've died, click on the **Account Deletion** checkbox so it appears checked.

SUMMARY

In this chapter we've seen how to research yourself on the Internet, and discover if there's a problem. If your accounts have been compromised, someone tracks what you've done, or someone uses the details of your life to steal your identity and ruin your credit, your reputation can be ruined quickly. By keeping what you do online private, monitoring activities related to your account, and protecting your digital presence and assets, you have a better chance of preventing your reputation from being damaged.

REFERENCES

BBC News, 2015, August 25. *Ashley Madison: delete tool detailed in latest analysis.* Retrieved November 20, 2015, from BBC: http://www.bbc.com/news/technology-34061938.

eMarketer, 2014, December 23. *Retail sales worldwide will top $22 trillion this year.* Retrieved October 24, 2015, from eMarketer: http://www.emarketer.com/Article/Retail-Sales-Worldwide-Will-Top-22-Trillion-This-Year/1011765.

Pew Research Center, 2014. *Social networking fact sheet.* Retrieved November 20, 2015, from Pew Research Center: http://www.pewinternet.org/fact-sheets/social-networking-fact-sheet/; http://www.pewresearch.org/fact-tank/2013/09/27/majority-of-online-americans-google-themselves/.

Beyond technology—dealing with people

9

INFORMATION IN THIS CHAPTER

- Netiquette
- Anonymity
- Annoying and Abusive People
- Online Chat
- Online Dating
- Meeting People in Person
- Protecting Yourself
- Creating a New Identity

One of the main reasons we go online is to interact with others. You may be playing games with others on sites or a game system, writing blogs to share your insight, posting pictures for distant family members, hoping to meet a special someone or share your deepest thoughts and desires with a stranger. Whatever the reason, whether the relationship is cursory or long-standing, you will meet people on the Web. These interactions can have different dynamics from the real world, and bring with them their own set of risks.

NETIQUETTE

There are rules of behavior for any social situation, including what to do online. *Netiquette* is short for network etiquette, and are conventions on socially acceptable conduct when engaging others on the Web. Just as there are socially agreed upon rules when talking on the phone (such as answering with "hello," and ending a conversation with "goodbye") there are similar concepts when using social media, chat rooms, and other Web-based technology.

The reason netiquette is important is because of the way most interactions are conducted online. If you and I had a face-to-face conversation, part of how you'd understand the meaning of what I said would be by watching my facial expressions, body language, and hearing the inflections in my voice. Since most online conversations are textual, these visual and audio cues aren't available, so you wouldn't be able to interpret what I really mean by a comment. If you posted a picture, and

The Basics of Cyber Safety. DOI: http://dx.doi.org/10.1016/B978-0-12-416650-9.00009-7

I commented "nice hair," you couldn't tell by simply reading the words if the statement was sarcastic, flattering, or nasty.

The rules of netiquette weren't invented by a single person. As with any social convention people organically come to agree on what is considered proper behavior as they participated in Bulletin Board Systems and later the Internet. Certain codes were developed over time, and were expected from others who joined after they'd been established.

Largely, the core rules of netiquette involve interacting with someone as you would want to be treated, but remembering that they can't actually see you. Some of the basic rules of netiquette you should be aware of include:

- Not typing in capital letters, as IT LOOKS LIKE YOU'RE SHOUTING.
- Remember where you are. The rules for your behavior depend on where you're posting, so look at how others are conducting themselves before jumping in. One room may allow rude comments and dirty jokes, while another will expect you to be on your best behavior.
- Respect the privacy of others. While you may not have a problem saying something about yourself, others might. Mentioning the name of someone's child, where they work, the state of their relationship, or other details, may offend the person you're talking about.
- Apologize for your mistakes, and forgive others. Just as you'd want someone to pardon your mistakes, excuse others when they make one.
- Use your power wisely. If you have the ability to perform an action that affects others (such as deleting their posts, kicking them out of chat rooms), don't let it go to your head. Don't do things to others that you don't want done to you.
- Be authentic and helpful. You may be an expert or be able to provide advice to others on a problem they're having. By showing you're helpful and knowledgeable, it will make everyone's experience a better one.
- You don't need to comment on everything! Some people feel the need to weigh in on every topic or post, regardless of whether they have anything relevant to say. If someone asks a question, and you can't help them, don't answer "I don't know." Simply ignore the post and move on.

EMOTICONS

Emoticons are small pictures or keyboard strokes that convey a mood or facial expression. For example, if you were to type :) it looks like a smiley face, if you'd turned your head. Similarly, :(looks like a frown, and :P looks like a silly expression of someone with their tongue hanging out. Some sites like Facebook, email, and chat programs will actually convert these into actual pictures of a smiley face, frown, or other image. They may also offer you the option of clicking on an icon to select a picture to include in your post, which helps convey a particular feeling.

When making comments, emoticons are useful in expressing your intentions, and will help a person realize you're joking or upset. However, you should only use them in informal conversations and emails, and not ones where you're trying to maintain a level of professionalism.

UNDERSTANDING THE LINGO

The longer you're online, the more you'll notice abbreviations, acronyms, and slang being used. In many cases, these are used to decrease the amount of typing required to write a text message, comment in chat, or respond to a particular post. Some of the common ones you'll come across include:

- A person may shorten a phrase to letters and numbers that sound similar or identical. "See you" is written as *cu*, "see ya" is written as *cya*, and "hater" is shortened to *h8r*.
- Acronyms may be used to shorten a phrase to a few characters. For example, *btw* is an acronym for "by the way," *lol* is "laughing out load," *brb* is "be right back," *imho* is "in my humble opinion," and *rotflol* is "rolling on the floor laughing out load." Acronyms are also used on sites to describe certain content, such as *FAQ* standing for "Frequently Asked Questions."
- Comments may be shortened to obtain information. For example, in chat rooms, a person might start a conversation with *a/s/l*, meaning "age/sex/location." What they are asking is your age, gender, and a rough idea of where you are. This is done to find basic information and determine if you have the basic qualities for further discussion. If they want to later engage in sex chat (discussed later in this chapter), they will do this to ensure you're of legal age, a gender they're attracted to, and (possibly) within a meeting distance. Often, location is merely asked as a springboard to start further conversation, such as asking "How's the weather there?"
- Comments shortened to hide information. You'll often people (especially teenagers) using terms in chat, texts, and posts that are used to hide what's being said from parents. Some of these include *9* for "parent watching," *99* for "parent gone," *PIR* for "parent in room," and *NIFOC* for "naked in front of camera."

While some terms have been around for decades, the language of the Internet does change with new terms appearing frequently. If you're unsure of what's being said, there are some sites that serve as a dictionary of Internet jargon, which you can use to decipher what's being said:

- Internet Slang (www.internetslang.com)
- NetLingo (www.netlingo.com)
- Urban Dictionary (www.urbandictionary.com)

ANONYMITY

Anonymity is the state of having your identity hidden, so it isn't visible to others. An Internet Service Provider (ISP) or a site you've logged onto may know your identity, but you want to remain anonymous to others, and not have personally identifying information shared with third parties. People may also want different levels of privacy for what they do online, ranging from a basic desire for confidentiality to complete secrecy.

Although we've talked about privacy settings throughout this book, staying anonymous online often goes beyond the basic settings. For most people, a need for anonymity often varies between sites and situations. While you always want personal, sensitive, and financial information to be kept private, there are moments when you may want to hide many or all details of your identity. You may setup an account to chat online with an alias, use online dating, or engage in peer-to-peer file sharing with torrents. In these and other circumstances, you may want a higher level of anonymity because there's a greater need for discretion or an activity presents greater risks.

THE EFFECT PERCEIVED ANONYMITY HAS ON PEOPLE

There are good reasons why people want to remain anonymous. Perhaps you've read an article, and want to make a comment, but don't want to get into a big discussion on how your views conflict with the norm or other people's opinions. In these cases, the site may allow you to post anonymously, so the site knows your identity, but it's hidden from others. If the ability to review a product or provide an opinion wasn't there, you might decide it's not worth weighing in with your opinion. While anonymity gives you the freedom to express yourself, it can also make you feel there's no culpability of your actions.

A price of anonymity is accountability. When people hide their identity or use an alternate persona online, they may feel they have freedom to say or do what they want. The person may post comments they wouldn't normally say to your face, visit sites, and view content they might otherwise never consider looking at, and do things that are contrary to their normal behavior. Because they feel no one knows who they are, the restraint of thinking they'll get caught or "what would so-and-so think if I did this?" is removed. The social constraints that keep their conduct and actions in check aren't there, and this can cause some people to act differently and take risks they wouldn't normally take.

BEING WARY OF OTHERS AND YOURSELF

The effect anonymity has on some people can be extreme. Some people will post inflammatory comments and derogatory remarks in the hopes of starting an argument, or simply to cause problems. Others may go a step further and bully another person, posting negative comments, creating rumors, and making their online experience a miserable one. Others may lurk in the shadows, watching what you do and post online, as they stalk you from a distance. The belief that they're hidden and disconnected physically from others who might hold them accountable can give these people a false sense of power.

While we'll discuss these and other threats later (in this and other chapters), you should be aware of how the perception of anonymity can affect you and others. It can make people engage in activities that they wouldn't normally do. While you would never shoplift a DVD from a store, you might feel free to download a movie without paying for it. Since it's online, you might view illegal downloads as a game or not entirely real because no physical items have been taken. Though others can't physically see or hear you, the rules of conducting yourself are often the same as real life. It may be tempting to bend your morals and beliefs, but it's important to maintain what you believe in, and remember that what you do online can affect someone else behind another computer.

THE FALSEHOOD OF ANONYMITY

Many people go online thinking their identity is already anonymous. They haven't logged onto an account or the site allows them to use an alias, and they believe no one can see who they are. In most cases, they couldn't be further from the truth. There are many ways that sites can capture where you go and what you do, including:

- When you visit a site, the Web server can retrieve your IP address, the site that you came from, the type and version of browser you're using, and a considerable amount of other information. Using the IP address alone, someone could identify who is logging in.
- Your ISP can analyze your activities, which may be used to see if you're downloading copyright materials with BitTorrent technology.
- Social media sites can also track you through the social network plugins on sites, where you can click "Like" or retweet.

This isn't to say that there aren't ways to maintain a level of anonymity online. There are ways to conceal your identity to a higher degree than normal so others can't see what you're doing online.

THE FLIP SIDE OF ANONYMITY

Just as many people bask in the belief that they're hidden online, there are many others who seek attention online. Social media has provided the ability to quantify the attention we receive from others, and get a perception (real or false) of our popularity. Some of the ways that this is done include:

- How many "friends," subscribers, fans, and followers we have on Facebook, YouTube, and other sites.
- The number of "likes" and comments posted in response to something we've said, and how many times it's been shared or retweeted to others.
- The number who have viewed your photo or video on Flickr or YouTube, or viewed your page on sites like Facebook and LinkedIn.

The ability to measure the attention we receive and influence we might have over others is both a positive and negative feature. If you post a comment, the number of likes you receive can give you an idea of what's appealing to your audience. More importantly, let's face it, this makes you feel good. You may also have social media accounts for your professional activities, where you write articles or make videos to share your expertise, share content others have created, or promote your business somehow. By seeing that a particular post is liked by a high number of people, you now have a good indication of what other content you should create and share in the future.

While seeing how people respond to your posts and the interaction of showing you like a post are beneficial, there are downsides to how social media quantifies your life:

- Quality of posts may suffer. Rather than providing accurate information or showing your genuine feelings, you'll see many people pandering to popular opinion, or posting items to solely generate likes and shares.
- Keeping score of your life. Some, especially children and teens, may gauge their popularity by how many people subscribe to their YouTube channel, become Twitter and Instagram followers, and so on. The scores become a measure of self-worth and can be seen as a warped reflection of how they're doing in life.
- Lowering security settings to increase the audience. If a person is obsessed with increasing the numbers of likes and followers, they may lower their security and privacy settings to increase the number of people who can see their posts. Rather than creating a new public account, they may make the mistake of allowing personal information to become visible by allowing everyone to see it.
- Adding people you don't actually know exposes you to new threats. Someone may be proud that they have hundreds of Facebook friends, but they don't actually know all of them. The number of friends and followers becomes a status symbol to some people, but adding all those people may have let in troublemakers, bullies, pedophiles, identity thieves, and other threats. You may have secured your settings so that personal information and private photos aren't viewed publically, but if you accept any stranger's friend request, you're giving everyone access anyway.

ANNOYING AND ABUSIVE PEOPLE

Dealing with the people you'll meet online can be a varied experience. You'll meet nice people in other areas of your country or the world, who have interests and outlooks similar to yours. You'll keep in touch with family and connect with friends you haven't seen in years, allowing you to maintain relationships that might have drifted or been lost. Unfortunately, there are also a lot of jerks on the Web. These are people who irritate, annoy, and anger you by the things they post and the comments they'll make. Even worse, there are those who are insulting, abusive, and even frightening.

As we'll see in the sections that follow, certain types of negative behavior are more prevalent among certain groups, so what you'll experience online may depend on your age, gender, and the types of sites you visit. While no one is immune to being the target of abuse, you should be aware of where and when you're more susceptible to it. By knowing this, you'll be more prepared when it happens, and better able to make an unemotional decision on how to handle it.

ONLINE HARASSMENT

Anyone can be the target of unwelcome behavior. Someone may inadvertently insult you, expose a secret you'd rather have kept private, or show unrequited affection. If it's an accident or wasn't meant to be malicious, you'll probably just blow it off. You might confront the problem, by letting them know they hurt your feelings, or that the comments were unwelcome. If someone challenges you, makes a rude observation, or says something you oppose, you might even be a little defiant and contest what they have to say. Where it becomes a serious problem is when the undesirable statements are repetitive, excessive, or extremely offensive.

According to a 2014 study by the Pew Research Center (Duggan, 2014), 22% of those surveyed experienced less severe forms of online harassment, inclusive to name calling and being publicly embarrassed. Of these, men are more likely to be the targets. In addition, 18% experienced more severe forms, inclusive to ongoing harassment over an extended period of time, sexual harassment, physical threats, and stalking. The study found that:

- 32% of men and 22% of women have been called offensive names
- 24% of men and 20% of women have been embarrassed online on purpose
- 10% of men and 6% of women have been physically threatened
- 8% of men and 7% of women have been harassed for a sustained period of time

About half of the people who were harassed didn't know who was responsible, because the aggressor was either a stranger or the real identity of the person(s) responsible wasn't known. This can happen if the person created a fake account, used an alias, or took other steps to hide their identity. Perhaps more frightening is that the other half were known to the victims. This means that the harasser had some kind of relationship with and/or felt so comfortable with bullying the person that they didn't even try and hide who they were.

Being the target of some kind of abuse can happen anywhere on the Internet, but the most common places may surprise you. Of those targeted by harassment, they reported the most recent incident occurred on the following types of sites:

- Social media 66%
- Comments section of a website 22%
- Online gaming 16%
- Personal email 16%
- Discussion site (e.g., reddit) 10%
- Dating site or app 6%

If you've ever been the victim of online abuse, you can see from this that you're far from alone. The perpetrators and targets of online harassment can involve any age, gender, social, or ethnic background, regardless of where they live or work. While younger Internet users have a greater chance of being targeted, this doesn't mean that older users should believe they'll never see or experience this kind of behavior.

TROLLS AND FLAMERS

As we've seen, the threat of harassment can come in a variety of forms, and there are different types of annoying, abusive, and menacing people you'll come across online. A *Troll* is someone who posts or responds with comments in the hopes of getting some kind of reaction. In doing so, they may make derogatory comments, or say something that will upset people. This may be some racist, sexist, or offensive remark that will draw others into responding.

The meaning of the term is similar to that of a *flamer*, which is someone who posts inflammatory comments in the hopes of inciting an argument. By posting something outlandish or offensive, called *flamebait*, the hope is that someone will then respond, possibly resulting in drawing in other users and resulting in a *flame war* where multiple people are exchanging arguments, offensive comments, and insults.

If it sounds like some kind of psychotic game, you wouldn't be far from wrong. Trolls and flamers generally fight with people as a form of entertainment, and enjoy the emotional responses they receive as a result of their posts. In a 2014 study on the behavior entitled "Trolls Just Want to Have Fun," it was suggested that people who enjoy and engage in this type of behavior have traits that show signs of "narcissism, Machiavellianism, psychopathy, and sadistic personality" (Buckels et al., 2014). In other words, they enjoy hurting people with their comments, so they do so as a way of having fun.

The way to deal with trolls and flamers is to look at what they want, and not give it to them. They are posting these comments in the hopes of getting a reaction, so don't give them one. If you don't respond, you haven't added fuel to their fire, and you've extinguished any flame war before it's begun. If you ignore them, you've won and they've eventually go away and bother someone else.

CREEPING

Creeping is the act of someone viewing another person's profile or page, and following their activity without their knowing. This isn't the same as seeing someone's posts appear on your wall, keeping up-to-date with a friend or family member's pastimes, or checking out someone you've just met to see if they're okay or a threat. When someone creeps a page, it's to watch what you're doing, without your knowledge, possibly for disturbing reasons.

A person will creep another person's page to monitor them. A jealous boyfriend, girlfriend, or spouse may watch their significant other's page to ensure they're behaving in a way that's expected. It's also common practice after a breakup. A 2012 study (Lukacs, 2012) found that 88.2% of people spent time looking at, analyzing, or creeping their ex's profile. If you think the easy solution to this would be to simply unfriend or block your ex, you'd be wrong. The study also found that those who'd been unfriended used another person's account (such as logging in with a mutual friend's account) to view their ex's activity.

While some sites like LinkedIn allow you to see who's viewed your profile, most do not. In many cases you won't be aware if someone's creeping your page unless you hear about it. If you hear the person is using another friend's account, you could unfriend or block their account, as we'll see later. If it's your understanding that they're using a school or work computer to creep your profile, you could complain to them. Using the computer in this way could be a violation of the school or employer's acceptable use policies, which could result in disciplinary action.

CYBERSTALKING

Cyberstalking is the act of persistent and unwanted contact from someone online. It may involve any number of incidents including threats, libel, defamation, sexual harassment, or other actions in which to control, influence, or intimidate their target. Stalking a person online may also involve stalking the person in real life. In many states and countries it is illegal, and could result in criminal charges as a named offence or under harassment and stalking laws.

There have been a number of prominent cases involving cyberstalking, including the incident involving actress Patricia Arquette. In 2011, she deactivated her Facebook account on the advice of her security people due to problems with an online stalker. She decided to only communicate with fans through Twitter and advised fans in her last post to only accept friend requests from people they know.

Cyberstalking doesn't only affect the rich and famous. According to a 2014 study by the Pew Research Center (Duggan, 2014), 18% of those surveyed said that they had seen someone stalked, while 8% reported that they had been stalked. It also found that women are more likely to experience online sexual harassment or cyberstalking then men. Of these, women aged 18–24 experienced a disproportionately high number of incidents, with 26% having been cyberstalked, and 25% being the target of sexual harassment. This isn't to say that men aren't targeted by this type of behavior. The survey found that 7% of men aged 18–24 reported being stalked online, and 13% experienced sexual harassment.

Because cyberstalking could ultimately result in violence, if you're a target it's important that you take action as soon as possible. Contact the police and report the crime(s) that have been committed. Gather as much evidence as you can about the incidents. This would include printouts or screenshots of posts and messages, documenting dates and times of incidents, and any other information you might have. You should also evaluate your privacy and security settings, and change the passwords for any email and social media accounts, in case the person has gained access to them. As we'll see in this and other chapters, many sites also have features to report harassment and other problems, possibly resulting in the person's account being disabled or removed.

PROTECTING YOURSELF

When you're faced with a problematic user, it can seem hopeless when you're staring at their annoying or abusive posts. As mentioned, if you feel threatened, then calling the police is an important step. If it hasn't come to that and you want to avoid potential problems, there are steps you can take. In addition to the preventative measures we've already discussed, you can limit your exposure to the person, seek support, and report problems.

Thinning the Herd

Every so often, it's a wise idea to go through the friends and followers you have and remove ones that have no redeeming value to your online experience. Perhaps they were added so you could have more neighbors in a game you no longer play, they used to date a friend but that relationship is over, you have a nasty relative who posts disagreeable things, or a friend you no longer want a relationship with. Ever few months at least, you should go through the friends you and your children have on Facebook and other sites, and remove ones that are no longer relevant or shouldn't be there.

For those you want to keep but limit access, you should utilize lists. As we saw in Chapter 6, Protecting yourself on social media, you can add people to the *Restricted* list in Facebook so that they can only see your public posts and the posts they're tagged in. People in such lists might be your boss, a family friend who isn't really a personal friend, and others you want to remain friendly with but limit what they can see. It may also include people you're having some problems with, so you can still see their page, but they can't see any of your private posts.

Unfriend, unfollow, unjoin

Limiting exposure to people who are annoying or abusive also involves removing them from your real life, and your online world. A good cull of the groups you belong to but no longer find relevant, and former friends who shouldn't have access to your life involves unfriending, unfollowing, and unjoining.

Unfriending a person on Facebook removes their access, so they'll only be able to view publically accessible content. The person isn't notified, so they'll only notice if they review their list of friends, or visit your page and notice the option is there to add you as a friend. To unfriend someone, go to your profile page, and click the **Friends** link on the navigation bar below your cover photo. When the list of friends appears, do the following:

1. Click the button beside the person's name that says **Friends**.
2. On the dropdown that appears, click **Unfriend**.

Just as you may have grown tired of a friend, you may no longer wish to be part of a group. To unjoin a group, you would visit their page, hover your mouse over the button on the cover photo that says **Joined**, and then click **Leave Group** on the dropdown that appears.

In some cases, you may not have added the person as a friend, but are simply following them. In doing so, you can see their posts on your newsfeed. In other cases, you may want to keep them as a friend or stay in a group, but don't want to see their posts anymore. To remove their posts from your feed, simply visit their page, hover your mouse over the button that says *Following* on their cover photo, and then click **Unfollow**.

Twitter also allows you to stop following someone. To stop seeing tweets from a particular person or group, visit their page, click on the **Following** button below their header photo. The button should now say *Follow*, indicating you are no longer following them.

Blocking people

Blocking a person prevents them from contacting you and removes their ability to see your profile and content. The ability to block someone is a common feature in many apps and social networking sites, allowing you to use their services without having to deal with unwanted users. The method of blocking someone varies from app-to-app and site-to-site. In the paragraphs that follow, we'll show you methods available on some of the most popular apps and sites.

Blocking in Facebook is done by clicking the downward arrow in the top right-hand corner of the top navigation bar, and then clicking **Settings**. Click on **Blocking** in the left-pane of the screen that appears, and you'll see a screen as shown in Fig. 9.1.

As seen in Fig. 9.1, Facebook allows you to block users, invitations, apps, and pages. The settings on this page include:

- Restricted list, where you can add and edit the people on your Restricted list, which we discussed in Chapter 6, Protecting yourself on social media.

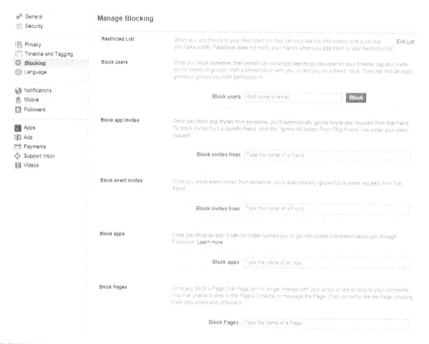

FIGURE 9.1

Facebook blocking.

- Block users, where you can add names of people you want to block, so they no longer see your posts, can tag you, invite you to events or groups, send messages/start conversations, or add you as a friend. The exclusions to anyone added is that they can still interact with you in any apps, games, or groups you're in.
- Block app invites, which will ignore any invitations to join games or other apps sent by the person.
- Block event invites, which will ignore any event invites from the person.
- Block apps, which prevents any apps from contacting you or getting nonpublic information about you.
- Block pages, which blocks any pages from liking your posts, or replying to comments, and prevents you from posting on the page or messaging it. If you've liked the page, this will automatically unlike and unfollow the page.

Twitter also allows you to block someone. In doing so, they can't follow you, send Direct Messages to you, add your account to their lists, tag you in photos, view your tweets, who's following you, who you're following, or your content (photos, videos, lists, or favorites). When you block the person, they won't receive any notification of it. To block someone on Twitter, you'd do the following:

1. At the bottom of their tweet, click the More icon (which is three dots).
2. Click **Block**.

On Instagram you can block someone so they can't see your profile or posts. You'd do this through the app, by tapping on their username to open their profile. Once you're on their profile, tap the icon with the depiction of three dots, and then tap **Block User**.

Snapchat also provides ways to block users. To block a user who's added you, so they can't view your stories, or send your snaps and chats, you would start by going to your profile screen. On this screen, **Added Me**, find their name and tap the gear-shaped icon next to their name, and then tap **Block.** To remove them from your list of friends, tap **Delete**. If you wanted to remove a person from your friends, you can tap **My Friends** on your profile, tap their name, tap the gear-shaped icon below their name, and then tap **Block**. There are times when you'll be in chat with someone and want to block them from there. To do this, you would swipe left of the user's name, tap the icon with three bars, and then tap **Block**.

While the steps involved in blocking a person vary between apps and sites, you will see similarities in the process of how to block them. To get detailed instructions on a app or site we didn't cover, you should check the help section for the site and search for how to block someone.

Does losing anonymity help?

You might think that a possible solution for getting rid of trolls and stalkers is to remove their ability to remain anonymous on sites. However, as we saw earlier, about half of the people experiencing online harassment were able to identify the person.

This is consistent with what can be seen on sites that removed anonymity. While you used to be able to post anonymous comments about a video on YouTube, in late 2013 Google forced people commenting on videos to associate comments with their Google+ accounts. If you visit YouTube, you'll still see plenty of nasty remarks being posted, showing that trolls have no problem with others knowing who they are.

If you're a blogger or have some other site you own and control, you may have the ability to ban commenters from responding to the content you post. On YouTube, when someone posts a comment, you'll get a notification that has an arrow in the upper right of the comment. Upon clicking this, you can choose to remove the comment, report it as spam or abuse, or hide it. If you choose to hide it from the channel, the user is added to the hidden users list on your channel, and he or she is blocked from posting comments on videos.

Bloggers and YouTubers also have the ability to manage comments that have been added, preventing them from being seen until they're approved. While it won't protect you from seeing any negative or derogatory comments people may post, it will save you possible embarrassment from others seeing them. By checking the settings available to you, you can limit the exposure of such comments, and report them as they come in.

Reporting abuse

As you've seen, there are mechanisms on sites and apps for dealing with annoying and abusive people, allowing you to minimize the exposure of their comments, make it so you no longer see them, or block them so that they can't bother you anymore. There are times when you'll want to take an extra step and report what they've posted. You can take steps to delete and remove links and content, and also report those posts to the site.

If someone has created a page, group, or profile that's designed to embarrass or harass you, you can report it on Facebook by going to their profile, clicking ⋯ , and then clicking **Report**. You would then follow the instructions to report the problem.

You can also report issues to Facebook through the following steps:

1. In your browser, go to www.facebook.com/help/contact/274459462613911.
2. Click the link that is most closely related to your problem. Options include **Someone is threatening to share things that I want to keep private** and **Other abuse and harassment**.
3. Follow the onscreen instructions to report the problem.

On Twitter, you can report abuse by visiting the person's profile, clicking the gear-shaped icon, and then clicking **Report**. You can then select that **They're being abusive or harmful**, and report the issue you're having.

If the problem is on another site, don't worry. Other sites commonly have links or contact email in which you can notify the site about a problem. In many cases, this is the domain name preceded by *abuse@* (e.g., abuse@myfakesite.com), but you should check the site to ensure this is the correct way of notifying them about an abusive user.

If you have the person's email address, you may be able to see the ISP they're using for Internet access. In such a case, you could notify their Internet provider of the harassment, in the possibility they will remove him or her as a subscriber. Without Internet, they won't be able to harass you online.

If you're experiencing any threatening comments, or are fearful for your safety, you should always contact the police so that the matter can be fully investigated and/or you can get help obtaining a restraining order. Don't dismiss abusive behavior, hoping that it won't escalate.

ONLINE CHAT

Online chat refers to any type of communication in which messages are sent in real time between two or more people. While discussion boards and email are used to post or send a message that may be responded to later, the various programs and protocols used for chatting allow people to send and receive messages instantly. Communication between those involved in a chat may be text-based or use streaming technology to allow people to actually talk (using their voice) and see one another via live video.

While chatting online can introduce you to people you never would have met, and may even provide a spirit on online community where the same people chat together regularly, it is not without its potential threats. Some of the things to remember include:

- You're talking with strangers, so be aware of what you say. Don't provide any personal information, inclusive to your name, address, credit card information, names of family members, where you work, and so on.
- Be careful of links. It's common for someone chatting to send a link, but this may download a potential virus or a site with malware.
- Disable automatic downloads, if that is a feature of the program being used.
- Leave your profile blank or enter false information.
- If you have problems, report them to the moderator or site. You can also log out, change your username, and log back in. Block or ignore (*iggy*) anyone who gives you a problem so that they can't contact you or see what you've typed.

PICKING AN ALIAS

When you chat online, you'll often use an alias. The alias is a username that others will see when viewing a list of people visiting a room, or when communicating with you privately. This helps to shield your real identity, so that people can't directly see who they're talking to. When choosing an alias, don't use any names that reveal who you are, where you work, your marital status, if you have children, or other personally identifying features. There are a number of sites that can help you create usernames for chat rooms and other purposes, including:

- SpinXO (www.spinxo.com)
- Cool Name Generator (http://cool.namegeneratorfun.com/)
- Name Generator (www.namegenerator.biz/screen-name-generator.php)

INSTANT MESSAGING

Instant Messaging (IM) is used to send messages in real time. Traditionally, this has been limited to text-based messages, although some sites and apps also have the ability to communicate with voice or video. When using IM, you would keep the messages relatively short to keep communication flowing at a reasonable pace. To use IM, you would have to install client software that used a specific protocol to chat with others using similar software. Some of the clients available include AOL Instant Messenger or AIM for short (www.aim.org), Pidgin (www.pidgin.im), and eBuddy (www.ebuddy.com/). These traditional IM clients have been overshadowed in recent years by the proprietary IM software included with phones and other mobile devices, such as Blackberry Messenger and Apple's iMessage.

Another popular method of using IM is with the integrated features in social media sites. Rather than install additional software or apps, you could IM using the chat features on sites like Facebook. In 2011, Facebook partnered with Skype (www.skype.com) to provide a video call feature. Rather than simply type your message, you could now choose to engage in video chat as well. To turn off this feature, you would do the following:

1. On the chat sidebar, appearing on the right side of the Facebook page, click the gear-shaped Options icon.
2. Click on **Turn Off Video/Voice Calls**. To turn off chat itself, you could also click **Turn Off Chat**.

CHAT ROOMS

Chat rooms are areas in which people can gather to engage in real-time conversations, generally using text-based communication. There are a number of sites on the Internet where you can find chat rooms focusing on various topics, interests, ways of life, or providing forums for general discussion, although other sites may only provide a single chat area. You may see forums for moms to chat, issues with sexuality, and so on, although these often go into more general discussion that don't reflect the room's name. In the *main chat room* there will be groups of people who are all chatting with one another, although two or more people can open a *private chat room* to communicate privately. Some of the chat sites on the Internet include:

- Delphi Forums (www.delphiforums.com), which provides multiple rooms. After setting up an account and profile, you'll be able to join the room(s) you wish and engage others in conversation. Some rooms require a 48-hour wait before you can enter, which prevents those who have been banned from a room just creating a new account and going back in.
- Chat Rooms Online (www.chat-rooms-online.com), which provides multiple rooms, but doesn't require creation of a profile if you go on as a guest.

Chat rooms generally have *moderators*, who are responsible for ensuring the rules of the room are followed. A variation of netiquette is used in chat rooms called *chatiquette*, which govern the acceptable behavior in most rooms. While some rules like not typing in caps are the same as those used in netiquette, there are others that are unique. For example, prior to going into private chat with someone, it's commonly expected that you should ask first in the main room. You may see someone ask you "can I PM you?" meaning they want to private message or go into a private room with you. Those who are bothering people in the room and ignoring the rules are often "kicked" from the room, and moderators may ban them so they can't reenter.

Different rooms may have different rules, so you should hesitate before jumping into conversation. Some rooms may strictly forbid offensive remarks and rude behavior, while others may have a more laissez faire attitude and let anything happen. *Lurking* is the act of not participating in the main chat room's discussion, but simply reading what's being said. By taking this step, you can see if the room meets your approval, and if the group that's on there seem like the kind of people you want to interact with.

While the people who go into chat rooms are predominantly nice, they also attract trolls and people who want to engage in cybersex, which we'll discuss later. It's important to remember that you don't really know who you're talking to, and that everyone's a stranger. It can be difficult to retain this mindset as you get comfortable. However, if you have a problem, feel free to use the button to ignore a pest and block any communication from them.

WEB CAMS

Web cams are cameras that are built-in or connected to your computer, allowing you to take digital photos or video of yourself. They may be used for video conferencing, taking pictures that can be used to update a profile, or used to create videos and pictures that can be shared with others.

Using a Web cam, you can put a face to the words as you're chatting, or conduct real-time conversations "face-to-face." This can be done using programs like Skype, which allows you to make voice or video calls. As we mentioned, sites like Facebook also provide the ability to engage in video discussions. If you have a camera installed, when you click on the name of the person you want to chat with, you would then click on the camera-shaped icon at the top of the discussion. A new window would appear allowing you to chat.

In general, you should never agree to engage in any kind of intimate act, remove clothes, or do anything on camera that might be considered embarrassing or incriminating if revealed to someone else. You should always go on camera with the thought that others may see it. If anyone does threaten to blackmail you, don't agree to their demands and contact the police immediately.

Even if you don't do webcamming, the webcam may still be used to watch or record videos of you. *RATting* refers to a Remote Access Trojan (RAT) being installed on a computer for the purpose of acquiring remote access of that machine. Once a RAT is installed, a hacker gains administrative access to the machine, and may gain control of your webcam. They can turn it on, watch you without your realizing it, and either live-stream or record what's happening for others to watch. To avoid having your system exploited and used in this way, you should have antivirus and antimalware software installed with the latest updates, and use a firewall. This will block and remove any known remote administration tools that may have been installed. If you have an external camera that plugs into your computer, look to see if the light is on showing it's been activated. You could also consider removing it when it's not being used. Obviously, if it's not attached, no one can use it without your knowledge.

ONLINE GAMING

The ability to communicate with others has been integrated into a wide variety of programs, including online games. If you go on Facebook, you may have blocked the chat feature, but people may still send messages to you in the various games you've signed up to play. The app may have a feature visit the playing environments of your neighbors or allies and send messages. Generally, this comes part-and-parcel with the game, and the only way to stop others from communicating with you is to uninstall the app.

Most games that are online and multiplayer allow voice communication with other players. This not only includes computer games, but also those designed for game systems like Sony PlayStation, Nintendo Wii, and Microsoft Xbox. While you're playing with others, you can talk to them and/or send text messages through the game system. While this has benefits in the game, it also exposes you to stalkers, trolls, and other potential threats that come from dealing with people online.

There are also virtual environments where you can chat. Massively multiplayer online role-playing games like World of Warcraft and virtual worlds like Second life (www.secondlife.com) allow you to create a humanoid representation of yourself called an *avatar*. Using the avatar, you can interact with other players, and talk online with them using voice or text-based methods.

Romance scams

While you might have to kiss a few frogs to find a prince, sometimes you just get warts. As you might expect, online romance has attracted criminals who use promises of affection and companionship for personal gain. A cybercriminal will review your profile to see what kinds of music books, and movies you like, review your posts and tweets, and determine your likes and dislikes. Using this, the scammer will pretend to have shared interests, make flattering comments, entice you with promises, post attractive photos that are supposedly them, and gain your trust. Once this is done, they'll ask favors, asking you to pick up or resend packages on their behalf, or request money to deal with a family tragedy or some other hardship. The cybercriminal may use chat rooms, dating sites, social media, or other sites to meet a victim.

According to the 2014 Internet Crime Report (Internet Crime Complaint Center, 2014), this scam generated 5883 complaints to the Internet Crime Complaint Center and resulted in victims collectively losing $86,713,003. While people from every demographic and both genders have fallen for this scam, women who are over the age of 40 predominantly fall victim.

ONLINE DATING

Online dating is the process of trying to form a relationship for romantic or sexual reasons. While you can meet people through social networks, chat rooms, or any other online venue, finding a relationship through online dating typically involves a site or app specifically designed for this purpose. In using a dating service or app, you may be provided with matchmaking where your interests and motivations are aligned with others who have similar interests. Others may simply provide the ability to peruse a database of people, or search on the basis of age, sex, location, and other factors.

Even though you may be taking steps to find Mr. or Ms. Right, not everyone uses these services for the same reason. Some of the steps you should take to protect yourself include:

- Try to be as anonymous as possible. Never give away information that identifies you, such as your surname, where you work, or other details in your profile or when initially making contact.
- Keep any contact information private, inclusive to your email, phone number, and address. The services you use may include temporary phone numbers for texting, internal messaging, or other features that allow you to communicate so they won't have access to you directly.
- Take things slowly. You may be excited at the prospect of a relationship, but you shouldn't be quick to reveal personally identifying information or sensitive details too fast. Remember the person is still a stranger, even though you may have exchanged messages or talked to one another.

TRADITIONAL VERSUS EXTRAMARITAL

Commonly, people use traditional dating sites in the hopes of finding someone to have a long-term relationship or sexual partner. While many of the people on these sites are single, there are also those who are married. A famous site that caters to extramarital affairs is Ashley Madison (www.ashleymadison.com), where single or married people can connect with other women or men. Couples also use the site to meet others to join them in discreet sexual encounters. If you think few people would consider using this service, you'd be wrong. It's a membership site that boasts over 42 million members across 53 countries. Of course, even if you aren't using a site that has the clear intention of being an extramarital dating service, it doesn't mean that the person you're meeting isn't already in a relationship.

Being in a relationship and using sites to find another partner opens you to the risk of being identified by someone you know. Other information included in your profile could also cause serious embarrassment. When Ashley Madison was hacked in 2015, there were details of people's sexual fantasies and interests included in the profile data. Once the hackers made this available for download on another site, members were identified, and according to the Toronto Police Department it led to two people committing suicide and others being victims of extortion.

Online dating provides a unique situation of balancing privacy with openness. When you are looking for a relationship online, the site may use a matchmaker algorithm to match you with someone, or people may browse profiles to find someone they like. To attract someone who's compatible requires you to provide honest information, which also makes it a useful source of intelligence for cybercriminals. As we discussed in Chapter 5, Cybercrime, someone may use this as the basis to obtain personally identifying information that can be used for identity theft and other crimes. It may also be used for webcam blackmail, extortion, and romance scams. It's important that you limit what you reveal, and think of how a piece of information may be used. If it personally identifies you or could be embarrassing, keep it private. You can always leave some mystery and reveal some details when you are confident you can trust the other person.

SITES

There are a number of dating sites on the Internet to meet with someone in the hopes of achieving a romantic or sexual relationship. These services may be free, cost a subscription fee, or provide some free access but provide other features at a cost. They also typically require you to create a profile and may require you to fill out an online questionnaire to obtain additional information so they might better find a compatible match for you. Most allow you to upload photos and videos to allow others to see what you look like. The features of dating services vary, with some providing the ability to engage in text-based chat, Voice Over IP voice chats, and webcam chats. Some of the popular sites include:

- eHarmony (www.eharmony.com)
- Match.com (www.match.com)
- Zoosk (www.zoosk.com)
- PlentyOfFish (www.pof.com)

If you think a traditional dating site is safer and more secure than nontraditional ones like Ashley Madison, you'd be wrong. In 2011, both eHarmony and PlentyOfFish were hacked. In the same year, a woman claimed she was raped after meeting someone on Match.com and sued the site, wanting them to do background checks to prevent registered sex offenders from signing up. After the suit was filed, Match.com announced it would screen new members. Regardless of the site you use, you need to be careful, safeguarding both your information and yourself.

APPS

Sites aren't the only method of meeting someone online. Apps like Tinder (www.gotinder.com) can be installed on iOS and Android devices. When you use Tinder, you swipe left on your device to review different people looking to meet, and swipe right to like them. If you and the other person both like each other, you can then message one another and see where things go from there. Who views your Tinder profile is anonymous, so you never know who views your picture and profile. Other popular dating apps include:

- Hinge (www.hinge.co)
- Coffee Meets Bagel (coffeemeetsbagel.com)

A common feature in dating apps is that they'll connect to another account, such as Facebook, as a form of verification. Of course, you could easily create a fake account. Some will also do this to gather additional information from your Facebook profile to provide additional details about your interests, people you both know, things you have in common, and so on. There are also apps that are put out by dating sites, extending the services to mobile devices.

MEETING PEOPLE IN PERSON

It can be exciting to take that first step of meeting someone in person, whom you've only known as an online entity before now. Making physical contact with a stranger, regardless of how long you've communicated online, is a major step that can have major consequences. When meeting someone in person, remember that your physical safety is your primary goal:

- There's safety in numbers. Meet in a public place, where there are lots of people around.
- Don't meet anyone in secret. Let your friends and family know who you're meeting, where, and when you'll be home. You should make arrangements to contact a friend or family member, so they'll know you're okay and got home safe.
- Don't rely on the person you're meeting. Use your own transportation to meet them, or have a friend drop you off and pick you up at a specific time.
- Bring your mobile phone, so you have a way to contact a friend or 911 if a problem arises.

While it may seem like a good idea to meet for drinks, alcohol can impair your judgment. Also, if the person has brought you an open drink, there's the possibility he or she may have slipped a drug in it. There are a number of drugs that can be used to inebriate or knock out a person, including those that are odorless and tasteless. You want to walk away from an enjoyable date, and not be the victim of a date rape.

PROTECTING YOURSELF

There are a number of steps you can take to protect yourself when using sites where you'll interact with new people. Some of these include:

- Limiting information. As we've said before, be careful about what you add to your profile and reveal in conversation with others. As we saw in Chapter 5,

Cybercrime, the details about yourself can slowly come over time, eventually revealing more than you meant to say. You should try and be aware of what you're saying, and think before you type.

- Keep your contact details private. Don't reveal your phone number, address, where you work, or other information that would enable a person to find you in person.
- Remember that some apps will connect with other accounts, such as Facebook, revealing people you're friends with, interests, and other details. Consider creating a separate account for dating and chat.
- Be careful of opening any attachments in messages, as they could be malware.
- Don't access your accounts from public computers, or with public Wi-Fi hotspots. It's possible that someone could acquire your username and password. Public computers and Wi-Fi could also be used to see what sites you're visiting and what you're doing, as you'd reveal your activity to anyone who might be monitoring the network or has a clear view of the computer screen.

CHECKING WHETHER A PERSON IS WHO THEY SAY THEY ARE

Just because a site doesn't do a background check on its users doesn't mean you can't. If you're interacting with someone on a regular basis, through a dating site, or considering meeting the person, you should research them as much as possible. This not only includes any profile on the site you're using, but other sources of information that may be related to the person. You can find a considerable amount of information on a person's social media accounts, search engine results, and other resources.

There are also online offender registries, such as those that allow you to look up registered sex offenders in a particular area. These can be useful in determining the threat level of a person, and cost nothing but your time. If you're meeting a person, you might also consider doing a criminal background check. While this may seem extreme, remember that dating services, apps, and sites don't do these. Depending on what you find about a person's background, you could be incredibly thankful that you took the time to check the person out.

Reviewing profiles

While we discussed creeping earlier, doing a little cyber-snooping can be useful in vetting a person. As you chat with a person online, you may find that they say things that are contradictory to what's on the site's profile, or other sites where they have an account. Someone may say they're single on a chat site, but their Facebook profile may indicate otherwise. Similarly, they may say things to impress you or falsely create an emotional connection, but checking what they've said on other sites may indicate their lying or grooming you for something inappropriate or illegal.

Image search

A useful way of determining the validity of a person is doing an image search. If someone has sent you a photo of themselves, you can upload it into a search engine, where it's compared to other photos found online. In using it, you may find the photo is a stock photo of some model, or on sites that are totally unrelated to who the person says they are. To do an image search on Google, do the following:

1. In your browser, to go https://images.google.com, and click the camera icon beside the search box.
2. If the photo you're checking is online, paste the URL into the box in the **Paste image URL** tab, and click **Search by image**. If you have a copy of the photo, click on the **Upload an image** tab, and then click **Browse**. Navigate to the photo, select it, and then click **Open**.
3. Review the pages that have matching images.

SUMMARY

In this chapter we've discussed some of the common practices and etiquette of interacting with people electronically, and the potential problems of communicating with others online. While most people you meet online will be genuinely nice people, there are those who can make things difficult and even dangerous. Now that we've looked at dealing with others, let's move on to Chapter 10, Protecting your kids, to find how you can protect your kids and other family members.

REFERENCES

Buckels, E., Trapnell, P., Paulhus, D., 2014. *Trolls just want to have fun.* Retrieved November 7, 2015, from Academia: https://www.academia.edu/6016545/Trolls_just_want_to_have_fun.

Daneback, K., Cooper, A., Mansson, S.-A., June 2005. An internet study of cybersex participants. Archives of Sexual Behavior 34, 321–328.

Duggan, M., 2014, October 22. *Online harassment.* Retrieved November 6, 2015, from Pew Research Center: http://www.pewinternet.org/files/2014/10/PI_Online Harassment_72815.pdf.

Internet Crime Complaint Center, 2014. *2014 Internet crime report.* Retrieved October 31, 2015, from Federal Bureau of Investigations: https://www.fbi.gov/news/news_blog/2014-ic3-annual-report.

Lukacs, V.A., 2012, August. *It's complicated: romantic breakups and their aftermath on Facebook.* Retrieved November 7, 2015, from University of Western Ontario: http://ir.lib.uwo.ca/cgi/viewcontent.cgi?article=1938&context=etd.

Protecting your kids

10

INFORMATION IN THIS CHAPTER

The latest generations are raised online, with children introduced to technology at an early age and growing up with it in hand. A child may begin using computers or other devices as young as preschool age, interacting with what's on a screen in schools, libraries, or at home. As they progress in age, they may be expected to do research online, and experience the peer pressure of having their own tablets or smartphones. It doesn't take long before they know their way around the Internet, and begin downloading apps or other files, playing online games, or interacting with others. Because of the prevalence of technology in their lives, it's important to establish restrictions, set expectations, and help them stay safe online.

PROTECTING YOUR KIDS

Even if your child knows how to use the technology, it doesn't mean they have the experience and maturity to deal with situations and people they meet online. Regardless of their age, what and who they encounter can be overwhelming. The use of smartphones, tablets, and other mobile devices also means that you may not be around when your child encounters problems. While technology has added a new

The Basics of Cyber Safety. DOI: http://dx.doi.org/10.1016/B978-0-12-416650-9.00010-3
© 2017 Elsevier Inc. All rights reserved.

layer of complexity to effective parenting, it doesn't make things hopeless. There are ways to monitor and maintain your child's activity, even when you're physically not there to help them.

Keeping kids safe online isn't a single-step process. As with anything in parenting, the restrictions you place on your kid's Internet usage when they're younger will change over time. As you work to raise responsible, selfregulating individuals, what you teach and supervise will change as they grow closer to adulthood, and you gradually shift control of their Internet usage to them. When it comes to Internet safety, you need to revisit things you've taught and change limitations on a periodic basis, keeping in mind the rules you set should be a combination of:

- Supervision—where you oversee, regulate and help direct their online activity.
- Education—where you teach them the dos and don'ts of online behavior, as well as the prevention and solutions to various risks so they know how to avoid and deal with potential problems.
- Tools—which consist of software, hardware, and settings that help you and your child limit risks and assist in monitoring online activity.

The Internet may expose your kids to an array of problems, and it can be difficult realizing that many of them are variations of what parents have contended with for generations. Your mother may have worried about an objectionable magazine under the mattress, rumors of a weird stranger hanging around the school, or being told about the school bully. The core problems and concerns of protecting your child are essentially the same in the real and virtual world. You need to teach children to be cautious and respectful of others, treat others as they want to be treated, abide by your family's values, and avoid potentially harmful material and situations. To keep them safe, you need to do everything you can.

A difference between your generation and today's is that kids have increased availability and access to material and interactions that may be unsafe and disturbing. They now have access to a greater scope of people and content. While it may have been unlikely that you had to deal with a school bully at home, view child pornography, or come in contact with identity thieves and sexual predators, these and other threats are a legitimate risk to a growing child with Internet access. This doesn't mean that the Internet should be avoided, just that you need to minimize the risks. Doing nothing only increases the likelihood of a problem.

PASSWORDS FOR KIDS

Basic security is the first step to protecting a child. As we saw in Chapter 2, Before connecting to the Internet, strong passwords are important to prevent unauthorized access to online accounts, software, and devices. Unfortunately, although children are taught how to use computers in the early grades of school, any passwords they're given are often generic, easily guessed, and often identical to other students. This means it's usually up to parents to teach children that they need to use passwords that are:

- At least 8 characters long
- A mix of uppercase letters (A, B, C,...), lowercase letters (a, b, c,...), numbers (0, 1, 2,...), and special characters (` ~ ! @ # $ % ^ & * ( )_ - + = { } [ ] \ | : ; " ' < > , . ? /)
- Don't contain words found in the dictionary

Coming up with secure and memorable passwords can be seen as a game for younger children, but if they have problems coming up with their own passwords, there are a number of kid-friendly password generators that can help:

- DinoPass (www.dinopass.com)
- Password Bird (www.passwordbird.com)

Children also need to be aware that passwords should never be shared. They may feel that a friend can be trusted with it, or be fooled or pressured into revealing it. They should know that under no circumstances should they ever share this information (except with you), or change the password afterwards without your knowledge.

If they're limited to only using a family computer, there are other options for security. As we discussed in Chapter 1, What is cyber safety?, fingerprint readers and facial recognition features (such as *Windows Hello* in Windows 10) can make it easy to login to a machine. Rather than needing to remember a password, you simply need to place your finger on a scanner, or let the camera on your computer recognize the characteristics of your face or eyes.

SEARCH ENGINES

Popular search engines commonly have settings that allow you to set your preferences when searching for content. By checking the options available, you'll often find settings that will filter your results, so there is less chance of violent, pornographic, or other adult content appearing in the results. While some adult text, images, or video results may still make it into the results, you'll usually find that they are drastically fewer than what you see when their SafeSearch settings are off. On Bing, you would turn on SafeSearch by doing the following:

1. Visit www.bing.com/account/general.
2. In the *SafeSearch* section, select the **Strict** option to filter all adult content from results, **Moderate** to filter adult images and video but not text, or **Off** to not have results filtered.
3. Click **Save** to save your settings.

On Google, you would turn on the SafeSearch settings by doing the following:

1. After logging onto Google, visit the settings page at www.google.com/preferences.
2. In the *SafeSearch filters* section, click on the **Turn on SafeSearch** checkbox so it appears checked.

3. Click **Lock SafeSearch** link next to this, and login if prompted. Confirm that you want to lock the SafeSearch settings by clicking **Lock SafeSearch**.

4. Scroll to the bottom of the page, and click **Save**.

KID-ORIENTATED SEARCH ENGINES

There are also search engines for younger children, in which filtering is on and can't be disabled, so that adult content isn't mixed in with the safe results you and your child are looking for. Some of the ones available for kids include:

- KidRex (www.kidrex.org)
- KidzSearch (www.kidzsearch.com)

PARENTAL CONTROLS

Parental controls are features or software that allow you to monitor and restrict what a person does online. There are a wide variety of programs that do such things as block and filter websites and content, record their activities, limit their time online, and view their browsing history and communications. While the features in parental control software vary, some will log keystrokes, take screenshots of what they're doing, log chats on various sites or apps, and record where they are by providing reports on the location of a laptop, tablet, phone, or other device. Some of the popular parental control software available include:

- Net Nanny (www.netnanny.com)
- Safe Eyes (www.internetsafety.com/safe-eyes-parental-control-software.php)
- CYBERsitter (www.cybersitter.com)
- WebWatcher (www.webwatcher.com)
- MMGuardian (www.mmguardian.com)

As we'll see in this chapter, parental control software is generally user friendly and fairly straightforward to use. Some, such as Microsoft's Family Safety, are free while others require purchase or a subscription to use all or any of the features. Some parental control software are designed for certain devices or platforms, so you may need to use different products if you're planning to install it on various phones, tablets, laptops, and PCs. For example, while Microsoft Family Safety is available for Windows Vista and higher, you'd need to install something else on your child's iPhone. Also, some products may have some features that work on a phone, but aren't available on tablets. Before deciding on a parental control product, ensure that the features available suit your needs.

The level of control you'll place on them will depend on their age, maturity, and any situations and issues your child's dealing with. If you think using such tools are a little extreme, and that you're one of the few thinking of using them, consider that in a survey of parents of teens aged 13–17 (Anderson, 2016):

- 39% of parents have used parental controls to manage their child's online activities.

- 16% have used them to restrict cellphone usage.
- 16% have tracked their child's location through monitoring tools.
- 61% have checked which sites their teen visited.
- 60% checked their teen's social media profile.
- 48% reviewed their teen's phone calls and/or messages.

While it is important to respect privacy, it shouldn't be at the cost of your child's safety. Let them know that in allowing them to have their own email account, phone, or other device, you're reserving the right to check how it's being used. It doesn't necessarily mean that you don't trust them, but you want to ensure they're safe, and there are strange and creepy people out there who could cause them harm. In doing so, parental control software can be useful in keeping an eye on your child when you're not physically able to supervise what they're doing online and who they're doing it with.

UNDERSTANDING WHAT THEY'RE USING

To keep track of what a child is doing, you need an understanding of what they're using. Once you know the apps they have installed, browsers being used, and devices they have access to, you'll have a greater understanding of how they're using the Internet, be better able to identify potential problems, and know what needs monitoring. A common feature of parental control software is the ability to control what apps are allowed on the PC, phone, or tablet, and may be used to see what's been installed.

As seen in Fig. 10.1, after installing Net Nanny on a tablet or phone, you can logon to their site to see what apps are on the device, and click on them to allow or block their use. By blocking an app, they're prevented from using it, until you change the restriction. You can also click on the **Click to Change** link in the upper right-hand corner of the screen to specify whether new applications are allowed to be installed, or if the child needs to contact you for permission to install something new.

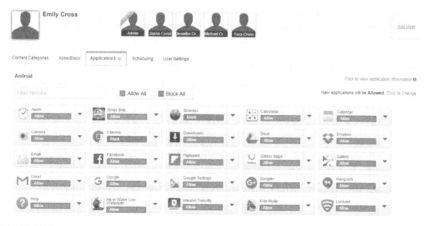

FIGURE 10.1

Net Nanny applications control.

In looking at the listing, you'll be able to see if they're using certain apps for popular sites or services. This may indicate a need to view their account and identify any issues that require a discussion or the need to block the app. Because sites aren't always accessed through an app, and most are commonly through a browser, you should also try and keep abreast of what's popular. For example, a study by Pew Research Center (Lenhart et al., 2015) shows the social media platforms most often used by teens are:

- Facebook (41%)
- Instagram (20%)
- Snapchat (11%)
- Twitter (6%)
- Google+ (5%)
- Vine (1%)

PARENTAL CONTROLS IN WINDOWS

While there are numerous products available that can be installed on phones and tablets, Microsoft does provide a free program and site that can be installed on Windows Vista and higher, and is included in Windows 8.1 and up. You would setup the Family Safety controls in Windows by first logging on with an Administrator account. As we saw in Chapter 1, What is cyber safety?, each member of your family should have their own account for Windows. Children can initially be setup with a child account or you can switch an existing account to a child's account. In Windows 8.1 you would switch the user account for your child to a child account by doing the following:

1. From the search screen, type PC Settings. When *PC Settings* appears, click **Accounts** in the left pane.
2. Click **Other Accounts**. When the list of current accounts appears, click on the account you wish to change, and then click **Edit**.
3. On the *Account Type* dropdown lists, select **Child** and then click **OK**.

Once a user is set as having a child's account, you can then set restrictions. As seen in Fig. 10.2, you can configure the account so your child has time limits, constraints on the websites they can visit, restrictions on apps they can use, and your ability to monitor them. The settings are adjustable to what you're comfortable with and feel is suitable.

To configure these settings for your child you would follow these steps:

1. Right-click on the Start menu, click **Control Panel**, and then click **User Accounts and Family Safety**.
2. Click **Set up Family Safety for any user**, and when the list of accounts appears, click on the account you wish to change.
3. At the top of the screen that appears, ensure that **Family Safety** is turned **On**.

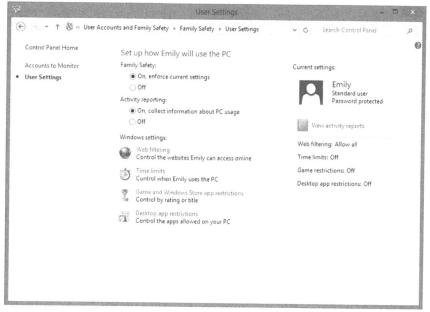

FIGURE 10.2

Windows family safety.

4. If you want to monitor what your child does on the computer, ensure that **Activity Monitoring** is turned **On**. Once on, you could click **View Activity Reports** to see when they've used the computer, the most popular sites they visit, their most used apps and programs, and a list of pages that have recently been blocked so they can't see them.

Filtering and blocking

In Family Safety, once you turn on restrictions, Windows will automatically turn on SafeSearch settings on the most popular search engines, including Google, Bing, Yahoo!, and others. As we discussed, this will prevent adult images from appearing in Web search results and image searches. You can also setup filtering and blocking to prevent access to sites with certain content. To do this, you would go to the Family Safety screen in Control Panel that we showed you earlier, click on the account you wish to change, and do the following:

1. Click **Web Filtering**. You'll now see options to either allow the user to use all websites, or so that the user can only use the websites you allow. Click the second option to filter what sites they can use.

2. Click **Set web filtering level**, and a page similar to Fig. 10.3 will appear.

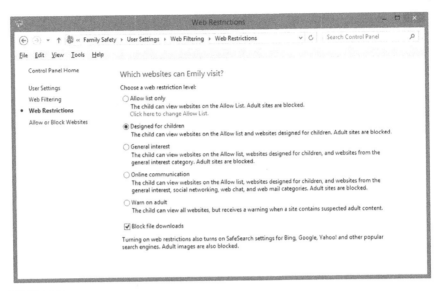

FIGURE 10.3

Web restrictions in family safety.

3. Click on a restriction level for your child. Each option gets progressively more permissive, so select the one that best suits the age and maturity of your child. Options include:

   a. **Allow list only**, which let's your child view sites that have been added to the Allow List. These are sites you've specified through the screen to allow or block websites. Adult sites are also blocked.

   b. **Designed for children**, which allows everything from the previous setting, blocks adult sites, and allows sites that have been designed for children.

   c. **General interest**, which allows everything from the previous settings, blocks adult sites, and allows sites categorized as general interest.

   d. **Online communication**, which allows everything from the previous settings, blocks adult sites, and allows social networking, Web mail, and chat.

   e. **Warn on adult**, which allows the user to view any site they try and visit, but will warn them if there may be adult content.

4. Click on the **Block file downloads** checkbox, so it appears checked. This will prevent the child from downloading files, which could contain viruses or other malware.

5. On the left pane of the screen, click **Allow or block specific websites**.

6. In the *Enter a website to allow or block* box, enter the URL of a website you want to allow or block. If you want to allow the child to access the site, click the **Allow** button. If you don't want the child to visit a site, click the **Block** button.

Depending on the button you clicked, the site will now appear below in either the list of *Allowed websites* or *Blocked websites*. If you made a mistake in adding a site, simply click on the site in the list and then click the **Remove** button.

LIMITING TIME AND THE TIMES THEY'RE ALLOWED ONLINE

Children spend a considerable amount of time on the Internet. One study of children aged 9–16 in 25 countries found that 93% of children go online at least once a week, with 60% of them going online daily or almost every day (Livingstone et al., 2011). A more recent study found that 24% of teens aged 13–17 were online "almost constantly," 56% were online several times a day, 12% went on once each day, 6% went on weekly, and just 2% went online less often (Lenhart et al., 2015). The lack of exercise, eyestrain, stress, and lack of meaningful contact with others, possibly resulting in antisocial behavior, can be a legitimate concern, and are only some of the reasons why you should limit their time on devices.

Many parents limit their kids' time online, and use such restrictions as a form of discipline. A Pew Research Center survey of parents of teens aged 13–17 found that 55% limited the amount of time or times their child could go online each day, and 65% have taken away their child's phone or Internet privileges as punishment (Anderson, 2016). Some of the ways you can set limitations is by explaining the risks associated with spending too much time online, finding activities that take them away from the Internet (such as sports, reading, hobbies, or family events), inviting their real-life friends over, and so on.

If you have a very young child, you can control access by keeping your tablet and phone out of reach, and by setting up passwords/PINs on the device to prevent access. As they get older, parental controls can be useful in limiting how long and what times your kids are allowed to go online and/or use the device. In doing so, you could allow them to use the computer or device during certain times and a limited number of hours on school days, and more time on weekends.

To setup time limits in Microsoft Family Safety, you would do the following after going to the Family Safety screen we discussed earlier:

1. Click on the name of the account you want to change, and then click **Time Limits**.
2. To set the number of hours the child can use the computer, click **Set time allowance**.
3. To set the hours, select the option to use the PC for an amount of time. In the **Weekdays** and **Weekends** dropdown lists, set the number of hours and minutes they can use the computer during the week and on weekends, respectively.
4. Click the back button to return to the previous screen, and click **Set curfew** to set when the child can go on the computer.
5. Click on the option to set the time ranges they're allowed on. When the grid appears, click and drag your mouse across the day and time periods. Areas that are marked will dictate when they're permitted on the computer.

DECIDING ON AGE APPROPRIATE LIMITATIONS

The ages and settings you configure are up to you, and you can set it to be as restrictive or permissive as you see fit. Parental controls commonly provide suggested settings based on age ranges, but you may decide to adjust them since you're the one who knows your child best. You may feel that time settings aren't necessary, certain apps are inappropriate, and certain types of filtered content should be allowed. These should be reviewed occasionally to fit your child best as they get older.

In deciding on what's age appropriate, you shouldn't let your child pressure you. You might hear the argument that everyone in their class has a tablet or phone and is allowed to use them how and when they want, or that they're the only ones who aren't allowed to play a certain game. Maybe it's true, but it isn't a compelling reason for them to have a device or access certain content. Just because other parents allow a young child to play Mature-rated games, watch Restricted or 17+ movies, or allow them to have their own Facebook and YouTube accounts (who have an age limit of 13 or older) it doesn't mean you should allow it. Even if it's true that other kids have or are allowed to do something, trust in your opinion of whether your child is old enough or has the maturity to handle it.

LOCATION OF COMPUTER

The location of where a child is able to use a computer, laptop, tablet, or other device can have an impact on their safety. If a computer, laptop, or gaming system has been setup in or near a common area of the house, such as a living room, your child will be less likely to encounter problems. You'll be nearby if they have questions, need help, or supervision, and your presence can be a deterrent to doing something that they know they shouldn't. The same also holds true for younger children being limited to using a tablet or other device at home.

LOCATION

As a child gets older and more mobile with devices, you may want to keep track of where they are, making sure they're really at school, a friend's house, or other places they're supposed to be. According to a survey released on 2016, 16% of parents have used monitoring tools on their teen's phone to track their child's location (Anderson, 2016). This may be done through features in parental control software, locator apps, GPS trackers, or antitheft software. Such measures not only help to ensure a child's safety, but are useful to anyone who's worried about losing or having their phone, laptop, or other devices stolen.

LOST OR STOLEN

When a computer or mobile device is lost or stolen, you can always go out and purchase a new one, but the information you've lost can be devastating. There may be photos that aren't stored elsewhere, music and books you've paid for, as well as other data that may be difficult or impossible to replace. Even worse, you could have credit card numbers or other financial data that could be used to make purchases and ruin your credit.

Protecting yourself involves taking steps before your computer or mobile device is gone. As we've discussed in previous chapters, physical security is important to make sure no one can easily walk off with a device and it's vital to use the security settings available on the devices, apps, and accounts to prevent unauthorized access. In addition, you should document the make and model of the device, as well as any serial numbers that can be used to identify it if it's later recovered.

ANTITHEFT

As we saw in Chapter 1, What is cyber safety?, phones and tablets have settings that control whether its location can be tracked, enabling apps and websites to show where the device is at a given moment. If turned on, the device may use a combination of data from your cellular network, Wi-Fi, Bluetooth, and GPS to determine where it is. In the case of a computer or laptop, connections to the Internet (such as Wi-Fi) may be used in making a rough estimate of its location. This data may then be used by apps that are installed, and sent to websites to provide location-specific services, such as finding your device when it's lost or stolen.

Many phones and tablets come with antitheft features that can be activated, allowing you to manage the device remotely and determine its approximate location. These features may include:

- Viewing the location, where it displays where the device is on a map.
- Playing a sound, which will ring or play a loud sound, helping you find it even if the sound is turned off.
- Locking the device, where you can lock the screen and optionally set a new password, preventing others from using it.
- Displaying a message, which allows you to show a custom message on the home screen, even if the device is locked, which can be used to provide contact information for returning the phone.
- Wiping the device, which deletes all data and settings from the device.
- Flagging the device as stolen, which deletes all data and settings from the device, and registers it as stolen.

While the features offered on your phone or tablet may vary, the native antitheft software on a device is usually free and may require activation. In addition to turning on the Location Settings on the device itself, this is done by going to the device manufacturer's or operating system's site to turn on and use the features. For example:

- If you have an Apple device, you can log onto iCloud.com with your Apple ID or use the Find My iPhone app. Once *Lost Mode* is turned on, any attempts to use Apple Pay on the device is also suspended.
- If you have a Windows Phone, you can log onto account.microsoft.com/devices and click Find My Phone.

- If you have an Android device, you can use Android Device Manager (www.android.com/devicemanager).
- If you have a Samsung device, you can use Samsung's Find My Mobile (https://findmymobile.samsung.com).
- If you have a Blackberry, you can use Blackberry Protect (http://ca.blackberry.com/devices/features/security/protect.html).

In addition to the native software on a phone or tablet, there are also software products that can be installed on computers, laptops, and other mobile devices. Using antitheft software, locator apps, or certain parental control products, you can view where it's located on a map and remotely lock it. Some products also provide features to log keystrokes, take screen captures, and perform other actions that may help identify who's using it and where it is. Antitheft software may also provide the ability to remotely wipe the laptop, phone, or other mobile device, so that they won't have access to its data. Some of the popular antitheft products available include:

- Lojack for Laptops (http://lojack.absolute.com)
- Lock It Tight (www.lockittight.com)
- Prey Anti-Theft (www.preyproject.com)
- Hidden (www.hiddenapp.com)
- Lookout (www.lookout.com)

Many antitheft products also include a spy cam feature, which will take photos of anyone in front of the device and save it to their website. This can be useful in showing who's taken a device and where it's located. You may find that someone you know has the device, such as a friend, family member, coworker, or fellow student, allowing you to recognize who has it. If you don't know the person, it can be used as evidence, and may help police discover who took the device.

Other apps and sites

Even if you don't have antitheft protection setup on your laptop or device, you may still be able to determine its location. Apps and accounts installed on the device that are allowed to access location information may send it via the Internet to their related sites. For example, if your phone has a Google app installed and an account setup, it can be used to send your location information to Google. Such data can be used to determine commute predictions, provide location specific advertising, and where the device has been or is currently located.

After logging onto your Google account, you can visit https://maps.google.com/locationhistory/, and (once turned on) see a map detailing all the locations you've been with your device. In the lower left-hand corner, you'll see an area informing you whether or not Location History is turned on or off. If you want to turn it on, click **Enable Location History**, and when prompted, click **Turn On**. To prevent Google from tracking you, you would turn off the feature by clicking **Pause Location History**, and then clicking **Turn Off** when prompted.

FINDING A DEVICE FINDS A PERSON

One of the easiest ways to find a device is to use a feature that shows the approximate location of the device on a map. As seen in Fig. 10.4, in viewing the location, a picture of where it is, the time it was located, and the accuracy of its location within a certain distance is displayed. By zooming in and out of the map, you can identify where it is, making it relatively easy to retrieve.

While such apps and sites can be helpful in finding lost or stolen devices, it's also important that they can be used to track you. Anyone with access to the site or software that shows a device's location could use it to see where you are, and possibly discern what you're doing. This can be useful if you're trying to see where your children are, or disconcerting and dangerous if a suspicious or abusive partner is monitoring your whereabouts. To avoid others from seeing you or your child's location, make sure that you've used a strong password that's changed regularly to prevent someone from logging in and seeing where you are at any given time.

An app's ability to determine your location is in your control. To see what apps are using location services, you should review the privacy settings on your phone. As we showed in Chapter 1, What is cyber safety?, if you don't want your location being available to any app, you can turn location services off. When installing an app, you may also be able to disable its ability to track you by not granting it permission to see your location. If you don't want your child adjusting these settings, parental control software often has a feature that prevents or limits access.

FIGURE 10.4

View location on BlackBerry protect.

Finding it safely

While antitheft software and location features can help identify where a device is, it's also important to remember that it shows the whereabouts of anyone who has it. A thief may be unwilling to part with his or her new acquisition, and could become violent. One of a numerous examples occurred in February 2016, when a 23-year-old man used an app to track his stolen phone to a church parking lot. Upon arriving, he used the app to make his phone ring, heard it inside a vehicle, and was shot and killed when he went to retrieve it (Beasley, 2016). If your phone is stolen, and you use such a feature to track it, always notify the police so they can recover it. Nothing is worth your safety, so let law enforcement take care of it.

REPORT IT STOLEN

Once you realize a computer, laptop, or other device is stolen, report it. Once reported, it may be returned to you if it's later found, and police will provide an incident or report number that you can give your insurance company. Beyond the police, there may be others who need to know it's missing. If it's a device that was issued to you by your employer, they'll need to know if there was corporate data on it, and the Information Technology department may be able to wipe it so any sensitive settings or data is erased. If it was taken at school, you'll want to report the theft to campus police or the school's office.

In reporting it lost or stolen, don't presume detectives are diligently working around the clock to reunite you with your property. An extreme example of how the theft of such devices are considered a low priority was when Joshua Kaufman had his MacBook stolen in 2011. Using antitheft software, Kaufman did his own investigation, found the person with his laptop, and still had difficulty getting the culprit arrested. The software took photos of 27-year-old Muthanna Aldebashi using the computer, logging onto his Google account, and showed email with the name of a cab company he worked for. After submitting the evidence to police, Kaufman found they were unwilling to help and ignored his follow-up emails. Writing about it and posting the pictures on http://thisguyhasmymacbook.tumblr. com and Twitter, his story went viral, and after Good Morning America contacted the Oakland Police Department, an arrest was finally made and Kaufman got his laptop back (Thanawala, 2011).

Even though your expectations may be low in reporting a stolen phone or computer, you can increase your chances of recovering it by working with the police. By using the antitheft software, you can lock the device so it can't be accessed by the thief, and tell the officer where it's currently located. Remember that police can't access this data without your help, so having it ready when an officer shows up to take your report allows for a quicker recovery.

Unfortunately, such tools only work if the phone, tablet, laptop, computer, or other devices can connect to the Internet. If the thief doesn't connect the computer to the Net and simply removes and wipes the hard disks, or removes the SIM card and prevents Wi-Fi access to a phone or tablet, the antitheft software will never receive any messages to lock, wipe, or reveal its location. In such cases, your only choice is to replace it or hope it's recovered.

You may also be able to increase your chances of recovering a device by registering them on sites that may be used by pawn shops, second-hand buyers, or police to identify lost or stolen items. When recovered, checking the database will identify you as owner, making it easier to return what's been stolen. Some of the sites available include:

- Immobilize (www.immobilize.net)
- CheckMEND (www.checkmend.com)
- Trace (www.tracechecker.com)
- Stolen Register (www.stolenregister.com)
- Stolen 911 (www.stolen911.com)

Also, don't forget that you haven't just lost the phone, but all the data on it. When someone has access to your accounts and sensitive information, you should take steps to change your passwords, contact banks, issuers of credit cards, and other organizations related to any data that may have been compromised.

Blacklists

If your mobile device is stolen or lost and irrecoverable, you should contact your carrier and report it stolen. In doing so, they can add the device's International Mobile Equipment Identity (IMEI) number to a national blacklist. The IMEI is a 15-digit number that uniquely identifies the device, and any IMEI that appears on a blacklist can't get service from carriers, and is blocked by wireless service providers. Essentially, the device is unusable because it can't be used to make calls or connect to the Internet.

If you're buying a used phone, it's important to check whether the IMEI has been added to a blacklist. To do this, you first need the device's IMEI number. On most mobile devices, you can dial *#06# to see a message that displays the number. You can also find a device's IMEI and serial number on the device by doing the following:

- On an iPhone, iPad, or iPod Touch, tap **Settings**, tap **General**, and then tap **About**.
- On an Android device, tap **Settings**, tap **About phone/About** table, and then tap **Status**.
- On a BlackBerry, tap **Settings**, tap **About**, tap the **Category** dropdown, and select **General** to view the serial number or **Hardware** to view the IMEI.

Once you have the number, you can then use various sites on the Internet to determine whether it's being sold legally. If you're purchasing a used iPhone, iPad, iPod Touch, or Apple Watch, you can visit iCloud's Find My iPhone (www.icloud.com/activationlock/), enter either the device's IMEI or serial number, and see if the activation lock has been disabled. If it was stolen, and someone used Find My iPhone to lock the device, it's unusable until the correct Apple ID and password have been entered. Many carriers and resale sites like Swappa (www.swappa.com/esn) also provide the ability to check the IMEI or serial number. Telecommunications sites in some countries may also provide the ability to check if a device is blocked by that nation's service providers, as in the case of:

- Canadian Wireless Telecommunications Association (www.protectyourdata.ca/)
- Australian Mobile Telecommunications Association (www.lost.amta.org.au/IMEI)

Remote wiping

When you're sure that the device is stolen or can't be recovered, there comes a time when you should consider wiping it. When you remotely wipe a device, it deletes any data and settings on the device and does a factory reset. This means that any apps or accounts that may be used in locking or locating it are erased on the device, and can't be used to identify where it is or protect it, so you should be careful when you choose to take this step.

As we've mentioned, antitheft features may need to be activated on a phone prior to using the features, so you will need to setup your mobile device first. For example, before you can remotely wipe an android device, you need to set it up to be locked and erased. To do this, go to the Android Device Manager site (www.google.com/android/devicemanager), and log in with the Google account associated with your device. Once you've selected the device you want to configure:

1. Click on Set up Lock & Erase
2. Click Send
3. Drag down the notification bar, and tap Android Device Manager
4. Tap Activate
5. Switch Remote Locate and/or Remote Lock and Factory Reset so they're enabled.

Once the Android device is setup to be remotely wiped, you can then erase it by going to the Android Device Manager site, clicking on the **Erase** button, and then confirming it when prompted.

It's important that you back up your computer and any mobile devices on a regular basis, and keep a list of accounts and passwords you use up-to-date. If you lose the device and need to wipe it, your files, apps, accounts, and other data will be erased. Even if it's later returned to you, anything on it will be gone. You'll want to have a recent backup and list of accounts and passwords stored in a safe location so you can use them to restore the data and regain access to any sites and systems you use.

Once you've wiped a device that's no longer being used or available to you, you should revoke its access from any online sites and services that use it. For example, you may have setup the phone or tablet to access social media sites through various apps, or work with particular accounts.

RESALE

A device being stolen isn't the only time you'll want to wipe a device. Prior to selling an old computer, laptop, phone, tablet, or other mobile device, you should remove any personal data that the new owner could use to access you or your child's online accounts or see sensitive information. For phones and tablets, you should backup your data (including any contacts), log out of any services like email or social media accounts, and remove the SIM card and any SD cards used for additional storage. Even though you're selling the device, you may be able to use the SIM and SD card on your new phone or tablet. Once done, you can wipe the data and do a factory reset, which essentially reverts the device to the state when you originally bought it.

Once you've wiped a device that you'll no longer be using, you should also revoke its access to any online accounts it may have been setup to use. For example, if you have a Google account, you would go to http://myaccount.google.com, and then:

1. Click **Sign-in & Security**
2. In the left pane, click **Device activity & notifications**
3. Under *Recently used devices*, click on **Review Devices**
4. Click on the device you want to remove, and then click the **Remove** button to revoke that device's access to your account.

You should also take steps to remove any data from laptops, computers, or storage devices (such as an external hard disk) before its resale or disposal. Taking the extra step of formatting the hard disk(s) will make sure any files or sensitive data stored on it are erased. Wiping the data correctly is important. Depending on how you format the drive, data may be left behind.

In Windows Explorer (or File Explorer), you can format a drive by right-clicking on a drive letter, and then clicking **Format** on the context menu that appears. Once done, a dialog box similar to what's shown in Fig. 10.5 should appear. In looking at

FIGURE 10.5

Windows format.

it, you'll notice that *Quick Format* is the default option. It's quick because it wipes the file table, but doesn't actually wipe the drive. If you uncheck the *Quick Format* option on Windows Vista and up, the disk will be formatted and overwrite all of the existing content with zeros.

Until data is overwritten it can still be recovered. Even if the drive is quick formatted, so long as the disk isn't used and data isn't written to it, you can still use recovery tools to unformat the drive and restore the data. For an additional measure of safety, you should use a tool that will overwrite data on the disk multiple times. Tools like CCleaner (www.piriform.com/ccleaner) can be used to securely erase the drive. Other tools like Eraser (http://eraser.heidi.ie) use different methods and patterns to overwrite data multiple times, making it impossible to restore. It also has features that allow you to schedule overwriting free space on your drive, so that any deleted files are securely erased at regular intervals.

TALKING ABOUT WHAT'S INAPPROPRIATE

The Internet is no different from any new environment. When your child was very little, you probably told them look both ways before crossing the street, and explained doing so might prevent them from being hit by a passing car or bike. You also probably explained the etiquette of human interaction by saying *please* and *thank you*, being mindful of others and wary of strangers. In the same way, children need to understand the risks, remedies, and acceptable behavior of being online so they can stay out of trouble.

Because children use computers and the Internet at an early age, it's wise to start training as soon as they begin using technology. If you think your child is too young, consider that a preschooler watching his or her favorite TV show will hear invitations to "visit us online" at a particular URL, or may even use a computer preloaded with children's sites and software at a daycare or library. Even though a child may have restricted exposure, they should understand that there are limits to when and how long they can use a device.

Letting them know what they can use on a computer or other device is also important to learn early. While you'll probably be sitting beside them as they interact with an educational game or site at first, eventually they'll need to know what icons they can click on and sites they can visit. As they get older, they'll realize there are sites and apps for specific age ranges and uses, and not all of them are ones that they're allowed to use. This can be helpful in starting a discussion on what's age appropriate, and talking about age restrictions and ratings on games and apps.

At all times, regardless of your child's age, they should feel comfortable discussing the Internet, problems they encounter, and feel free to ask for help. Staying supportive and positive will help them in keeping the lines of communication open as they get older. You should also realize that any discussions won't be a one-time thing. You'll often need to repeat the information, allowing them to soak it in over time.

Your child isn't the only one you should discuss the rules with. You should let any babysitters, parents of your child's friends, and others who may look after the child know about the limits you've imposed. Doing so will add consistency in what the child is allowed to do, regardless of where he or she is.

SETTING EXPECTATIONS

As your child gets older, they should have a clear understanding of what you expect from them online, your values, and what's considered appropriate. They should also have an understanding of what's age appropriate for them, and what they shouldn't show a younger brother or sister. While they'll come to realize that what's forbidden at one age may be permitted later, they should know that some rules apply to any age and that you follow similar rules. These include:

- Don't reveal passwords, and use secure passwords, as we discussed earlier.
- Never share personal information online. This includes addresses, school names, where they currently are or will be later, phone numbers, birthdates, age, and so on.
- Realize that a person may not be who they claim to be online. Just because they say they're a friend-of-a-friend or someone they know may not be the case.
- Acceptable sites. A younger child should be limited to a list of specific sites, but they should understand that as they get older, certain kinds of sites or content are never allowed.

By setting boundaries before they get their own accounts or devices, you'll be better able to set expectations, modify settings, and install software to monitor and protect them. Once they have their own accounts and devices, you'll find you're in for a more difficult time-changing settings and monitoring the way it's used.

Conduct

As we saw in Chapter 9, Beyond technology—dealing with people, there are expectations on how to act online. Netiquette shows us the accepted behavior in dealing with others, and they should know that there are trolls and other abusive people who may make things difficult for them. They should know what you expect from them, and what they can expect from others.

A person's conduct also relates to how they present themselves online. Impersonating an older person can attract someone who thinks you're of age, inviting discussion that isn't suitable for a child, and possibly accessing content that may be disturbing. One study found that 44% of online teens admitted to lying about their age to access a site or sign up for an online account (Lenhart et al., 2011). It's important they understand that sites put such limitations in place to protect those under a certain age from viewing inappropriate content.

Your child should also know what's appropriate to post and share with others, including anything they write, photos, videos, and other content they create. Once online, it can be difficult to remove and may be available for others to see in years to come. If it violates the policies of the site being used, it could also result in their accounts being disabled or deleted. At all times they should go with the philosophy that if they have to hide what they're doing, they shouldn't be doing it.

Content

While parental controls can block and filter certain content, it doesn't mean your child shouldn't have an understanding of what they are and aren't allowed to view. Explain to your child why the settings are as you've configured, so they know to avoid certain sites and apps that you've deemed inappropriate. After all, just because parental control software prevents them from visiting such sites on your computer, doesn't mean they're blocked on a friend's tablet or a public computer (such as one at school or a library). Explain your concerns with certain content so they know what to avoid.

As we saw in Chapter 5, Cybercrime, a common target of identity theft is children. Let your child know that it's important not to share personal information. They should know that emails, online forms, questions asked when creating an account, and even surveys or questionnaires may be phishing expeditions designed to provide details. To prevent particularly sensitive information like national identification numbers (e.g., Social Security Number) from being shared, keep such documentation out of their reach. If they don't know it, they won't be tempted to share it. (Lenhart et al., 2011).

Teens may also use various tools to send texts with photo or video. For example, Skype (www.skype.com) is popular with Web chatting, while apps like Snapchat (www.snapchat.com) allow you to send an image or video that the recipient can only view for a certain period of time (such as 10 seconds or so) before disappearing. Because people using Snapchat believed the photo was deleted and gone forever, the 2014 hack dubbed the "Snappening" in 2014 was a surprise to many when thousands of images were stolen and leaked on the Internet. Being that a large portion of Snapchat users are underage teenagers, the seminaked or naked photos appearing online were a shock to many. Even if the software streams video or promises to delete or make an image disappear after a set time, the seconds its visible is often long enough to make a screenshot of it.

Your child should also know that just because someone said something, it's not necessarily true. Anyone can create a blog or web page, and appear like they're giving expert advice. If they were looking for information about how to deal with personal problems, how their bodies are changing, relationship advice or other facts of life, they could get skewed facts or inaccurate details. Let them know that you're available as a resource, and they can talk to you or get your opinion on the articles they read.

Contact

Most parents want to know who their child associates with. You might have conditions on meeting their friends before they go out, and meeting the parents before dropping them off at a sleepover. The question is, do you really know who they're associating with online?

Even though many social media sites may have age limitations, many parents allow an underage child to have an account. A child may have their own Facebook account or YouTube channel under a false age, so they can associate with classmates or share homemade videos. If they do, you should have an agreement with them so you can monitor their account, and preview any content they publish. You should also do such things as:

- Make sure they know that just because someone asks to be a "friend," they may not be. Don't blindly accept friend or buddy requests. For younger children, they should ask you first if they can accept.
- A person may pose as someone they aren't online. A person seeming to be a child could actually be an adult with a fake profile.
- Make younger children understand that many people have the same name, so they shouldn't make or accept friend requests without talking to them at school or by calling first.
- Even if it is a friend, someone else could be using their account. Their real friend may have lost a phone or had their account hacked, meaning a stranger is actually texting, or it could be the friend's sibling or someone else posing as them.
- Never agree to meet anyone online, or do anything that makes you feel uncomfortable.
- If it is a friend of your child that you know, and they've made arrangements to meet, always meet at a safe location. Again, it could be someone posing as them.

It's wise to review your child's friend list occasionally to ensure they are people you know. If your child has 300 friends, chances are that they aren't people they know. Going over the list will help you understand who their friends are, where they met, and how long they've known each other. For younger children, you should limit it to trusted relatives and only friends of theirs that you know. Anyone you're unsure of, or who is posting questionable material should be removed.

CYBERBULLYING

A few decades ago, a child might be limited to being bullied on the playground or the walk home from school. Once in their house, they had the comfort of knowing they were safe until the next school day. With the Internet, those days are long past, and a bully can torment your child online, no matter where they are or what time it is.

Cyberbullying is the act of harassing someone online, and may take the form of aggressive comments, offensive names, or embarrassing someone on purpose. While the act of bullying is most associated with children and teens anyone can be the victim of online harassment. If you think that it's a limited problem, consider that even if your child isn't bullied directly, they can still experience the cruelty second hand. In one study (Lenhart et al., 2011) it was found that 88% of teens using social media had seen someone being cruel or mean to another person, with 12% of them saying they witnessed it frequently and 15% saying they were the target.

The effects of bullying can last for years after its ended, and have a negative impact on a child's confidence, self-image, and feelings of self-worth. They can experience anxiety, depression, and other psychological effects, and in the most extreme circumstances even have thoughts of selfharm or even attempt/commit suicide. This isn't intended to frighten you as a parent, but to provide a better understanding of the need to step in and help, so the child isn't left to fight his or her own battles.

If they encounter someone bullying or pressuring them to do things they shouldn't, your child should have a clear understanding that they should immediately come to you. When they do, keep a clear head. If the bully is someone your child knows in real life, you can try and get others involved. Since schools commonly have anti-bullying policies, you should check the website of your child's school district and review the policy. Once you know what they can and should do under their policy, let the school know about the problem. You should also keep a record of any incidents, just in case you need to contact the police. Depending on your child's age, the police could intervene and talk to the bully's parents, or possibly charge the teen bully with harassment, threatening, or assault if that's occurred.

For online bullying, take screenshots of any incidents that show your child is being harassed. These can be used to backup any claims and shown, if necessary, to the school or police. Even if you don't know a bully in real life, you can block the person from contacting you and report them to the site. In doing so, their account may be disabled or deleted. Let your child know that they shouldn't engage the cyberbully online, or react in any way, but should work with you to save the evidence and not to delete it. This may also help the child feel that they're fighting back with you as an ally.

In talking to your child, let them know that bullying of any kind is wrong. While making a cruel comment to a post may seem funny, and joining in the mob mentality may make you feel part of the crowd, it's not acceptable. Even though it's online, it affects someone in real life.

CALLS

Today, a bully can use a variety of tools to harass someone. One study found that after ending a relationship, 22% of teens experienced their ex using the Internet or cellphone to call them names, put them down, or say cruel things about them. Fifteen percent said their former partner used such technologies to spread rumors about them (Lenhart et al., 2015). Bullies may also use various technologies to automate the process of harassing someone.

While you may have made one or two prank calls to someone, there are free and commercial sites that allow you to send a recorded prank call from a phone number that's not your own. Some allow you to enter someone else's number, while others will send it from an anonymous number. Using this, the cyberbully can enter your phone number, click a button, and the service will repeatedly call you over and over again a set number of times.

By using features that may be already included on your phone, or contacting your phone service provider for help, you may be able to use features that will block such calls. There are services that will block a number you specify, or any numbers where the number is unknown, unavailable, or private. They may suggest you dial *60 and set up call screening, which allows you to block numbers from calling you. The phone company may also suggest you trace the call by dialing *57 the next time you receive a prank call, and following the recorded prompts. In doing so, police may be able to use the information to arrest the person harassing you.

The site the bully is using may also have features to add your number to a do-not-call list. By visiting Stop Prank Calls (www.stopprankcalls.com), you'll find a list of links to a page on the most popular prank call sites, where you can enter your number so no more calls are sent from the site. If you know the bully's number, add their number as well. This will prevent them from sending a prank call to their phone, having it forwarded to an IP phone, which then is set up to call you. The bully could have your phone number or theirs removed from the do-not-call list, but most sites will only remove it for a fee. If they try again, it can become a costly endeavor for the person harassing you.

Sites that make such anonymous calls aren't the only issue with unwanted calls from a bully. If the person has setup an IP phone number, you may find it difficult to track where the calls are coming from. Unlike a landline, you can purchase a phone number with an area code corresponding to other locations throughout the world. For example, Skype allows you to purchase a number that allows local calls for area codes in different countries. Similarly, if you have a Gmail (www.gmail.com) account, you can use Google Phone to make calls. If this is the case, and the person is switching between numbers, you may need to attempt blocking several different numbers.

Another option is parental control software or call-blocking apps, which you could use to create a whitelist of people who may call the phone, and/or a blacklist of blocked numbers. If all else fails, you could simply get a new phone number. If you keep the number private, and don't share it with anyone associated with the bully, they'll be unable to call.

ONLINE PREDATORS

An *online predator* is someone who sexually exploits a child over the Internet. The pedophile may lure the child gradually through gifts or affection; coerce them through threats or extortion, or other methods where the predator will attempt to get what they want. This may be an attempt to get the child to pose for suggestive or explicit images, or meet in person so they can be sexually abused.

Because a pedophile targets children, he or she will be aware of the latest fads, music, and interests of an age group they're interested in. They may spend significant time getting to know the child, and because they know what the child likes, can pose as one online. By talking to the child in chats, messages, or comments in posts, he or she will get to know the child, build trust, and lower inhibitions. Because a child may be curious about sex, the predator may share child pornography with them, introducing a sexual aspect to the conversation and/or finding what he or she likes. He or she may then ask your child to take a similar picture of themselves, engage in video chat, or meet secretly in person.

While most pedophiles are adult men, they can also be female. They may be strangers, but may also be someone you know, such as a bodyfriend or relative. The threat of your child being approached sexually online can also occur with someone closer to your child's age. For example, someone in their early twenties may seek out a young teen, or an adolescent may desire a young child. To protect your child, you should be aware of anyone your child is interacting with online, and certain signs that they're at risk, such as:

- The presence of child pornography on the computer. The predator may introduce such imagery to convince them that sex between a child and adult is normal, to engage in a sexual discussion, or get the child to take a nude or seminude picture of themselves.
- The time your child spends online. Because adults generally work during the week, the time spent finding children is often limited to the evening and on weekends. A tendency to go on the Internet after dinner and on weekends may indicate they're spending time with an adult.
- Sudden gifts, packages, or mail from someone you don't know.

Another indication that something's wrong is seen in the calls they receive, and discussions they're having. Phone sex may be a precursor to trying to meet the child for real sex, so review numbers on your child's phone and to your house. Look for sudden phone calls from numbers you don't recognize, long distance numbers, or calls from adults asking to speak with your child. Also, try to listen to how they're responding to audio conversations on game systems where headsets are used to chat, as well as audio or video chat to determine whether they've taken a sexual turn or they're responding to odd questions. If they suddenly turn off the monitor, or take action to prevent you from seeing or hearing what's being said, it can also indicate they're involved in a sexual conversation.

Children targeted by a sexual predator will often become withdrawn from the family, and distance themselves from those they previously trusted. The child may have been told to keep a secret, the predator may be working to cause discord or drive a wedge between the child and family, and/or the child may have already been victimized.

To protect your child from online predators, you can use parental software to monitor their internet activities and check their accounts manually, which allows a greater chance of detecting a problem early. You should also talk to them about any suspicions or concerns you might have. If they know about a potential danger and how online pedophiles work, there's a greater likelihood that they'll be able to recognize the threat before it goes too far. They should know:

- Never give out their phone number, address, or other personal information to anyone online, and never agree to meet anyone they've met online. If they do, a virtual threat may become a real one.
- Never download files or pictures from an unknown source.
- Never reply to messages that are suggestive, indecent, or mean in any way.
- Trust their instincts. If they suspect a problem, are asked to do anything that makes them uncomfortable, or told not to tell or trust their family, they should end any communication and tell their parents, a teacher, or another responsible adult that's around.

If your child is contacted by a sexual predator, you should report it. Contact the police, and report it online. In the United States, you can report it to the National Center for Missing and Exploited Children (www.missingkids.com), while in Canada you can contact the Canadian Centre for Child Protection (www.cybertip.ca). Your child should know that if they were targeted by a sexual predator, it's not their fault and nothing they did was the cause of it.

PRIVACY

Everyone has an expectation of privacy, even children. These expectations grow as we mature, but as we saw in previous chapters, the reality of privacy on the Internet may not match a person's expectations. Regardless of whether you're the parent of a young child or teen, they should understand that what they say and do online may not necessarily be private.

If you're using parental controls or other monitoring software, it's important for your child to know that you have the ability to see and limit what they're doing even if you're not physically there. They should know that you're not necessarily doing this because you don't trust them, but to help them if they encounter any problems. For example, if they were bullied, any logging might help prove there's a problem to police or teachers. Similarly, blocking certain sites will protect them from seeing disturbing content, and lowering the risks of getting malware. They should also know that you're willing to discuss any restrictions, so that you can compromise without jeopardizing their safety and the security of any devices they're using.

Just as you might reserve the right to go into their bedroom, they should understand that any technology and accounts they use will also be open to your review. If you feel they may be at risk, you may feel the need to review their email, contacts, friends on social media, and other aspects of their life online. If you're concerned that doing so is being overprotective, keep in mind that 43% of parents of teens know the password to their kid's email account, and 35% know the password to at least one of their child's social media accounts (Anderson, 2016).

Your child should also understand that you're not the only one who can see what they're doing online, and the lack of anonymity they have. If they're using a computer at someone else's house, there's no way of knowing if there's a keylogger installed, which can capture any passwords or other information entered. Schools and libraries may also monitor what's happening on the computers they use, allowing them to log the sites they visit and other activities. Let them know that you're not the only one who may be watching.

You should configure the privacy settings on any social media or other online accounts your child uses. You should review these settings with them, and understand that these should be changed, and no personal information should be added to profiles. If you don't require them to check with you before creating new accounts, it's especially important they learn how to do it themselves.

SUMMARY

Understand that kids accept technology and have a good understanding of it. In discussing it with them, you may find they even know more than you. Even if they seem to be an expert on how to use it, it doesn't mean that they're able to handle the social interactions and problems they may encounter online.

As we saw in this chapter, there are a number of tools you can use online to protect your child and the devices they use. These include parental controls, antitheft software, and other software that can be installed to provide security. Combined with this is a need to talk to your children, and make them understand the basic steps in keeping themselves safe online, so they know the pitfalls and possible solutions available to them.

REFERENCES

Anderson, M., 2016, January 7. *Parents, teens and digital monitoring*. Retrieved April 1, 2016, from Pew Research Center: http://www.pewinternet.org/files/2016/01/PI_2016-01-07_Parents-Teens-Digital-Monitoring_FINAL.pdf.

Beasley, D., 2016, February 22. *Alabama man killed after tracking stolen cell phone with app*. Retrieved March 1, 2016, from Reuters: http://www.reuters.com/article/us-alabama-crime-idUSKCN0VV2GS.

Lenhart, A., 2015, April 9. *Teens, social media & technology overview 2015*. Retrieved November 27, 2015, from Pew Research Center: www.pewinternet.org/files/2015/04/PI_TeensandTech_Update2015_0409151.pdf.

Lenhart, A., Anderson, M., Smith, A., 2015, October 1. *Teens, technology and romantic relationships*. Retrieved April 1, 2016, from Pew Research Center: www.pewinternet.org/files/2015/10/PI_2015-10-01_teens-technology-romance_FINAL.pdf.

Lenhart, A., Madden, M., Smith, A., Purcell, K., Zickuhr, K., Rainie, L., 2011, November 9. *Teens, Kindness and Cruelty on Social Network Sites*. Retrieved September 8, 2015, from Pew Research Center: www.pewinternet.org/files/old-media//Files/Reports/2011/PIP_Teens_Kindness_Cruelty_SNS_Report_Nov_2011_FINAL_110711.pdf.

Livingstone, S., Haddon, L., Ólafsson, K., 2011. *Risks and safety on the internet: the perspective of European children. Full Findings*. LSE, London: EU Kids Online. Retrieved November 21, 2015, from The London School of Economics and Political Science: www.lse.ac.uk/media%40lse/research/EUKidsOnline/EU%20Kids%20II%20(2009-11)/EUKidsOnlineIIReports/D4FullFindings.pdf.

Thanawala, S., 2011, June 1. *Photos from stolen laptop lead to man's arrest*. Retrieved November 23, 2015, from The Seattle Times: http://www.seattletimes.com/nation-world/photos-from-stolen-laptop-lead-to-mans-arrest/.

Index

Note: Page numbers followed by "*b*" and "*f*" refer to boxes and figures, respectively.

Printed in the United States
By Bookmasters